COLLARED BY GOD

THE REMINISCENCES OF AN ORDINARY PARSON

By
Paul S Duffett

COLLARED BY GOD

THE REMINISCENCES OF AN ORDINARY PARSON

By Paul S Duffett

First Published 2007 by kenandglen.com
Avenida Rusia 19, Las Atalayas
12598 Peñíscola, Castellón, Spain.

Written and Compiled by Paul S Duffett
Copyright © 2007 Paul S Duffet

The moral rights of the author have been asserted. All rights reserved. No part of this publication may be reproduced, stored in a retrieval system or transmitted in any form or by any means, electronic, mechanical or otherwise without the written permission of the Publisher.

ISBN 978-0-9556753-3-1

Contents

Chapter 1	The Child is Father to the Man	1
Chapter 2	Home and Family	8
Chapter 3	Hallo Mr Chips	15
Chapter 4	The Sublime and the	28
Chapter 5	..... onto the Ridiculous	39
Chapter 6	Back to Alma Mater	55
Chapter 7	City Parish - the halcyon years	63
Chapter 8	Abantu Bazula	76
Chapter 9	Charless Johnson's Hospital and Lukas Meyer	107
Chapter 10	Old Blighty!	134
Chapter 11	The Place of Resurrection	155
Index		178

CHAPTER 1

THE CHILD IS FATHER TO THE MAN

A friend sent me one of those cards for my birthday with information about all sorts of rather useless facts. For example, the best actor in 1933 was Charles Laughton for the film 'Private Life of Henry Eighth', a dozen eggs cost about 1d in the USA and on this day in 1893 the first motor-driven vacuum cleaner was patented! Amongst the famous people born on October 3rd the one I like most is Cherokee Chief John Ross. The most satisfying historical event was the reuniting of East and West Germany in 1990. Of course one must also admit that a certain man became Chancellor in Germany in this particular year but I prefer to recall that Jack Crawford won the Wimbledon men's title!

My sisters – who are all older than me by 10, 8 and 6 years respectively - tell me that when I was a baby one of them tipped me out of my pram coming down the steps of our first home in Horndean in Hampshire and that I have never been the same since! The house was in Five Heads Lane which twisted its narrow way up to pretty Catherington and the Church where I was baptised and where the Vicar – I later discovered – not only liked the ladies but also shouted and thumped the pulpit a lot. Our home was semi-detached and on a slope opposite a shop the Proprietor of which fell in love with my Aunt Margery. My parents wondered why she suddenly took an interest in tennis which she played on the recreation ground next door to the shop! My parents had moved there from Upper Norwood where all my sisters had lived as children and had John Amiss as a neighbour.

What Father was doing moving south I'm not sure, although he had been born in Fareham and had met Mother in Portsmouth where Grandad had a Greengrocers shop. He had been given permission to sell bananas in the first world war! This meant he had worked very hard as he was the only greengrocer given this privilege and had died of a stroke at the age of 63 years, before I was born. So had my other Grandfather who was a painter and decorator, although for years I thought he was the landlord of the pub next door - this was a family joke as he spent so much of his time in there! I don't think he was a very nice man. Father never spoke much about him and the only thing concrete I can remember being told was that in his will he had left only a pair of binoculars to my father 'which he had once borrowed and never returned'! I can't remember my maternal Grandmother either. She died when I was about 3 years old. However I was told that she delighted in combing my 'golden curls' as Mother called them! That just leaves my paternal Grandmother. When we moved on to the main road, about which more will be said later, she came to stay with us because of the war, living in the Drawing Room. I remember her as an upright Victorian looking lady with a bun. She was kind and I think little trouble to our parents. The one vivid thing I do remember about her is that she would say she was going to the bottom of the garden to look at the cows. This meant, I discovered, that she needed to pass wind. Considerate, no doubt! I can just remember when she died. I wasn't taken to the funeral but I can clearly recall my Father dabbing his eyes with a handkerchief. He really did love her.

We left Five Heads Lane and moved into a new 'ribbon' development on the A3, the road between Portsmouth and London. I had however prior to the move disgraced and half-amused my Mother. As she was showing off her first born son to a neighbour the lady leaned approvingly over the pram only to hear me say 'bugger off!' I was 2½ years old when we moved and I laid the foundation stone for our new house. The house cost Father £850 which must have been more than a year's wage for him then as I remember his salary going up to £1000 nearly ten years later. Where he got the money for the house from I can't guess. Perhaps he took a loan. Anyway it was a fine house. First there was a big garden stretching to the main road in the front, with a shingle drive bending right out of a green gate past the neighbours' houses and a little twist to the left out on to the road. At the back there was a lawn and then a little orchard with 5 apple trees beyond which was a vegetable patch. The border was a hedge over which Granny could see her cows! They produced milk for farmer Pearson who lived on the corner of the Causeway and delivered the milk himself. As I said the £850 not only bought all this land but also 4 bedrooms and a bathroom upstairs with a handsome hall downstairs and 4 other rooms – a sitting room, dining room, kitchen and the drawing room used only on special occasions or for Granny and later my youngest sister and her husband to live in. The dining room was known as 'the breakfast room' for some reason and we ate most of our meals there. Breakfast was eaten in a hurry before running for the No. 41 bus and lunch (which was called dinner) during the holidays was always at 1.00pm with tea at 5.00pm - bread, jam and delicious cakes. Supper was usually a light meal of Welsh Rarebit, the favourite and a cup of Ovaltine to help us sleep. Supper was eaten in the sitting room listening to the radio. In winter there was always a roaring fire, the only form of heating of course. Meals had to be eaten in silence especially when Father was present and he was quite nifty with a knife which would be rapped over our hands if there were any signs of what he thought was bad behaviour. The breakfast room had a hatch through which plates and food would be passed from the steaming kitchen. This hatch was once the means of a prank on my part! When my middle sister was courting I would open it at regular intervals on some pretext to see if I could spy what they were up to in the dark. I was aged about 9 years then and she was the first one to be married in December 1944 at the age of 19 years. There was one other 'small room' downstairs at the end of the hall near to the stairs. I can just remember some interesting behaviour on my part as this room contained a potty upon which I was put to perform at regular intervals. Mother would return to her duties in the kitchen and I would have to shout 'finished'. Often she couldn't hear me so I would manoeuvre myself on the object pulling it forward like a 'Go-cart' across the wooden floor of the hall often to meet a flummoxed Mother coming the other way.

    The sitting room was the scene of my first terror. This room was used by my parents at the weekends for a snooze after lunch and I was wont to play with toys on the floor, or so I am told, speaking in whispers to my soldiers or whatever it was I was trying to organise. Mother would often pretend to be asleep so she could listen to this. On one occasion an argument began between Mother and Father and as I was only 3 or 4 years old I probably wasn't aware that this was a common occurrence. They both had fiery tempers! On this particular day I heard Mother say that she could knock Father down anytime. He stood up inviting her to do so. She hit him with a couple of quick jabs to the chest whereupon he unleashed a pretty fierce straight left and knocked her down sending the chair she had been sitting on backwards. She got up in floods of tears and ran from the room. This set me bawling, running to Father for comfort and clinging on to his legs. The door suddenly swung open and in rushed Mother wielding a carving knife. Father backed towards the window with me bawling even more! Mother shouted something like ' I've a good mind to stick this into you' and then marched out of the room again. Perhaps my screaming had saved him! I remember Mother coming back into the room to console me. The damage had been done however and I remember sometimes waking up in bed to hear them arguing in their bedroom next door whereupon I would shake with fear or get a knot in my stomach. Their quarrelling was to end in divorce but over 30 years after that particular incident.

Nevertheless there were plenty of happy times. I remember the sense of security that accompanied the sound of the boiler being raked out in the mornings and the regular pattern of wash-days. Father loved special occasions. At Easter time he would boil the eggs for breakfast in cochineal which turned them blue. And around December 15th he would get out the decorations from the hall cupboard and stand on a ladder fastening the runners across the room and the baubles around the lampshades or wherever. Because of the war Christmas dinner was usually a cock-bird although we must have had a turkey once because on this occasion someone at the table noticed the carcass in the hatch moving! Father jumped up and discovered our little dog having leapt on to the hatch from the kitchen side busy inside the now empty bird!

The garden was lovely to play in and as I grew up and befriended neighbouring children we took full advantage of it. The house was given a special name – 'Dajocopa' – the two first letters of each of the children's names and I'm sure that both parents wanted it to be a happy family home. Father was keen on gardening and a ready learner. Our next-door neighbour, an Ernest King, was also a keen gardener and they were great competitors. Each season they would try and outdo each other in the size of their onions, tomatoes, carrots, cabbages and marrows. One year the winning carrot –but only just- was 14" long! The favourite however was runner beans. Father made long sticks and bound them together at the top and planted out the little seedlings brought on in the cold frame. They grew by the bag-full and our next-door neighbour had to accede the crown on this vegetable even though his name was King! I wasn't much help to Dad. At the age of 4 years I once followed behind him as he planted lettuce seedlings pulling out what he had put in, much to the amusement of my older sisters. The other job I was given and found boring was to take all the caterpillars off the cabbages. At that time the whole of the front lawn was given over to growing cabbages as part of the 'Dig for Victory' campaign ordered by the Government during the 1939-1945 war. Our neighbours on the other side were a single mother and her daughter Tessa who was a year or so older than I. We became firm and inseparable friends. Across the main road were woods stretching for miles around; now they are smart housing estates built in the 1960's and 1970's. As woods they were magic and our favourite haunts were the two ponds. One pond we called 'Lily' because of the beautiful white and yellow flowers floating on it's surface and the other much larger pond we called 'Boating' – this was much deeper into the woods. Here Tessa and I would go by ourselves to spend time imagining great journeys or to build some private 'Wendy House'. Our parents never had to worry about us.

And so the war came. It was the same year that Portsmouth won the F.A. cup as I sat on my Uncle's knee soaking up the excitement. It was my Father's knee that I sat on to hear Mr. Chamberlain make the sad announcement at 11am on September 3rd. For a while nothing seemed to happen until gradually the news worsened as one country after another fell to the Nazi scourge. One warm, cloudless autumn day I was playing in the garden as usual, when I was distracted by the whining and wailing of aircraft overhead and looking up I could see them weaving in and out, some trailing smoke. It looked like a weird ballet dance. When I asked my Mother what was going on she replied 'It's a dog-fight'. It was of course the Battle of Britain. Father joined the Air Raid Personnel and was appointed Head Warden. He, Mr. King and others would go out at night checking to see that no-one had forgotten to black out their windows and that generally 'all was well'. This check was usually uneventful. However one evening a 'floating mine' became entangled by its parachute on top of the 'Gales Ales' Brewery in the village. It sounded as though a bomb had landed next door and the A.R.P. were suddenly shaken out of their lethargy. Soon after this a more serious incident occurred when one of these nasty things landed in a near-by field. An unfortunately zealous lady warden ran towards it thinking it was an airman in his parachute, only to be blown to smithereens. This happened near the little copse that was clearly visible from our back garden.

Then came the bombing of Portsmouth. The dockyard was the main target but the whole city suffered terribly. I stood out in the garden on January 10th 1941 and watched with horror as the flames and smoke rose from just 10 miles away. Father and the other A.R.P. Wardens had been called to the aid of the Services trying to prevent the spread of fire from the incendiary bombs and assist the civilians caught up in the devastation. He was there all night and came home exhausted and in modern day colloquialism 'traumatised'. Two further events happening later in the war remain fixed in my memory. One involved us leaving our house at night to stay with friends in the village. Mr. King, our next-door neighbour, had heard a big thump at around 2am and on investigation had found a hole in his garden. He called in his Boss and together they decided this hole might be an unexploded bomb. We had to be evacuated to friends in the village. At dawn the disposal people arrived and discovered that it was an enormous lump of clay thrown up by a stray bomb some half-a-mile away. The second memorable event occurred during an air raid. We were used to the siren wailing away and we would gather under the stairs in the hall where it had been made comfy to lie down under blankets. This particular night we were startled by a gigantic explosion that rattled the windows. I remember Mother rushing to the pram to pick up my baby brother Christopher who had been born in 1942. We waited tensely. Suddenly there was another bang as big as the first followed quickly by two more just as loud. We thought our end was coming! Then followed an eerie silence. We learnt later that it was an enemy plane that had been shot down crashing with a full load of bombs about three miles away. We went to see the crater it had left some time later. It was enormous! Of course there were lighter moments as well. The A.R.P. had a lot in common with the television programme 'Dad's Army'! On one occasion Father and Ernest were on a regular tour of duty in the village during an air raid. There was some activity. The anti-aircraft guns were popping off and the dull thud of bombs could be heard. They took shelter under a tree just as a much louder explosion occurred. Ernest felt something hit his neck and shouted 'I've been hit by shrapnel!' Father leapt forward with his A.R.P. torch. All that could be found was an acorn lodged in Ernest's collar!

There is a lot more that could be said about the war and how it affected us all but I am running ahead of myself because I had started my education two years before the war had started. Our parents believed in education - at least for boys! It may have been their way of making up for what they had had too little of. Father had left school at 12 years of age beginning work as a Draper's boy for 12d a week. He was an avid reader and had worked his way up the ladder. I never thought of him as an uneducated man. Mother, I think, had a little more formal schooling but was needed to help in the business and no doubt the home as well. She had been to a 'Secretarial School' and was competent at shorthand and typing. Anyway they had decided to send my three sisters to a private school. It was called an 'Academy for Young Ladies' and was run by a Miss. Hall who looked like a typical Victorian schoolmistress – bun and all! I discovered in later years that she was a single mother (you would never have known). The tiny Academy was at Waterlooville about three miles on the way to Portsmouth. This meant catching the No. 41 bus as I have previously mentioned. Helpfully it had a tiny Kindergarten attached to it and it was to this that I was duly sent at the age of 4 years. My only memories of it are not academic ones, although somebody had obviously taught me to read as a year later I was told that the neighbours next door but one had asked if I would go over and read to them. I learnt later that the Gentleman of the house, who looked so serious and important, was in fact the Editor of The Portsmouth Evening News. He told my parents that he was suitably impressed! What comes immediately to mind were two of the bus journeys. On one trip I won 3d for a 'dare' that I should kiss a pretty little girl called Biddy. This must have gone to my head as one day later I spent half of my bus money on sweets. Perhaps I thought there would be another chance to win it back! However, as I was short on my fare money the bus conductor put me off a stop short of my usual one and so deposited a howling child over half-a-mile from his home. My other memory can only be described as disturbing! There was a young lady on whom I had a crush. I hope this is not unusual for a 4 year old? I remember I used to hug her raincoat in the passage-way. The only other aspect of this relationship that I can remember is an occasion when she accompanied me to the toilet, I think I may have had difficulty in undoing my buttons. Her red face remains fixed in my mind! I've sometimes wondered whether there was any other reason for my crush on this poor girl.

    Sister Daphne was a star of the school concerts as elocution was her forte and Miss. Hall prided herself on teaching her young ladies 'proper English'. I stayed at that school until I was nearly seven and then it seems there had been some discussion about a 'boys only' education for me. Mother in particular had notions above her station! HER son deserved a superior education. I think this was her thinking but perhaps I am being unkind here. Another reason which was communicated much later to me was that Father feared that without boys to play with at home I may become 'effeminate'! Anyway it was decided that I would go to a preparatory school in the nearby town of Petersfield. This must have been quite expensive for my parents. The route there was by the afore-mentioned No. 41 bus leaving at 7.55 in the morning. There was then nearly a mile walk from the bus stop to the school which was an ordinary four-bedroomed house slightly adapted to accommodate 20 Boarders and 20 Day Boys. Officially it was the Prep. School for Churchers College, a minor private Public School founded by Captain Churcher of the East India Company in 1722 for the education of Officers' children. At the turn of the century it had moved from a much smaller and more beautiful building nearer the centre of the town to it's present site on the A3 towards London in an area of great scenic beauty. The rear of the school looked out over the South Downs and provided space for a fine cricket field and two rugby pitches. Even the Prep School had an adequate soccer field which was used for cricket in the summer. The Prep School hadn't been in existence long and was run by a man who had lived in South America for some time and was now in his late 30s. He was an excellent sportsman, especially at cricket, but taught football and boxing as well. He wasn't a bad Teacher either and I remember he was first-class with the cane!

So began my daily trip, arriving home about 4.45pm. Not a lot comes to mind of those long days except of course my foundation in education which is never lost. There are bits of 'The Brook' and 'Morte D'Arthur' by Tennyson I can recall and we learned the traditional songs such as 'Hearts of Oak' and 'Jerusalem'. Each day would begin with an act of Worship and I could recite the prayer of St. Loyola after a little while......'Teach us good Lord to serve thee as thou deservest. To give and not to count the cost....' And so on.

These are amongst the first conscious words of belief that I can recall. I suppose that belief in God was taken for granted but I don't remember my parents ever speaking of it. I know that Father and his brother, the jovial Uncle Cleeve, were confirmed and had sung in a church choir as boys, being punished once for playing marbles during the Service. I also know that Father persuaded Mother to be confirmed after they were married in St. Cuthbert's Church, Portsmouth. I know too that my sisters were Confirmed. On one occasion Coral, my youngest sister, invited me to go with her to Church and I refused saying I had enough of that sort of thing at school! I must have relented once though, as I recall being severely reprimanded for copying the Vicar's gesticulations during the Sermon! On the whole though Church was for Christmas only and sometimes for Easter also. No doubt Father had a guilty conscience but more of that later. I never consciously believed but on the other hand even at this early age never rejected it either similar to most children of my generation.

I must have missed Father as he seemed to be away a lot and would even telephone at the weekends to say he was in South Wales or the North of England and couldn't come home because of work there on Monday. Mother seemed to accept this as normal. I don't know whether it was his absence which led me to make up stories but there was one at this time which lived with me for several years! I was travelling home on the bus and for some reason told the Conductor 'I have a garden you know'. 'And what do you grow?' asked the Conductor. 'Eh....carrots, cabbages, lettuce and potatoes' I replied. 'Do you grow them from seed?'. 'Yes, of course'. 'And how deep do you have to put the seeds?'. I thought for a bit, 'About 9 inches' I said. It was some time later that I realised I had been caught out and felt ashamed. Several years later when I was a Day-Boy again (having been a Boarder for nine years) I caught the bus home and the same Conductor was there. As he looked at my season ticket he said 'Have those seeds come up yet?' We both laughed!

As I previously mentioned the school was very traditional with great emphasis placed on the three 'Rs' and plenty of Sport. Although I am naturally left-handed a teacher by the name of Miss.Olsen tried forcing me to write with my right-hand. This didn't last too long – fortunately! The discipline was fierce and on one occasion I hit a boy who was hurting another boy much smaller than he. He cried loudly and went to the Master on duty who told me to report to the Headmaster. The Headmaster at that time was doing something over in the senior school and I was far too afraid to enter those awesome courts!

Anyway I believed I had only punished a 'bully'. As it was about time to go home I ran away from the Master on duty and off down the road towards the bus-stop. As I looked back I could see him going through the gates towards the senior school. The waiting until the next morning was agony! However nothing happened the next day, or the next, or indeed for two whole weeks. Each day was torture going to school and waiting for the inevitable summons! Then just when I was beginning to think it had been forgotten the announcement came from the Headmaster himself. I was given four strokes of the cane. But the psychological punishment had been the worst and I never knew if that had been deliberately the case.

On the whole my time at school passed smoothly enough. One amusing incident comes to mind although it was not so funny for me at the time. The bus ride home took two different routes depending on whether you caught the bus on the hour or the half-hour. If it was the latter the bus-stop was a little farther from home. One particular day I felt an impending crisis, I must have eaten something that gave me tummy-ache! As this bus took me to the furthest away stop I began to run home to prevent disaster from striking. Who should be walking towards me but our kind neighbour Ernest King! Of course he greeted me asking how I was and how school was going? As I stood there I knew it was too late and could feel my pants beginning to fill up. There was nothing to be done and as I stood helplessly trying to be polite there was a gentle plop and a dollop of 'you know what' fell onto my shoe. Mr. King looked down in silence and then said 'I think you'd better run home as quickly as possible'. Of course running wasn't wise and eventually I limped into the house and began to cry!

Two years passed very quickly and I was surprised to learn just before my 9th birthday that I was to become a boarder. I was never told the reason for this decision. After all school was only a short bus journey away with a healthy walk at the end. Whether I had not made as much progress as I should have, or whether there was more money available I never knew. I can only guess! Certainly the fees would not have been cheap. It could have possibly had something to do with my brother Christopher who was born on June 6th 1942 – twenty years after the birth of his eldest sister! Maybe it was felt that as Mother was entering her forties she would only be able to tackle one boy at a time – especially as Father was away such a lot. Anyway I was suitably given new clothes and a tuck box with which to begin the school year. It was the most important and the most difficult moment of my life so far.

CHAPTER 2

HOME AND FAMILY

The title of this chapter is misleading. As I hope you will soon understand it alludes to Churchers College and not to 'Dajocopa'. For reasons which will become apparent the community of school took the place in my mind and heart of what most children would call home and family – for better or for worse.

The start of those years was painful. There were tears on leaving home and every night for about two weeks thereafter. The school itself was full and so I was boarded out. My hosts were very kind but to a boy of 9 years they seemed ancient. The man was a retired Teacher of English at Churchers and his wife, Mrs.Piggott, was about the same age as her husband. They had a son who was quite well known as a Professor of Archeology at Edinburgh University. I was grateful to him for his possession of a series of 'Biggles' books which I was allowed to read at my leisure. They lived about three-quarters of a mile from the school and every evening after 6.0'o clock supper at school I made my way 'home' down the hill. It was painful for me that on my way down the hill I passed a gate leading into a field with a marvelous view of the South Downs and I felt that just over those gentle hills was my real home. Every evening I stood by the gate and cried for the security and warmth which my Mother especially gave me. Like most young lads I soon recovered but I am sure that was the start of a kind of depression that was with me for much longer and has returned to haunt me often throughout the years.

It was about nine months before a place was found for me to board in the school and by then I had experienced another incident with the Headmaster - this time to do with cleaning my teeth and brushing my shoes! Mrs. Piggott had asked me if I was cleaning my teeth and shoes every day and when I replied that I was she produced a dry toothbrush and a clean bootbrush and informed me that this was to be reported. Sure enough a few days later I was summoned to the Headmaster's study. I was to be punished, I was told, not for failing in personal cleanliness but for telling lies. It was four strokes of the cane again. When the time came I wasn't sad to be leaving the Piggott's home! There were four of us in the little dormitory up at the house and my first recollection is that every evening after supper and washing, Matron would inspect our hands and ears and we were then expected to kneel by our beds for five minutes of Prayer. I have thought about this since and I don't think I found it unusual so I must have known something about prayer. I duly asked the Almighty to bless my parents, aunts and uncles, sisters, brother and probably Peter the dog which I had been given as a Christmas present the year before. It never occurred to me to pray for the Teachers or my fellow pupils! Nevertheless I have sometimes wondered whether this little piece of discipline formed the basis for a future Spirituality. God heard those prayers and gave me the grace to think of prayer as a natural part of living.

Mentioning Peter the dog gives me the opportunity to introduce the person who gave Peter to me – Audrey Osborne. Audrey was brought up in the Portsmouth area, probably on the Isle of Wight, and had lost two beloved brothers in the first world war. This left her with the inability to go into a church building without crying. She had grown into a fairly tall young lady with lovely red hair and she and Father had been friends – probably even boy and girlfriend – in their teens. They met up again when Father began to travel for 'Chavent Fils', a firm specialising in ladies clothing, and Audrey had a job at Handleys store in Southsea, now Debenhams. She had climbed the career ladder and was by this time Manager of the Furs Department. She was certainly around in the early 30's as Daphne, the eldest of us children, remembers her presence at weekends when Father started the Horndean Tennis Club. He would give tea parties for his customers all of whom were 'trendy' ladies. Mother made the tea with delicious scones and Daphne recalls lots of laughter on these occasions. My first memory of her was as the 'auntie' who took me for a walk one Sunday morning to the nearest shop on the edge of the village and bought me an ice cream. Then there was the gift of the puppy which means that she must have been with us for Christmas. This would have been after the bombing of Portsmouth and our dear neighbours – the Kings – offered her a room, probably at Father's request. I also remember one evening when it was already dark and I was playing in the hall. The sitting room door opened and out came a frightened looking Audrey followed by Mother looking furious. The front door was opened and Audrey was pushed out with the angry words 'And don't you ever darken this door again'. I suppose she never did! I know that the Kings then asked her to leave and that was all I really knew about the relationship at that stage. I also remember going to a football match in Portsmouth with Father and afterwards being taken for a short drive and told to wait in the car on my own. Father seemed to be gone such a long time that I began to panic and cry. When I later discovered that Audrey lived close to the football ground I realised that Father could well have stopped the car outside her house. I also suppose Audrey could have been the reason Father couldn't come home some weekends because of 'work' although I am fairly sure that other 'customers' delayed him for probably the same reason! Audrey would have been considerably better paid than Father and may have helped him with my Boarding Fees for all I know. Apparently Father had made her a promise that he would leave home when I was 15 years old. This promise was revised when Christopher was born to when he was 15 years of age! I have always had a sneaking admiration for Audrey in that she agreed to this and sacrificed so many years of her adult life because of Father. She became an increasing factor in our lives as the years progressed.

But – the school bell had gone! Life was a round of meals, lessons, sport and sleep. Speaking of rounds brings to mind the early morning obligatory piece of behaviour which was actually known as 'going around'. In alphabetical order boys had to visit one of the only two available toilets in order to become 'regular'! As far as I can remember this worked pretty well and you considered yourself lucky if your surname began with the letter A, B or even D rather than Z! Everyone had the opportunity to go between breakfast and the beginning of lessons – a slot of 45 minutes to share between 30 of us. The meals were standard war-time bread and stodge and the lessons of the old fashioned ' up front and copy down' method with a lot of 'rote' learning for tables and the like. Sport was something I began to love as I grew older. At football I played in goal for the school team and at boxing, which I didn't really enjoy, I was matched with a lad called Issacs who was taller than I was and had a straight left like a sledge hammer! It was good news when he left and I was matched with someone more like myself as I had an interest in wanting to stay out of harms way for as long as possible! When in the Top Form he and I were matched in an exhibition bout for visiting parents and friends. I can still hear Father shouting 'Go on, hit one another!' Cricket became my passion. One day I was trying to figure out one end of the bat from the other when 'Greasy', the Headmaster, came up to me and squatted down to position my hands and legs correctly. He had his 'hooker pipe' in his mouth as usual. He then demonstrated how to keep the elbow bent and straight forward so that one could play a straight bat. He went on to explain that if the bowler pitched a ball up to you then you played forward but if it was short pitched you should move back to meet the ball as it rose, hopefully not too high, towards you. From that day I never looked back! Every day during the summer term I would be out practicing with friends, and even at home, I would spend hours throwing a tennis ball against the garage door and hitting it back in imaginary matches between famous teams whose players names I soon learned by heart. The school didn't play many matches but every year they would play with the Junior School for Bedales which was about 3 miles away in Steep village. In my last year I went in first and scored top score of 11 out of our majestic total of 32! I then took 7 wickets, including a caught, and bowled at full length for 4 runs with slow left arm leg breaks and they were all out for 26. I felt prouder than ever before or since! We always wrote home to our parents every Sunday – another school rule – and my letter that Sunday was a full record of the match with my bowling analysis in full! We were privileged to play our matches on the edge of the Upper School's field near the score board and so were allowed to use that as well, with our scorers sitting inside the little box and someone outside putting up the big metal figures. 'Greasy' was no mean cricketer himself and I was once in seventh heaven as I saw him score 100 for his team against the Upper School first eleven and then bamboozle their batsmen with his crafty spinners. He was my first hero when it came to cricket even though he was mean with the cane!

Our lessons were designed to prepare us for the new 11 plus examination introduced by the famous Butler Education Act of 1944. We were the first group of pupils in Britain to sit them and I think they wanted us to succeed! They consisted of a number of Intelligence tests as well as the usual English and Maths exams. The Intelligence tests were made up of shapes and symbols of different sizes which one had to combine according to the instructions. Not too difficult really. Before the final year started I was summoned into the part of the dining room at home that served as Father's study where a desk was covered in papers and bills. The Headmaster had sent the Term's report as usual and I had come bottom out of a class of 17. The Headmaster had written on the bottom how disappointed he was as he knew I was capable of doing better. Father was less than pleased. Money didn't grow on trees and I had better pull my socks up and so on! On my return to school I discovered that I had been made a Prefect and being thus encouraged I was determined to work hard and do my best. Having a little power went to my head!

One of our common activities to pass the time was a joint walk on Saturday afternoons. Can you imagine 30 energetic boys being conducted in a crocodile by one Teacher, especially if she were a woman? A new member of the staff was the sister to the Headmaster and she was newly married and living locally. She was younger than her brother and one day we took full advantage of her inexperience. I was the ringleader and at the end she was in tears. I knew of course there would be repercussions and this time it was a lecture on being responsible accompanied by 6 of the best! Greasy must have been angry that day and afterwards I went to the bathrooms to wash my face with cold water. I was feeling faint and I remember the room swimming round and the next thing I was waking up flat on my back on the floor. I guess I had fainted with the fierceness of the caning. I never dared to tell anyone this had happened! Perhaps it had beaten some sense into me after all as at the end of that particular term I was top of the class!

The Top form were made to feel special by having their own classroom in an annexe at the end of the old driveway from the front gate. Perhaps it had been the original garage. It was called the Art room and all the Art classes for the school were conducted there but apart from this it was the sole property of the Top Class. It was just about big enough for 17 desks to fit in and for the Teachers to still be able to pass between checking the exercise books and so on. One Maths Teacher was rather portly and I would amuse the other lads by pushing a compass into her back end whilst she was bending over to mark the book of the pupil in front of me. Fortunately it never penetrated far enough for her to feel it!

One day we were being taught by 'Greasy' when a boy called Rait interrupted his flow by saying 'Excuse me Sir but what is that aircraft outside? I don't recognise it.' If anyone could identify the type of aircraft by its noise it was he. This was his hobby. The Headmaster immediately went outside to look. It was certainly a very low and noisy aircraft. Almost at once there was a sudden silence – the engine had cut. 'Greasy' came charging back into the room his face as white as a sheet shouting 'Under your desks.' I knew straight away what it was as we had been told that the Doodle-bug engines cut out suddenly. It was this Nazi rocket carrying a pile of explosives. I remember thinking how well we all fitted under our desks – just enough room to squat and be completely covered. Then I started counting as we had read that it took thirteen seconds from the moment of cut-out to explosion. I had reached twelve when there was a dull thud. Of course as the Bug had stopped and cut its engines above us it had continued to drift about three miles away and had dropped its explosives harmlessly into a field. However a few weeks later we were awakened by an enormous explosion and thought one must have landed nearby, perhaps even on the local town just down the road. When we got up in the morning we were told it had dropped into Poole harbour about 25 miles away as the crow flies. The water had caused the sound to reverberate enormously. Naturally we were excited as well as nervous fearing that we might be hit by one of those awful V2s when they eventually started terrorising London.

The school holidays were such fun. The girl next door had been joined by another girl called Patsy who had moved in just down the road. The three of us invented horses and cantered around the place talking to these imaginary beasts and making horse noises. If for some reason the girls were not available to play I would be a soldier with my imitation machine gun. I more than once 'shot up' the house next door giving Elsie King the fright of her life as she stood with her back to me at the kitchen sink! Then the Americans arrived. They came with their tanks and personnel carriers and parked on the grass across the road. One day I was given a tour of one of their large tanks and some very sweet tea in a big mess can. On another day one of the soldiers gave me a tin of the grease used to keep the machine parts in good order, and taking this home the only use I could think of for it was to cover the wheel-barrow. You can imagine Father's remarks when he next went to do some gardening!

1944 marked the first big celebration in our now completed family. Joy, the second eldest was married in the Parish Church of Catherington. She was able to loan a wedding dress through an organisation called 'Women of America' and when it arrived on the wedding day it had in it a label saying it was from a high class New York shop. It was very beautiful and helped Joy to look the same. Barry, her husband, served in the Fleet Air-Arm and was tall, dark and handsome. Father looked suitably proud and Mother cried. The Vicar was in his element especially dancing with all the girls at the Reception which took place at the pub just down the road from the Church. They left for their Honeymoon on the local bus! Housing was very hard to come by and they began their married life in a converted railway carriage which hadn't been converted that well as the water came from a pump outside and other facilities were very rudimentary! I used to enjoy going to visit them as it was such an adventure. I remember helping Barry to wash up one day and having a philosophical conversation with him which was a new experience for me. He was that kind of a bloke – always thinking about things. There is a past tense about that comment as the marriage came to a sad ending when after the war ended Barry became a Teacher and fell in love with one of the Staff. To escape this situation he re-joined the Fleet Air-Arm and failed to make it one day coming in to land on an aircraft carrier off the coast of Korea during that nasty conflict. However before this sad turn of events Joy and he had two lovely boys and I was privileged to be asked to become Godfather to the younger one, Peter. The service took place at Catherington and I affirmed promises that I hardly knew the meaning of – in words, let alone in life! Nevertheless there was a certain solemnity and seriousness which affected me and I did try to follow my promises through by taking an interest in his development.

Other happy events included a holiday on Hayling Island where we often went on Sundays in the summer as a family. We hired one of those charming huts right on the beach and Mother would make wonderful egg salads. There is a charming photograph of us all there in about 1937, including Mother's sister and her husband - plus a few of Father's 'customers'! One of these 'customers' was married to one of my Godfathers. The great attraction of Hayling Island was that Aunt Edna, married to Mother's brother Bill, owned a large house on the island just about 400yards from the sea which they had turned into holiday boarding for Bed and Breakfast. However this holiday was different. I must have been about ten years of age and Uncle Bill was away somewhere for a few days and it was decided that I should 'Auntie-sit'. It was the autumn time and there were no visitors with the beaches deserted. Building intricate systems of canals in the sand was great fun. One day a middle-aged gentleman came along and sat on his walking stick watching me. He was interested in hearing what I had built and why and left saying that when the time came for me to choose a career I should be an Engineer! When I was not building in the sand the empty tennis court proved an excellent place to have football matches as the tennis ball would bounce off the wire at different angles so enabling me to score goals from all directions. One evening after supper Auntie and I listened to a radio programme called 'The Man in Black'. The idea of this programme was to terrify the listeners with ghastly tales of mystery and magic. This particular day the story was about a mummified hand that appeared suddenly through a window at night. After Auntie and I had gone to bed the wind got up and I awoke suddenly to hear the window rattling. The fright made me want to go to the bathroom and on my way there a terrified looking Auntie was coming unsteadily along the corridor towards me. She looked as white as a sheet and we consoled each other with nervous laughter.

The best times were Christmas when the whole family would descend on Bill and

Edna. They were festive occasions with parties and good meals. We played games such as 'Murder' and 'Going on Holiday' where you had to dress up from a suitcase full of clothes, run to the other end of the room, undress and put the clothes back in the case before the next person in your team did the same thing. Of course we played Charades as well.

One holiday, for some reason, we stayed in a hotel and although it was lovely and comfortable it wasn't nearly so much fun! The garden of this hotel was full of laurel bushes which were excellent for playing soldiers in. For a reason I cannot remember only my brother Christopher and I were there that year. Probably by this time Daphne was in the WAAF working with radar, Joy was a nurse at Emsworth and Coral was working at an Infant School in Purbrook. This holiday marks the first time I can remember being in a Church with Mother. It may have been Christmas or the Sunday after but the Church was larger than Catherington's with a lofty roof and bright light streaming from winter sun through high windows. Whether the acoustics were especially unusual or the Vicar had a knack of projecting his voice I don't know but suddenly, before anyone appeared, I heard this loud voice coming from what appeared to be the timbers of the nave roof and I was overcome with awe! I never dared to ask or tell anyone of this Epiphany experience.

The war continued to have its unique effect. I hated the Germans and prayed for their defeat by the heroic Allies, including the Russians about whose politics I knew nothing. We children became involved in the war effort in our own way. One day I hit on the idea of a garden party and together we arranged to sell whatever our mothers and neighbours could give us. We used the King's back lawn as it was much more spacious than ours. Our parents invited their friends and tea and cakes were provided as well. It was very exciting for the three of us and we collected £2 and 10 shillings for the Red Cross who wrote us a very polite letter of thanks.

The last term at Prep School was drawing to a close. One May day a small group of us were marched over to the big school to take the 11 plus examination. We had been well prepared and it was quite enjoyable. I remember Father arranging for me to take the Entrance Examination for Portsmouth Grammar School just in case I failed the 11 plus. Fortunately this help was not needed and it was announced that in September 1945 I would be attending class 2b at Churchers.

The days that summer were full of excitement. First there was the end of hostilities in Europe with people flocking to a great jamboree on top of Portsdown Hill with its wonderful view of the Solent. Barry took a trumpet with him and blew the thing every minute to add to the noise of jubilation! Our trips to Hayling Island continued throughout the hot summer. On one of these trips, when the waves were choppy, Father and Uncle Bill had with them a rowing boat and kept pushing it out from the shore whilst attempting to climb into it only to be thrown out time after time! Of course they were encouraged by the on-lookers with much laughing and cheering. In August came the end of the war after the terrible bombing of Horishema and Nagasaki - V.J. Day. The relief was enormous in my young and fearful mind and much to my gratification the front garden was returned to grass. No more picking off the caterpillars from the cabbage leaves!

Just before the new term was to begin Father took me to a shop in Waterlooville. He knew the proprietor well so probably did business with him anyway. It was here he bought me my first suit as this was required for Sunday wearing at Churchers. It was grey with a bluish tint. Afterwards we went across the road where my brother and I were photographed together. It was a sort of 'coming of age' ritual and now I was prepared for the bigger world. The social life of our 'gang' – Tessa, Patsy and I – was enlarged by the arrival of new neighbours next door but one, the Hawkeys. Christine was 2 ½ years my senior, Jo 2 years younger and Roger just over 3 years younger. At last I had a boy to play with and what's more one I could boss about! They were to become very much part of my life during the following six or seven years.

CHAPTER 3

HALLO MR CHIPS

On October 3rd 1945 I was 12 years of age and the school term had begun in the September. It must have been late in the month because on the 15th September (the anniversary of the Battle of Britain) Daphne was married to Jock Brown in our Parish Church at Catherington. Jock was a Squadron Leader who had been decorated for his bravery and very hard work. They had been courting sometime and once I remember going with them for a walk in the local woods and Jock giving me 6d. to go away and buy an ice cream! About the wedding I remember little except being asked to look after Uncle Cleeve, which meant replenishing his glass whenever needed! I must have done this well as it transpired later that going home he had stood on the wrong platform and begun his journey to Portsmouth via London! Where his wife was during this episode remains a mystery. I think Jock and Daphne began their married life together in Scotland, perhaps at Ochiltree near Kilmarnock. They came south later which was nice because it made them more accessible. I visited them a few times before leaving for South Africa and Jock recounts the story of my first visit. He came to pick me up from the station but I wasn't there! Eventually a message was relayed that I had travelled on to the next station, about forty miles away, with my nose stuck in a book!

At last the time came to leave for the 'Big School'. There must have been about thirty of us in all who turned up – nervous, shy, a little scared – small fry in a big pond! The rambling Victorian building along the London road as you leave Petersfield and on the outskirts of the village of Sheet was as old-fashioned inside as its exterior purports. The walls were different shades of heavy paint, green, brown and very off-white! The wooden corridors were long and echoed like a prison when the doors were slammed – which was often. The stairs were stone-worn by the countless feet of past pupils over many years. Upstairs were the dormitories, one having twenty beds and the other three having thirty beds each, or thereabouts. The Boarders were accommodated according to age.

However before one was allowed into this monument to antiquity there was a sort of 'half-way house' called Mount House across the road from the main school and up a little rise – hence its name. It was a nice house really and must have been bought as extra accommodation by the school when it became popular just before the war. It housed some thirty of the youngest pupils. There was a Matron, Miss.Tribe, who inspected teeth, hands and ears every night. There was also a House Master who lived in with his family and a bed-sitter for another Master who shared the duty of keeping discipline. The first was a bit of an ogre but the other was a mild man, the latest acquisition to the Staff and therefore younger. He used to let me listen to the cricket commentary from Australia crackling over the radio at 8.30 in the morning. Breakfast was in the house but everything else was over in the Big School. We came over the road at about 7.30pm after homework, or Prep as it was called, and got ready for bed. Lights went out at 8.30pm and life was very regulated. Sometimes we would come over the road earlier after supper and we could then play games or read. It was then that I learned to play Bridge. The kindly young Master taught three of us how to play and we would sit night after night like old hands playing away! I have always maintained that I never improved after those days!

In the mornings there was a twenty minute Assembly at 8.45 and once a week we would have Hymn Practice. To begin with this practice was led by one Basil Harwood who is credited with a Hymn in the Anglican Hymn Book. However after a short time his place was taken by a Mr. Lane, whom we called 'Larry the Lamb' because of his frequent laughter which sounded rather like a 'Baa'! He was a most skilful musician and conducted local choirs and orchestras as well as playing the organ at the large Parish Church in Petersfield. I think I learnt more Hymns from him than anyone else. The practice was to sing all the Hymns for the coming week so we in fact sang each Hymn twice that week. He liked the grand tunes as well especially the Welsh ones. I think he made my introduction to Churchgoing in later life much easier and I must have imbibed a lot of Theology without realising it. His wife also taught but she should never have taught growing boys! She was far too kind and gentle and we made her life a misery. One day I and another boy hid under the stage smoking all the way through the music lesson. I felt really sad one day a few years later, and perhaps guilty too, when I heard that she had been suffering from depression and had taken her own life. She, like her husband, was a brilliant pianist and their children turned into fine musicians too. The Roman Catholics and Jews – of whom there were one or two – had to stand outside during the Assembly. The Staff sat on the stage of the Hall in their gowns and the Head Boy stood by the door and shouted 'stand' as the Headmaster approached. After the Hymn there was a reading from one of the Gospels and every boy had a copy of a little Gospel supplied by the Gideons and given out with the Hymn Books as we went to our places. One of the Prefects read the Bible and then the Headmaster would read Prayers from some Anthology after which we all sat for the notices (No graffiti on the toilet walls, etc.). Sometimes there were awards to do with Sport. 'Colours' were awarded for good performances at rugby or cricket and if someone had scored 50 or over in a school match he was given a cricket ball.

The Hall was a grand room with oak paneling all around the walls and a lofty beamed ceiling. High on the back wall were panels with the names of all the Headmasters of the school and all the rugby and cricket Captains from 1900. On one wall one of the previous Headmaster had hung a couple of his own watercolour paintings. His name was Hogarth and he was a very fine Artist. The stage was high and large and was further enlarged in 1947 in order to produce Gilbert and Sullivan Operas. At that time there was a Headmaster called Schofield who was a Scientist and a Graduate of Clare College, Cambridge. He fancied himself as a Producer of Gilbert and Sullivan and the first he produced was' Iolanthe' which was such a success that 'HMS Pinafore' followed the next year. I was given a part as one of the Admiral's many sisters and aunts! It was great fun and fired my ambition to act on the stage. There must have been a bit of a break from these ambitious productions because the only other one I can remember was 'The Pirates of Penzance' in which I played the part of the Pirate King and strutted about the stage wearing fearful Pirate's garb and carrying a big flag bearing the skull and cross-bones symbol! The years in between the Gilbert and Sullivan productions were taken up by Shakespeare directed by the English Master, the eccentric Mr. Kershaw. He didn't know much about directing but was under strict instructions from the Headmaster! I managed to secure small parts in these productions until one year the Headmaster decided to produce a comedy in which I played a larger part! I forget now what it was called but it had very little literary merit!

It was very popular nevertheless including as it did quite a lot of slapstick and some quite funny situations.

Under the 1944 Education Act Churchers had been designated a Grammar School with direct aid from central Government. This was probably done to prevent it from dying on its feet! Most of the Staff had been there for a long time and were past their prime. I was put into what was called the 'A' stream and one of our first lessons was given by the 'old' Headmaster, Hogarth. We were terrified! He came swinging into the room with a swagger, his gown flowing. The Roll was called and I could hardly answer for my dry throat. Then he swept a pencil out from his jacket like a Magician. 'What is this?' he asked. I know, I thought, this is an English lesson and he is testing our grammar….that's easy! So I piped up 'A noun, Sir'. I had jumped two places ahead for him. His answer came like a machine gun. 'Stupid boy, it's a pencil!' I was silenced for the rest of the lesson. It was the only time he ever taught us.

After that we had 'Gus' Kershaw who desperately tried to put Literature as well as Grammar into our heads. He had a small beard which he often stroked especially when he was thinking. He also had a very worn rubber slipper which he would produce from his pocket to punish 'stupid boys'. This would happen several times a lesson and one got the impression that he rather enjoyed it! In fact when he was the Boarding Master on duty he would often chase little boys down the corridor and take them by the ear to his room where he would apply the afore-mentioned punishment. He was one of the remaining eccentrics still on the Staff but he had a very kind heart and was extremely erudite in both English and Classics. When I failed Latin at 'A' Level he took me under his wing for extra tuition for which Father paid. I had to pass in order to gain a place at Oxford and I had to translate a piece of Latin unseen at the Entrance Examination to Keble College. He was very diligent and patient with this Latin 'thick head'. In fact it turned out to be something of a miracle as when I went to sit this examination, there in front of me was the piece of Virgil I had worked on that week and 'Gus' had corrected for me just the night before! You can imagine my amazement! I made only one mistake and at my interview afterwards the Warden asked me if I shouldn't be reading Classics instead of English! I didn't have the courage to tell him the truth! Unfortunately Gus had a very sad ending. When I returned to England after five years in South Africa I heard that he was in a hospital for people with mental sicknesses and so I went to see him. I was appalled to see this erudite man surrounded by others who looked, walked and sat, as though they had been sick for many a year. We sat outside on a pleasant autumn day and chatted about what I had been up to. I couldn't detect any change in him except for some long pauses. He was dressed much as he had always been with a safety-pin holding up his trousers and a yellow waistcoat just that bit too small for his bulging tummy. Then suddenly in the middle of a conversation he said 'Can you hear the Church bells?' I couldn't of course. Then he added 'We had better be careful what we say because Canon Brown is hiding behind the hedge.' I felt so sad for this scholarly man whose hard work had helped me win a place at University. One of my old school pals had become a Doctor and I went to see him saying that I thought Gus had little chance of recovering, surrounded as he was, and wasn't there some alternative for him from being herded with others in a vast ward. In those days there wasn't but thankfully later ideas changed this method of care. I'm sure Gus would have managed better in some 'half-way house' but the changes came too late for him and he died a lonely man. Towards the end of his career Gus had become close friends with the Latin Master, Mr. Ives, known to us as 'Snoopy'. This was, as far as I know, before the advent of the famous cartoon character! 'Snoopy' had suffered a very unfortunate accident on a motor bike at some stage and was bent almost double with his chin touching his chest. He had to swing his whole body to look upwards or around. He was another kind man and a diligent Teacher. He had favourites of whom I became one and he had this rather embarrassing habit of putting his arm around your shoulder whilst marking your exercise book and giving you a little squeeze before moving on down the row. But it never went any further than that little squeeze. He was a very keen photographer and liked to take photographs of the boys at Athletics events (this may have been connected with his fondness of squeezing but no-one ever commented on it as such!). As I was keen on Sport I was given a number of photographs of my efforts at high and long jumping and including one of me winning the cross-country, which I still have today. As far as I can remember he was the only person to talk seriously with me about my future. He suggested that I should aim at becoming a Sports or English Teacher and that Loughborough College offered excellent opportunities to train in both. This was in fact what I had set my heart on from about the age of 14 years. He was also very patient with my faltering efforts at Latin. After failing Latin 'A' Level I had to return for a third year in the Sixth Form and retake it. Half-way through the year there was a mock examination and my mark was 4%! He sent a polite letter to my parents saying that although 'Paul works hard he doesn't seem to have a brain for Latin'. That was when it was decided that I should have extra tuition for two hours a week. When the 'A' Level results came out we were all biting our nails. The pass mark was 33% and I had got 36%. Another little miracle!

As mentioned earlier Gus and 'Snoopy' became good friends and sometimes went together to Winchester Cathedral for Choral Evensong. At some point Mr. Ives bought a house in Sheet just down the hill from the school. This must have provided a haven for Mr. Kershaw away from the noise surrounding his tiny bed-sitter full of books in the school. Gus was also President of the School Debating Society and every so often a debate would be held with the senior boys taking turns to try out their skill at public speaking. These evening sessions were held in the Library after Prep and were open to anyone who wished to attend. This gave some verisimilitude to what was going on and we would clap or occasionally 'boo' the speakers. This kind of thing interested me as I progressed through the school and eventually I became Chairman and it was then that someone suggested we set up and run a trial. The idea was that someone would steal the Detention book in which was recorded every misdemeanor and the name of the culprit. The deed was arranged between Gus and someone else and I was to be the Prosecution Lawyer. There were a number of suspects whom I was to question, also bringing in any witnesses I chose. Naughtily I hit on a cunning plan! I arranged for someone else to steal the book first and then built a case to prove that the person I suspected had originally been chosen for the deed had in fact stolen it after all! When Gus, as the Judge, gave his verdict he found this poor lad guilty. Of course Gus was not at all pleased when he realised he had been double-crossed. I also found it frightening that such a miscarriage of justice could take place if the argument was put across strongly and passionately enough and there were false witnesses who were prepared to perjure themselves.

One other member of Staff who loomed large on the screen was 'Charlie'. He was the French Master and not at all enthusiastic about his subject. He would arrive late for lessons and had no sense of discipline being far too kind to ever want to punish anyone. The only thing I can remember about 'Charlie' is his writing on the board 'Charlie is my Darling' and then tracing this phrase through Latin, French and German to prove the point! I also failed French at 'A' Level! However Charlie was deeply committed to the Cadet Force and had, at 19 years of age, been the youngest Colonel in the First World War. He had been Gassed. Once a week the C.C.F. (as it was called) would parade and Charlie could be seen marching behind his troops with the school band in the front. This was usually to practice for 'Founders Day' when the whole school would march into Petersfield for Service at the Parish Church. A special Preacher would be invited for the occasion and one year we had the Bishop of Oxford who had himself been a pupil at Churchers for just one year. Otherwise the Corps would be practicing for the great day of 'Inspection' held once a year. For this some of Charlie's old cronies would come from Aldershot or Bordon and be regaled with plenty of booze over lunch prior to the afternoon parade. One year the Inspector was Sgt. Major Brittain who became famous for his loud voice in one of the 'Carry On' films. More will be said about a certain parade later but for now mention must be made of Charlie's wife. She was as stout as he was thin and she felt sorry for the starving boarders. It was probably her suggestion that her merry husband get together with three senior boys and play bridge once a week in the little office that was his Corps. H.Q. The time came for me to join this elite band. What we really looked forward to was the excellent apple pie that Mrs. Charles provided each week plus the odd glass or two of 'The Major's' gin! It was my first experience of real grief when Mrs. Charles died suddenly – probably of a heart attack. The whole school turned out for her funeral and the silence of those 400 boys was awesome. The Major battled on.

In my last year I was chosen to be Head Boy and just before this happened Charlie came to see me. He said that it had been suggested that I be considered for this position and that the Staff would be deciding at the end of Term. He said he would be delighted to vote for me as he was the House Master for Drake House, the one I belonged to, but he couldn't in all conscience vote for someone who was not a member of the Army Cadet Corps. What a bribe! For reasons I never quite understood I had declined to join the A.C.C. Probably because of my rebellious nature, or because I was a loner, or probably just my desire to avoid hard work – like the Assault Courses! Anyway his slyness at getting a new recruit was matched by my duplicity at wanting to be Head Boy – whatever the cost! So I joined up at once and within three weeks was made a Sergeant! We all knew Charlie to be a likeable rogue.

Once the Rugby team had a match near London and it was decided that after the match we would 'hit the town'. Charlie was the Master accompanying us that day and some of us decided to go to the Windmill Theatre where the models paraded nude. As we queued for entrance we noticed a familiar figure joining the back of the queue. It was the Major himself! We both pretended not to notice each other. I last met him when he was taken into hospital in Midhurst with T.B. He was so pleased to see me and expressed his joy when I told him I had decided to be ordained. 'By Jove' he said 'I'm sure you'll be a Bishop by the time you reach 50'! It was typical of his generous heart and commitment to his pupils, and perhaps also to his lack of judgement! He always aimed to please and often did. I don't think he left the hospital alive.

There was one Master I could never get on with. He was nick-named 'Tut' because if someone made a mistake in class he would say this word with such sarcasm. He walked mincingly and had a light almost effeminate voice. You can guess what we also called him! In actual fact there was no evidence in support of what we thought about him but he did entertain some of the senior boys to tea in his little flat – and always in twos or threes. It was common knowledge however that he liked to have his feet scratched! . He was very popular with many of the boys but he never seemed to like me and made this very obvious with his sharp tongue.

The second Master I had a problem with was the one who was the Boarding Master for Mount House. He taught Maths and was very strict and once caned me so hard it was sore for days. He also was very angry with me when he discovered a notebook which I had found lying about and had commandeered for my private cricket game. It was based on a code. All the letters of the alphabet had an equivalent number, the most common being '0' up to the 'q's' and 'z's' equaling '6'. One or two letters meant 'out'. I drew a score card on the page and had a match, usually between England and Australia, or two County sides if I knew their names. Hours were spent on this idle pastime and the purloined notebook was probably full when discovered on a window-sill by Mr. Cottle. 'I bet this is your work, Duffett' he shouted. 'It's a disgrace and I've a good mind to cane you. What have you to say?' I was terrified and can't remember how I attempted to defend myself. Anyway he pocketed the book and stalked off. He probably showed it to the others in the Staff Room.

Another Master who was tough on discipline was the Science Master, known as 'Stinks' of course. He was short in stature and had a loud voice. One day we were told that his only daughter, aged about eight years, had died of Meningitis. There was a real sense of grief throughout the school that day. They later adopted a boy who became a friend of my brother Chris in later years. He never seemed able to settle to much and eventually made a name for himself by flying out of the country to Cyprus.

The Headmaster never quite won the respect of the boys. I suppose this was mainly because his only interest in Sport was an academic one. The previous Headmaster would often be seen taking a cricket ball at practice and complete with suit and gown readily bowl a few at the batsman. But Schofield didn't really know one end of a cricket bat from another. He also had an unfortunate voice! Father once told me that he had spoken with the Curate at Sheet Church, a man called Slack whom Father called 'Slack by name and Slack by nature', and this Curate had said that Schofield would have made a good Headmaster for a girls' school! This probably affected my judgement thereafter! However being an academic he did a lot to improve the school standard and was a good administrator. He was also a good man with a fine family. When he retired he played the organ in his Parish Church until the day he died. He and I had one big row but more of that later.

The Staff totaled about 50 in number. There was 'Wally' the Polish Woodwork Master and 'Holy Joe' who taught Divinity. He was a Plymouth Brethren and somewhat scorned by the majority of the Staff and was much teased in class. For some reason I used to stand up for him, maybe there was something about being on the side of the 'under-dog'. When he offered a prize to the sixth form for a Christian essay I went in for it and was delighted to learn that I had won. My elation was short lived as I discovered I was the only entrant! There were a few ladies on the Staff and they were much respected. Most were 'jobbing'

Teachers who got on with their work making the minimum of fuss, went home at the end of the day and came back the next morning.

Sport was very important to me and I discovered that I could run across country faster than most. I'm sure my height – I was 5'6" at 12 years old – had something to do with it. To maintain a standard required practicing two or three times a week and I think it was my way of dealing with stress and loneliness. Certainly out there among the hills of Hampshire one experienced the beauty of nature and the thrill of being able to win the four or seven mile races through mud and rivers, over the stiles and up one very steep hill! Then there was my passion for cricket. I played for the school at every level from 'Junior Colts' to the First Eleven and in my last year was Captain of a team which was beaten only once in the season. In fact I was one of the youngest ever to play for the First Team, being 15 at the time. Then I hit a low patch however and scored 0 and 1 in successive matches. The next match was with 'The Old Boys' and I was dropped. It was also the weekend before the 'O' Level exams started on the Monday. I sat at the lunch table disconsolate and unable to eat. I left before the pudding and went out to the field, sat down and cried my heart out. It must have worried the Head because when someone told him he telephoned my parents who promptly came up to the school and then he asked the Team Captain to play 12 a side so that I could get a game. What a spoilt brat! I think I scored only one.

We were the first group to take the new 'O' Level exams and again I think we were privileged. I managed to get an average of 60% in 10 subjects, including Latin! The decision was that I should take English, French, History and Latin at 'A' Level.

The school holidays continued to be full of fun and with Tessa removed by her mother and Patsy disappearing from the scene too, I spent more and more time with the Hawkeys. We enjoyed dressing up in different clothes from their attic and there was always football and cricket on the back lawn. Roger recalls that we went to Fratton Park to see Portsmouth play sometimes – I was actually there in 1949 with 50,000 others when they won the Premiership! When we came home from these matches we would copy the goals which were scored that day. Once Father and my brother-in-law, Chris, came over and joined us for cricket. I remember this because Father hit my bowling for six and I lost my temper and bowled him a bouncer!

When the girls were free we also played together and Jo was the first girl I kissed. On one day we used the head of a Bison, which had somehow found its way into the attic, to frighten passers-by. We put it on a stick and raised it above the hedge making suitable accompanying noises! We also used the trick of leaving a package on the path outside for passers-by to pick up. Inside would be nothing but rubbish! Once I was showing off again and jumped from the top of a stepladder breaking my arm which necessitated a visit to the local hospital for a plaster.

There would always be a cup of tea and some cake from their mother, Daisy, and sometimes the sun would be going down before I returned home. One evening I had either stayed longer or gone back after tea for some reason or another and the time passed. I remember only Christine being there and by that time I was impressed by her intelligence as well as her pretty face. So time had passed without us noticing the clock when suddenly there was a knock on the front door. Christine answered it and came back very red-faced. It was Mother, without teeth and complete with night-cap. 'Do you know what time it is young man?' she asked crossly. It was 11.30pm and I tried to look penitent as I left immediately with my tail between my legs.

1947 was the year of the big freeze with snow and ice from Christmas through to the end of February. I joined many others in the school by getting Chicken-pox. There was a pleasant Sick Room and there I stayed until Father came in his Austin 16 to pick me up. The roads were deserted and the climb up Butser Hill was something of a feat. Nature looked permanently frozen with the trees shimmering in the white light of the winter sun.

Also in 1947 I was Confirmed. I think I had asked Mother about this and she had said she didn't see why not. There were about twenty of us more or less the same age and we had to meet up after the day's lessons were over and be lectured to by the local Curate. I can't remember one thing he told us! He was a nice young man but had the unfortunate habit of saying 'er' after every few words in his sermons. On one day we counted 60 of them and I don't think we were very attentive to his lessons. It was part of the culture of those times though so we just put up with it. The Confirmation Service however was something else. There was a reverent atmosphere with parents packing the little church. The Bishop was younger than expected and had been a Naval Chaplain during the war winning the respect of the soldiers on board the 'Queen Mary' which had been commandeered as a Troop Ship and had docked in New York over Christmas. He had been born into a well-educated Scottish family and had served as a Chaplain to Trinity Hall, Cambridge. He had also won respect as an Explorer when he went to the North Pole in 1937 with, amongst others, Augustine Courthold. He had been the Chairman of the Church of England Youth Council and had become a Bishop at the age of 41 years. He was a good and holy man. One phrase of his sermon stayed with me – 'The Christian life consists in practicing the presence of God'. The laying on of hands with the words ' Defend O Lord, this Thy child with Thy heavenly grace' seemed very solemn and beautiful. I found it all very moving but would have struggled to express this in words at that time. Mother said many years later that she knew then that I would end up as a Priest. It was tradition that following your Confirmation you could attend the Holy Communion service at 8a.m. once a month. Most of the boys wouldn't bother as this meant getting up half-an-hour earlier than usual but for some reason I always did. Whether it was conformism or because I enjoyed the service, or just the challenge of doing something different I really don't know. The kindly Bishop came just once more to preach to the Boarders and I was very impressed that he remembered my name saying 'Hello Paul' as we left the Church. It gave me a real thrill that the Bishop had taken the trouble to learn MY name! It didn't occur to me that as he was standing next to the Priest he could have been told any of our names.

The big event of 1948 was the wedding of my third sister Coral to Chris Tulitt, who had recently qualified as an Architect. Coral had studied at the College of Art in Portsmouth and they met there. So for a third time we all assembled in All Saints Church and at the Pub in the village. Memories of it are hazy, except for the unfortunate occurrence of the trick played by Chris's friends on him. They spiked his drinks, which resulted in a much shortened Bridegroom's speech! For a while they lived in our Drawing Room. It must have been very hard for them.

My growing awareness of the deeper questions of life came together with the opening vistas of English Literature, Shakespeare first. The class readings we did were allowed to get as dramatic as possible and afterwards we were asked to comment on them. The loneliness and prevarication of Hamlet, the self-awareness of Richard the 2nd, the cruel cynicism of Richard the 3rd, the patriotism of Henry the 5th, or the ambition of Macbeth and so on. The characters began to come alive and the magnificent language took a hold on my imagination. It confirmed the truth uttered by Horatio to Hamlet that…..'there are more things in heaven and earth than are thought of in your philosophy'. Then we studied Milton and the Romantics for 'A' Level. Whatever one thinks of Milton as a Theologian there is no doubt that he is amongst the greatest of Christian poets. The gigantic sweep of 'Paradise Lost' or 'Samson Agonistes' and the artistry of his crafted sonnets fires the mind. Perhaps amongst the Romantics it was Blake who intrigued me the most. His fertile mind and imagination made for a sense that he was knocking on the door of infinity. He had a mission to get people to believe that they could know God through their imaginations. It was exciting stuff and I drank at the river of these delights. When revising for the 'A' Levels I would sit on the school fields reading for hours, completely carried away. I found myself becoming a pantheist like Wordsworth. 'The Prelude' were my Hymn and Theology! 'The unfettered clouds and regions of the heavens, Tumult and peace, the darkness and the light, Were all like the workings of one mind, the features, Of the same face, blossoms on one tree, Characters of the great Apocalypse, the types and symbols of Eternity, Of first and last, and midst and without end.'

This was accompanied by my love of nature, running and walking – and my first love affair. I suppose I had thought of Christine as my girlfriend for some time. We had shyly attended the Portsmouth High School end of year dance and shuffled around the floor a few times but we were both too shy to start a physical relationship. I admired her greatly as a friend and she seemed to trust as well as like me and there it rested. Then I was invited to attend a performance at Petersfield Town Hall of 'Tobias and the Angel'. There I saw Elisabeth Alexander - an angel acting! She was the Head Girl of Petersfield High School and as I was the Head Boy of Churcher's it seemed only right that we should get together. I can't recall how it happened but before long we were head over heels in love. This involved visiting her at her home at the foot of Butser Hill and going for long walks both by day and night, the sun and moon alike adding to the romance. Somehow I procured a book on sex by Dr. Kinsey and read it avidly, mostly on top of the bus going home as I was now a Day Boy for my last year! This reading encouraged a certain amount of 'experimentation' although this was very innocent at that stage. Still we learnt to kiss and seemed hardly capable of doing much else when we were together - even sitting at the back of the top deck of the bus on the way home from the cinema. She was a lovely person and our relationship lasted into my first year at College. In fact it produced one strange occurrence of precognition. One day I felt sure that she had come to Oxford and I had merely to go into the city to meet up with her. I did this and we did meet up! There had been no arrangement made between us in advance! I was invited to the 'End of Year Ball' at Goldsmith's college where she was training to be a Teacher and at this Ball she was invited to dance by a man some four years older than I. The problem was that he could dance and I couldn't…….and soon after that Elisabeth and I stopped seeing one another! It was the end of my world for about a month. I remember overhearing Reverend Bill Rees at Blendworth speaking to Mother and saying 'how lovely first love is. Such a pity it always has to end.'. My depression at that time was full of hopelessness.

Some time before all this happened there was another strand of my life emerging, It must have been in 1947 that it began because that was when my Godfather went for a swim in Alexandra Bay and drowned. Just before this tragic event a letter arrived from him asking me about myself and how I was getting on. I recall that I wrote to him and mentioned that I had started reading the Bible, a passage at a time before falling asleep at night. Whether this was because he had asked the question or not is not clear in my memory but he did write back to say he was pleased that this was so.

Soon after that I began to get up on a Sunday morning during the school holidays and walk the two miles to Blendworth Church for the 8a.m.Holy Communion. It made me feel so good! This was when I began to admire the Vicar – a young Welshman called Bill Rees. I particularly liked the way he said the Prayer of 'Humble Access' – the Prayer just before Communion. It may have had something to do with his Welsh accent! Soon afterwards he asked me to join the Youth Group meeting once a week in the village hall and it wasn't long before I was elected as the Leader. Not that I recall doing much! What does come to mind is that another member, who also sang in the choir was Charmione May – she later went to Drama School and appeared on television. It was probably because of this involvement that the following happened.

One day Mother asked me what I would do if I failed to get a scholarship to University as there was no money available to pay even the smallest of the fees. I thought for a bit and then said 'I think I might like to be a Parson'. She was surprised but I think secretly delighted as 'The Church' had status and social importance! So she replied 'Let me phone the Vicar' who then arranged to see me. It was early days he thought but if this was to be then it would work out so. He suggested that I see the Bishop for an initial interview. Consequently it was arranged for me to spend a weekend at Bishopsthorpe, the official residence in Fareham. I arrived there off the bus with my little suitcase very nervous and shy. The first thing to happen was that the Bishop and I were to say Evening Prayer together in his private chapel. Fortunately there was an understanding Chaplain because I didn't know my way around the Prayer Book and had to be helped. I had arrived about 5p.m.and supper was after the Prayers. Other visitors began to arrive. When I got to the dining room I was met by two gentlemen who turned out to have accompanied the Bishop on one of his Polar Expeditions. One had been Captain of the ship and the other was no less than Augustine Courthold, the silk stocking magnate, who had distinguished himself by staying alone in an igloo for a record length of time. The conversation was mostly beyond my ken! However at one point Courthold drew me into the conversation saying that he understood I intended to be ordained. He then proceeded to warn me against it by saying he had a son who was a Priest and that in his opinion he was over-worked and under-paid! The Bishop said nothing only chuckling in a way that was characteristic of him. Nothing more was said on the subject.

The next morning being a Sunday, breakfast had to be early as the Bishop was off somewhere. Beforehand he invited me to walk with him in the garden. He said that he understood that it was early days yet and asked me about my immediate future. I was able to say that I had by then obtained a place at Keble College. He advised me to postpone this and do my two years National Service first because it would probably take me two years to decide whether I had a vocation in the Church or not. He also said that he would like me to go into an Infantry Regiment so my calling could be tested! I knew at once that I could not give up my Oxford place being far too insecure to relinquish it even temporarily. However I did feel that something important had taken place and that the Bishop's interest in me was entirely personal and without any bureaucratic hoops.

The next event has always left me with an ambiguous feeling. The school sports had taken place and I had successfully broken the half-mile record but the mile event had been postponed for two weeks. As the exams were over this meant there was plenty of time to practice. The mile was five laps of the grass field and the record was 4 minutes 52 seconds and I thought I could better that. John Veitch was my closest rival and the competition between us was tense. On the day of the competition we were suddenly told there was to be a dress rehearsal for the coming inspection of the Cadet Corps. This would take place at 11a.m. and the race was to be run at 12 noon. It was a hot July day and those of us competing in the race felt it was unfair to expect us to stand in the hot sun for an hour just before running the mile. There was also added pressure as the winning of the School Cup would to be decided on the outcome of this race – if I won, Drake House won the cup, if John won Rodney House would win the cup by a couple of points. John and I decided to go and see the Headmaster and ask if the day's programme could be changed. The Headmaster called the Sports Master in and the problem was discussed but he was adamant that no alteration could be allowed. Colonel Charles was then consulted but he was of the same opinion. We remained firm in our claim that it was unfair to hold both events on the same day let alone the same morning so we left the meeting angry and disappointed.

Perhaps it is worth mentioning at this point that I was coming up to my nineteenth birthday and some weeks before I had been spoken roughly to by a Bus Conductor. I had responded by telling him that he wouldn't have spoken to me in that way if I hadn't been wearing a cap and I threatened to take his number and report him!

So following the above mentioned meeting we were left as two 'angry young men'! After the dress rehearsal for the Corps inspection we went into the changing room still angry at being made to run under these circumstances. The blood must have rushed to my head and I suggested to John a plan that could wreck the race if we joined hands so all four House representatives finished the race at the same time. This plan was enthusiastically agreed and you can imagine the scene with the whole school assembled to watch the race. The Staff were enraged, the Prefects went on strike and John and I were summoned to appear before the Headmaster who, white with anger, dismissed us on the spot! After lunch I told the gathered assembly what had happened. There was pandemonium! John and I left but I heard later that the boys were herded out of the school building onto the Sports field in case they started damaging the building and its contents. We now had to think what to do next. Father was an acquaintance of Mr. Gammon, Chairman of the Governors, and I knew where he lived as one of his sons had been a friend of mine when he attended the school for a couple of years. I suggested to John that we go to see him. He lived by Petersfield Lake about ten minutes walk away. Fortunately he was at home and looked very surprised to see us. When we had explained he left the room and made a telephone call to the Headmaster. When he returned he told us that he would ensure we were given a just hearing of our case so we thanked him and left. I think that visit saved our day because the Headmaster was taken aback to realise we were prepared to go on fighting our cause. Coming home I found dear Mother in a state of great anxiety. What had been going on? The Headmaster had telephoned her to explain what hadn't happened and she in turn had phoned Bill Rees, the Vicar, for advice. He suggested that I go to see

Sixth Form Valedictory Luncheon 31st July 1952 outside the Red Lion Hotel in Petersfield
Left to right: Neville Hill, Neil Tidmus, John Vetch, Peter Randall, Kenneth Shipman, Paul Duffet, Raymond Corkell, David ????, John Nixon, C Townsend and Peter Symonds.

him. I gladly agreed as I was beginning to wonder what the future would now hold for me. So for the second time in six months I found myself in the Vicar's study! He was very wise and said 'You have shown the courage of your convictions. Now if you really want to be brave the manly thing would be for you to apologise for taking the law into your own hands and causing so much disruption to the school.' I was ready to do almost anything to get back into school and put the whole sorry incident behind me. The message was relayed to the Headmaster by Mother and he agreed as long as my apology was made publicly at Assembly. The next morning found me nervous but determined. I can't remember exactly what I said but I do remember feeling embarrassed and sheepish as I stood before the whole school. Everyone was relieved and I was re-instated as the Head Boy for the remaining three weeks of term.

And so the nine years of being a Boarder and the one year as a Day Boy ended on a sweet and sour note and it became clear later to me that I had invested most of my energies during those years in the school and it had been for me a home and a family. Even now I have a residue of deep attachment for the place – something of me has remained there. Probably becoming a big fish in a small pond had gone to my head and done me no good but without those experiences there is no knowing where I would have ended up! It certainly formed in me some good and permanent ways, some of which were to find their fulfillment in the next phase of my life.

My last day was typical of the 'too big for your boots' syndrome that I had acquired! I arranged for our sixth form group to have a farewell lunch at the 'Red Lion Hotel' in Petersfield and before we went to our lunch four of us knocked on the front door of the Girls High School. It was opened by a gasping Headmistress and when we asked if the girls could come out to play she slammed the door in our faces! It was time for us to leave Secondary Education!

CHAPTER 4

THE SUBLIME AND .....

The summer of 1952 included a sixth form conference organised by the Bishop of Portsmouth at Canford School set in its beautiful surroundings of Dorset. It was even more beautiful than Churchers with a building like a manor house and lawns with great oaks and elms flowing away from the building into the distance. There were about 100 of us there and the Staff was made up of junior Clergy (most of them sporty) from the Diocese. One of the Lecturers was the retired Vice-Chancellor of Cambridge University, Canon Charles Raven. It was Bill the Vicar's idea that I should go and it was at very little cost. Charles Raven was just the man for such a gathering. He loved students and had a vast experience of them. He was a Physicist by profession and had written several books on the subject of Science and Religion. He had also been instrumental in the founding of the 'Workers Educational Association' and was a dedicated Socialist, so much so, that it was said of him that he would have made an outstanding Archbishop of Canterbury but that no Prime Minister would appoint him! He was also a well known Pacifist and had the largest private collection of insects in the world. He could talk about them for two hours without a note! Undoubtedly he was a great Preacher, also without a note, and to this day I have never met anyone to match his command of the English language. He had a beautiful voice and a commanding presence and whenever I heard him I felt I was listening to pure poetry such was the craft and skill he displayed. You can believe how he had these 19 year-olds eating out of the palm of his hand! Somebody had persuaded Elisabeth to go as well and although we slept in different dormitories and in different buildings this didn't prevent long, late walks under the harvest moon. The nights were balmy and there was no 'policing' of the school because as far as I know there was no need to. We were all in bed by midnight partly because we were up for Chapel at 8a.m. and kept busy until 9.30 at night. After supper there was a Barn dance in the school hall and we were taught Scottish reels (the Bishop being a keen participator) as well as the Virginia Reel and the Gay Gordons. It was all great fun and mostly innocent. Canon Raven was something of a mystic having seen the glory of God in a fish and chip van in Liverpool! He was also Liberal in his theological views – he was President of the 'Modern Churchmens' Union' but in those days I didn't understand about such things. His sermons on the 'Cosmic Christ' blew my mind and I can still feel the excitement with which they left me! On the Friday we all returned home tired and weary but ready to revive the local Church, only to find of course that no-one was really interested! One other thing I did that summer during the long holiday before University began was to go with some Teachers and boys from an East-End school for their first look at the sea at Southend. How this job came my way is lost in the mists of time but I do remember there was an interview for it. It was fun and my job mainly consisted of sitting with these 25 ten and eleven year old boys in the evenings whilst the Teachers went to the local pub. The Teachers also invited me to join in their fun and one thing looms large! One of the younger female Teachers invited me to go for a swim one night and I thought this was quite an innocent thing to do so I was surprised the next day to overhear one of the male Teachers telling her off for doing it.

Which reminds me of another incident a year earlier. This would not have been remembered but for something Father said later. It was discovered that I had something called a 'rumbling appendix' and was not allowed to play cricket until it had been seen to. Fortunately there was an eminent Surgeon living in Petersfield who was prepared to perform minor operations on a Saturday. It was arranged therefore that I should have 'the grumbler' removed. This was duly done and I was enjoying my convalescence when one night I was awakened by a young Nurse who said that she was alone on duty and felt lonely. I read nothing into this and we chatted for about an hour and then she left and I went back to sleep. I later heard Father comment to a friend of his about the operation and then say 'One night he was awakened by a Nurse who said she was lonely. They chatted for an hour or so. There must be something wrong with the boy!' It was only then that I realised things could have been different. I consoled myself with the thought that this was quite alright because I was in love with Elisabeth anyway!

A more intellectual pursuit was when I went into Winchester to be interviewed for a 'County Scholarship'. This entailed sitting in front of a group of County Councilors and answering questions. I remember only one of the Councilors. He was a Mr. Lubbock, the Chairman, and he lived in a big house in Sheet. I remember him because he had been to a Speech Day at the College to give away the prizes. Again I was blessed to be one of the lucky ones and was awarded a scholarship worth £590 a year (about £5000 now). This was for books, clothes and other 'necessary expenses'! All the tuition and accomodation was paid for by the State. It was time to open a Bank Account and I bought a new blazer and had the Keble College badge sown on to it!

The Oxford term started on my birthday, October 3rd. but 'Freshmen' were expected to be there three days before to 'settle in'. I went up by coach carrying my over-size suitcase. It is quite a walk from the bus station to Keble which is almost at the end of the city and I arrived sweating and a bit bemused. The College dates from 1874 and was built in red-white and blue brick in true Victorian style. It is said that Ruskin, the eminent Art Critic, was so disgusted with it that he gave up his daily walks in the Park opposite. There still exists, I believe, a society of which the qualification for entry is simply to show that you have taken an original brick from Keble's structure! It was a revolutionary College in both style and practice. Built as a memorial to the great churchman and poet it was the first College to have an egalitarian ideal. All the rooms were built to be the same size so the costs could also be met by the poorer students. The Chapel is the most amazing piece of Italianate Victoriana in existence and is in essence the Cathedral of the High Church Oxford Movement. It replaced a much smaller and more ordinary building which in its turn gave way to an enormous Library. The Oxford Movement, which changed the character of the Church of England for ever, really began as a protest against the Government interfering in the Church's right to decide its own future. Its inauguration by John Keble was a sermon delivered at the University Church of St. Mary's in 1844. In the little Lady Chapel of the Keble Chapel where there was a daily Holy Communion Service hangs the original painting of 'The Light of The World' by Holman Hunt. He painted another for St. Paul's Cathedral when he heard that people were being charged to see the original. There is no charge today! In my day it was threepence!

I was shown to a room in the Chapel Block on the first floor overlooking the road and opposite a house used as offices. There was an open fireplace in which a College

Servant, called a 'Scout', had prepared a fire. The ablutions were along the corridor and my little bedroom had a wash stand on which stood a large jug filled, I discovered the next morning, with hot water by Bill when he arrived at about 8.30 a.m.knocking on the door to awaken me. The Dining Hall is the largest in Oxford with a massive top table on a dias and long Refectory tables to seat the 400+ students. Meals were served by the College Scouts and one never had to fetch anything for oneself! At all meals one had to wear the College gown which was a short black affair put on over a coat or pullover. 'Scholars' and 'Exhibitioners' wore long gowns. This gown had to be worn to all lectures and tutorials and whenever one was in town at night. Reading English meant that I was assigned to a Mr. Rice-Oxley and that turned out to be a great disappointment! He had a sinecure and knew it. He was laziness personified. On one occasion he fell asleep during a tutorial whilst I droned on reading an essay, easy to do no doubt but very unprofessional. He had hardly any comments to make on his students' work. Each student in the group felt the same about him, furious and sick at the same time! It wouldn't happen now. Our year group was made up of five very different blokes. There was Jeremy, the 'Exhibitioner', who had been to Portsmouth Grammar School. He was clever but also rather lazy with a laid back charm which would melt anybody. David Judge was the joker in the pack who often had us in stitches. He had a slight contempt for almost everything. John Batstone was a hard worker and a good medium fast bowler soon finding his way into the first cricket eleven. David Stevens was a kind gentlemanly type who also eventually decided to be ordained. He also played for the Keble first cricket team. I played a few times but never scored more than single figures. They had all done their National Service and so I was given the nickname of 'Junior'. My first impression was of a very free and diverse society.

There must have been nearly 100 cards or flyers on my table when I arrived advertising everything and inviting one to become a member of 'The Shooting Club' or 'The Socratic Society' or whatever. It was all rather daunting and I didn't venture into any of them except 'The Freshers Squash' put on by the University's Christian Union and the Drama and the Athletic Clubs. The College Chaplain invited me to a pub lunch but he was such a shy man that this was very embarrassing. Still there were plenty of friendly chaps around. One of my first invitations was to dinner at Wycliffe Hall, the Theological College down the road. Bill, the kindly Vicar from Blendworth had written to the Principal of his old College telling him of my arrival at the red-brick monstrosity about half-a-mile away and Professor Thornton Dewsbuury sent me a note explaining he would meet me at the main door at 7p.m.on the agreed day. I had no idea who he was at that time and only discovered later that he had been a founder member of 'The Oxford Group' later to be renamed 'Moral Rearmament'. Sitting on the other side of me at dinner was Cyril Tucker, the Chaplain of Wadham College. He soon discovered my interest in athletics and offered to train me for the half mile. I learned later that he had won a Blue for this event!

We met our Tutors. There was some doubt about who would teach Anglo-Saxon as it was a requirement at Oxford then that students reading for the 'Honours' English Degree also learn about the history of the language and sample some of its ancient texts. We therefore had to study 1000 lines of Beowulf, the first recorded epic poem in 'English' Literature. Its language was quite unrecognisable, being a kind of mixture of Scandinavian and Germanic dialects. So for us it was like learning a new language!

It was eventually decided that we would be tutored by the son of Professor Tolkein - who later became famous with the publication of 'The Hobbit' and was responsible for lecturing on Middle English texts like 'Sir Garwaine and the Green Knight'. His son was charming if a little effete! We were rather ordinary chaps and he seemed to think we were not quite up to scratch. Things went quite well for a time until one night at about 7p.m.on a dark November day we were ushered into his little flat by a sepulchral voice and found him stretched out on a sofa with a wet cloth covering his brow. He was obviously under the weather and his voice sounded strained. We sat quietly down to begin translating our set texts. None of us had done much work. The atmosphere became more and more tense until at last he put down his book and in an almost pained way said 'Go away, you are getting into my hair!' Our exit was prompt, almost like a stampede down the stone and twisting staircase. We never returned there!

The next term we were told that a Mr. Miller would be our guide into the mysteries of Anglo-Saxon. He lived a little way up the road which meant about a ten minute walk. He was a gentle and kind man but something of an eccentric and open to teasing by cocky undergraduates. He took it well but sometimes it became a little embarrassing.

I wasn't surprised when the following term we were again assigned someone else! The only problem was that we were horribly behind with this part of our syllabus. My fellow students were scandalised when they heard that our new Tutor was a Miss. Cramp! Firstly she was a woman and secondly we would have to attend her lessons at the Ladies College across the road from us, St. Annes. A revolt was in the offing as we turned up one day at the College and were ushered into an enormous sitting room. The appointed time passed and there was rebellious talk. Then the door opened at the far end of the room and a sweet looking lady about the same age as my senior colleagues put her head nervously through the crack. 'Are you waiting for Miss. Cramp?' she asked in a charming voice. When we replied in the affirmative she sailed into the room her gown flowing. 'That's good. I am she and I am pleased to meet you.' Our eyes widened and we were lost for speech! She was something of a martinet but mellowed under the quiet teasing meeted out by David and we started to realise that we could do Beowulf after all. We even organised an Anglo-Saxon 'Verb Drive' with cards made out of paper. One term I went up early to complete some work that 'Rosie', as we called her, had given us. On entering the door of the Bodlein Library the first person I saw was John who had had the same idea! In the end we all did well in that exam called A4 – one of the 13 we had to take in our Finals.

One of the outstanding Lecturers of that day was C.S.Lewis, already well known for his broadcasts and his books. His great expertise was Poetry and particularly that of John Milton. His delivery was clear and precise and very easy to take notes from. His lectures on 'Paradise Lost' fired the imagination with desire to delve deeply into Milton's great mind. His lectures were later made into a book. One could hardly fail that exam with such help. Perhaps the greatest Lecturer of all was Maureen Gardiner who made Shakespeare live before our eyes. We had to be acquainted with all his works and specialise on a few of them. Together with Shakespeare we also had to study other Elisabethans. When it came to revision I made sure that I had read through Spencer's Epithalmion twice. If you are aware how long that particular work is you will understand why I trouble to mention this fact, or feat!

Most mornings were taken up with lectures between 9.30 and 12 midday and after lunch it was time for sport or walking. I joined the cross-country Club and two or three afternoons a week I would run, mostly alone, for about seven miles across the lovely meadows towards Woodstock and return, tired and ready to enjoy a hot bath in one of the ancient baths in which one could lie outstretched for as long as one liked. Afterwards it was time for pints of tea and a few cakes. On Saturdays there were matches against other Colleges. Once we went to Cambridge and ran against Peterhouse having a pint by the river before and another after a bite at a pub 'The Blue Boar'.

During the first term of the second year I went in for the Cuppers cross country race between all the Colleges and came 35th out of about 300. Chris Chataway, who was soon to become a world record holder was at the finishing line and said 'Well done' to me as I finished. The next week I found that I was entered for the trials to see whether I could qualify for one of the University teams. I finished last in a tough race at 35th and as they only took 28 for the three teams that was that for me. Also in the second and third years I was Secretary for the College Club and organised matches, one of which was against Churchers. We won because one of our best runners came with us but I was beaten into second place by the reigning school champion. Towards the end of the year I was told that I had been awarded a 'Tortoise Tie'. This was the University cross-country Club tie and a great honour for me at that time. I wore it so often that I wore it out within a few years!

The walking and talking was mostly done with Owen Whitney and thereby hangs a tale! I first met Owen sitting opposite me at the lunch table. He rudely interrupted me when I said something about the Church or Christian faith by saying something like 'That's a load of old rubbish'! This sparked off a discussion which continued over coffee in his room afterwards then followed by a walk out into the countryside. He was educated at Midhurst Grammar School and the Headmaster was a prominent Historian and a paid up member of the Communist Party. He seemed to have been pretty good at imparting his ideology to his students. Owen had an old school friend at Balliol, a scholar, who was also a member of the Communist Party.

The 'Establishment' in all its forms was therefore distinctly unpopular with Owen. The Politicians and Church Leaders of the time were to be ridiculed, the world wars were the plans of 'Capitalists and Fascists' and Wilfred Owen was the Saint of the abused Soldiers! Another side to Owen was his passion for music especially Mahler and his 'Song of the Earth' was played most mornings as a kind of ritual. But Owen made me think and for a time tore my faith to shreds. I spent six months as a reluctant atheist and stopped attending Chapel and Church services. In fact I recall one particular moment during a vacation. There was a Teacher at the school across the road from home in Sheet called 'Broadlands' where I was given a temporary job as a Student Teacher. One of the other Teachers invited me to go for a drink in his flat situated in a very large house on the edge of the village. We sat and talked the time away and both concluded that God did not exist. As I walked home the clock on the Church struck midnight and I felt rather like Faust! The most interesting point of this story is that I didn't meet him again for another six years and when I did we were both wearing dog collars and had such a good laugh about it!

So Owen and I became good friends and he was admitted as one of our 'circle'. Not that it was always smooth running! One evening I threw a ' China Tea Party' as I reckoned I couldn't afford Sherry. Owen arrived rather the worse for wear. He behaved reasonably well until he decided to stand on a chair and read from St. John's Gospel which he had spotted on my bookshelf. It caused some laughter and for me a bit of embarrassment but it was harmless fun! He once insisted that I went with him to a meeting of the University Communist Party. I found it very childish. Someone would say something about one of the leading Politicians of the day and everybody else would burst into raucous laughter. It didn't seem quite serious really. He did come with me once to Church actually and afterwards said rather sadly 'You will never be satisfied until you become a Clergyman!'

He also occasionally crept off to the leading Roman Catholic Church in the city because he said he loved the music. He had a German girl-friend whom he had met in one of the vacations. She was an au-pair in Midhurst and she came up to Oxford a couple of times when they would spend most of their time entwined in each other's arms! He, like me, had a series of girl-friends and eventually, true to character, he married a Catholic girl who was a niece of T.S.Eliot. I heard from her some years later when she asked if I would give evidence to the effect that Owen was incapable of being faithful in marriage. He had left her for someone else! It was not the first affair he had had and she wanted an annulment. I felt that it would have been disloyal to him to write something like that and also that the Catholic Church was trying to 'have its cake and eat it' by not facing up to the issue of divorce. Perhaps I should have written the letter because when I returned from South Africa in 1979 and enquired about him I discovered that he had committed suicide at the age of 47years, after having got his Secretary pregnant whilst married to somebody else. There was always something depressive about Owen and this had apparently increased a great deal as he had grown older. A sensitive man there was a kind of inevitability about the tragic outcome of his life. Did his old Headmaster have some responsibility for that? Certainly his parents whom I had met once seemed to be very ordinary working people living in a terraced house in one of Midhurst town streets. He did me a great service really by forcing me to think out my faith for myself.

In the summer of 1953 I returned to the sixth form Summer School at Cranford. The first day and a half were really misreable as I tried to distance myself from the lectures and worship but Canon Raven was on his best form and I just couldn't resist his brilliant speaking and enthusiasm for the Faith. At the end of the second day I said my first real prayer for months, 'God you seem to want my attention and I'll give it to you.' Thereafter I was a lot happier in myself. By this time my romance with Elisabeth was off and at this Summer School I met Sylvia from Petersfield. She was planning on becoming a Teacher and had not yet applied for the training. She lived with her parents in the street leading to the station about ten minutes fast walk from our little house in Sheet. The rest of that summer holiday was mostly spent at her home and walking back to my home rather late! She had an Uncle who had just retired as a Priest and as he had never married was living there also. He had spent most of his Ministry in Canada. The term in Oxford began in early October and Sylvia and I wrote to one another but I don't think she visited until the next year when the time for the May Ball came round. Keble had a Ball with Acker Bilk playing (of 'On the Beach' fame). There was also Fish and Chips served in the 'News of the World' paper at 5.0 a.m. I remember my sister Coral and her husband Chris also came. Our relationship was rather intense and suddenly in my final year she ended it. I found this hard and feeling much depressed I went to see her Uncle. He asked if I hadn't noticed that she was feeling trapped. Obviously I hadn't but with this news I just had to accept the break. It was probably just as well as my finals were beginning to loom rather large.

I had been fortunate enough to live in the College for the first two years but for the third year I had to find digs. Mother's bridesmaid, Gladys, who lived in Southsea had remained a friend of the family. She was the widow of my God-father who had tragically drowned in Egypt many years before and she lived with her brother and sister-in-law. She had another brother who had never married and who taught in Headington about three miles from the centre of Oxford. He had bought his own house there, small but detached and with three bedrooms. It was arranged that I should stay there for thirty shillings a week. This included breakfast and a Sunday lunch - he was an excellent cook. But I think I ate most of my lunches and suppers in town probably at the College. We didn't see a great deal of each other as he left early for school and I would get up about 8.30a.m. and make my own breakfast before getting the bus into Oxford. Apart from being rather far out of town it was an excellent arrangement. In fact when it came to the summer term I gave up going in to the University almost entirely, revising for six hours a day, having lunch at the little café around the corner and doing some walking or jogging for exercise.

Before that, the autumn term of 1953 was a momentous one for me. Sitting at my desk one evening there was a knock at the door and in came one of the students whose room was along the corridor from mine. His name was David Simpson and at the time of writing he has just retired from a number of years as the Dean of Canterbury Cathedral. He invited me to attend the University 'Mission' organised by the Evangelical Churches in Oxford. It was being led by a Dr. John Stott who was then in his early '30s and a Curate at the famous London BBC Church, 'All Souls', Langham Place. I was told he had four first class degrees and was a brilliant speaker. So already being interested and at that time still confused about who I was -- and whose I was -- I decided to go. There had been a University 'Mission' the year before put on by the Student Christian Movement with Archbishop Michael Ramsey as the Leader. I had been a couple of times but found him rather difficult to follow and perhaps a bit dry. The 'Mission' services this time were held in St. Aldates Church where John De Berry was the Vicar. The church was packed each night and the addresses full of intelligent, expository preaching with an appeal at the end for people to make a commitment to Jesus Christ. I think it was the second to last night that grabbed me. John spoke about the claims of Jesus as presented in St. John's gospel with special reference to the 'I am' sayings:- I am the bread of life; I am the way, the truth, and the life; and so on. He explained that for him these sayings could only be said by someone who was either true or a megalomaniac and did Jesus' other teachings make him appear mentally deranged? If they are true then they are unique and require a response from human beings. There was no sitting on the fence possible. At the end he asked us to pray a prayer of commitment if we chose to. He began with the verse in the Book of Revelation where Jesus as High Priest is pictured standing outside the door of the Human Life, knocking on the door and asking to come in. He says 'If anyone opens the door I will come in and eat with him and he with me'. The prayer of commitment which John asked us to repeat after him included the invitation to invite Jesus into our lives to live there as our Lord and Saviour. On doing this I knew without doubt that Jesus had accepted my invitation. I had from then onwards a desire to follow and serve him. After the service those of us who made a commitment were given some literature and counsel about the way forward. One piece of advice which has never left me is to spend some time of each day in prayer using the Bible in a 'quiet time'. I started the next morning using the copy of St. John's Gospel given to me the night before, as I did not at that time have a bible of my own with me. That was soon corrected and I also bought a copy of the Inter-Varsity Press Bible Commentary which stayed with me for about thirty years until it was replaced by the revised version which I still have and use. Attendance at St. Aldates every Sunday followed and I was encouraged to join the 'Oxford Pastorate' whose Chaplain at that time was Cyril Tucker who was already known to me. The Pastorate ran Bible Studies at Cyril and Kathleen's home every Sunday afternoon followed by tea, always an attraction to hungry undergraduates! I went there when I could.

I remember one study which fascinated me given by Stella Aldwinkle, a Philosopher, on an ' Ontological approach to God' – far above my head but mind stretching. She also organised a prayer time on Fridays at the Cathedral between 1 and 2 p.m. which she called 'Scars' and this was a time of silent prayer for the re-unification of the Church. I found these times a great blessing and attended regularly with about twenty others.

The next big question was what to do with my life. As already stated the Latin Master at Churchers (Snoopy) had suggested that I teach. He had at first suggested that I should be a Physical Training Teacher going to learn at Loughborough College. This was later revised to being an English Teacher at a Secondary School. At Oxford there was a Department of Education where those with a degree could attend for one year and at the end receive a Certificate for Teaching. I had been to the Department for an initial interview and had been told that if I passed I would be given a place there. Now I wasn't sure if that was what I wanted to do! Perhaps I should work with a Missionary Society and teach in Africa or India. I spoke to Cyril Tucker about this but I can't remember whether he gave any useful advice. There was also the possibility of Ordination. After all I had already thought about this but I was becoming increasingly unsure. During one vacation I had gone to the Vicarage in Sheet and asked Ben Forster, the Priest in charge, whether I could use one of the rooms for revision purposes. The rooms looked more spacious than at home and there were more signs of books and study around so I thought it would be easier to concentrate there. Fortunately he agreed and I spent the first morning with Milton or whomsoever it was I had to write an essay on. As I left for lunch Ben said 'When are you going to decide about ordination?' I think he must have been shocked by my reply of 'I'm not going to be bloody ordained!' as I stalked off in a huff. Obviously the whole question was worrying me! It was really a question of identity and I hadn't much of a clue as to who I was. My role models were Bill Rees, Lancelot Fleming, the Bishop of Portsmouth and Ben himself. The difficulty was that they seemed to me at that time to be 'ideal people' – how on earth could I live up to their apparent standards? I was only too aware of my own weaknesses. On the other hand whenever I heard of Clergy who 'Let the side down' so to speak, I felt very threatened. I knew I didn't want to be like that! Also I felt that there were distinct 'types' of Clergymen. They seemed like black mice in their cassocks and I wanted to be me! So the question remained suspended – yes I did but no I didn't.

A friend called David who had made the commitment at the same time as I had was having the same problem. We decided to join the University Christian Union more because we felt others would see that one could still drink beer and be in the Union! We were determined to 'find ourselves' but oh, still a long way from doing so.

The Oxford Pastorate ran some great events in the vacations and in the winter of 1953 I went with about 40 other Oxford and Cambridge students to Lee Abbey in Linton, North

Devon. Lee Abbey was an old hotel that had been used as a military hospital during the war. Afterwards it was abandoned and became dilapidated. A group of Christian men had put their heads and money together and bought it as a Christian Conference and Renewal Centre. It still flourishes today. In those days it was a bit primitive but as students we loved it especially with the sea nearby and those wonderful walks around the cliffs to Linton. Our job was to assist the Staff in return for which we were given free board and lodging. In the evenings we would assemble around the enormous log fire in the great sitting room for an Epilogue Service and well known Preachers would teach and inspire us. My first job was working in the fields scattering the ash from the large boilers which kept the place warm. I worked with a Canadian member of the Staff and he would drive the tractor. Our first attempt failed miserably as we threw the ashes against the wind! We needed a good wash when we returned for lunch.

Before going to Lee Abbey I had participated in a Pastorate 'Mission'. This had meant travelling to Plymouth with about 100 other students from Oxford and Cambridge and being put up in private homes for ten days. The 'Mission' was in two Parishes one of which was St. Andrew, the city centre Church, and the other a smaller 'daughter' Church called Christchurch I think. The city had been terribly bombed in the war and still looked like a big bomb site. Our work was to visit homes up and down the streets and encourage people to attend the meetings held every night in the Church Hall. At these there would be shown films called 'Science and Faith' which was about the bloodstream or the eye showing just how amazing life is both for humans and nature in general. Then one of the Pastorate Team would speak about the claims of Christianity. The meeting would end with an appeal for commitment asking people to say a prayer and to stay behind after the meeting and speak to one of the more experienced students about what to do in the future. My memory of this time is vague but I do remember how I enjoyed visiting people in their own homes and how willing they were to discuss their beliefs, or lack of them!

At the same time I was there my sister Joy married Robert Smith at Tor Point Church, just across the water. Robert was a P.T. Instructor in the Royal Navy and at that time stationed in Dartmouth. I was privileged to be asked if I would 'give her away'. There were just four of us at the ceremony and I remember the Priest was very short-sighted. It was reported that he once shook hands with his wife at the Church door welcoming her as a new member of the Congregation! We had a very good meal afterwards at a Plymouth hotel. Joy and Robert started their married life in Looe.

These student 'Missions' continued and the following year I travelled to Walthamstowe where we were based at St. Mary's Parish Church and were welcomed by the Vicar, Canon Drewitt. I remember his name because he was responsible for a teaching on Scripture which has always stayed with me. He spoke about the Gospel of John, Chapter 3 and the interview Jesus had with Nicodemus. Although I had been reading the Bible daily since the commitment made at St. Aldates Church I had probably not thought about this passage at all deeply, or maybe not even read it before. I had never heard that people could or even should be 'born again' but as he spoke I was quite sure that he was describing something that had happened to me that night. My life had taken a completely new turn and I had discovered that it was possible to know God in a personal way. It was strange to discover that my own experience was confirming what Jesus said should be the experience of all who believe in him.

Two other events stand out from that 'Mission'. One was speaking with a girl of about my own age on how to be a Christian. She had appeared at a lot of the meetings held in the Church Hall and spoke with me several times. After one such talk – the last! – the Vicar of St. Aldates, Keith De Berry, took me on one side and suggested that perhaps her motives in singling me out for chats might not have been simply for spiritual help. It was a shock to me and I think I avoided her after that. The second event was Maureen. I don't know how this started and I may even have been staying with her family but anyway it was decided that we should meet up again after the 'Mission' was over. So began a friendship which lasted for about a year. It is remembered mostly for the trips I made from Liverpool Street station by train in the days of the slow steam locomotives threading their way through the grime soaked tunnels billowing smoke. Also for the diminutive home Maureen and her family lived in. The relationship ran into problems mainly because she was three years older than me and it became obvious she was thinking of a more permanent relationship! The burden was lifted by my good mentor Cyril Tucker. Maureen came to Oxford for a weekend and on the Sunday we went together to the Bible Study and tea in Cyril's home. During the following week I met him at the Iffley Road Athletics track and I asked him what he thought of Maureen. His immediate reply was 'Not your kind of girl Paul' which confirmed what I had been thinking. She was as sweet about the decision to end our relationship as always. It was just as well as the climax of Finals was fast approaching!

My 21st birthday came soon afterwards and we celebrated at home with a dinner made by Mother and about twelve of us crowded round the dining room table. Not a single girl was invited! It was a conscious decision on my part as there was to be a time of celibacy! This might work better for me! Mother and Father gave me a lovely 'wide-margin' Bible for a present which was most useful for making notes in. It is still one of my prized possessions. It probably cost the equivalent of £25-£30 in today's money.

Work became more serious as Finals approached. My routine of revising in my 'Digs' at Headington and having lunch at the café over the road was a very pleasant one. My friend Brian, at Wadham, advised me to put as many of my notes as possible onto postcards and really absorb what was there. The other invaluable tip I was given was to learn several quotations by heart, to write them down immediately at the start of each examination and then work them into the answers. And so the day arrived! We had been given so many 'dummy runs' that one couldn't be anything other than well prepared. Also I was one of those 'odd' people who actually enjoyed exams! We had thirteen papers in all, mostly lasting three hours each, spread over a period of about two weeks. There was great relief and rejoicing when they were over.

It had been a momentous three years. Would I have done it differently? Perhaps if I had done my National Service first I would have made more of University life, the Clubs and social life for example. But then I might have got out of the way of studying and been unable to keep up with the work. I always knew that I was a 'slogger' rather than a 'scholar'! The fact that I started straight from school did mean that I still had hold of the discipline needed for study with almost no supervision. Except, that is, for Rosie Cramp without whose support the Anglo-Saxon / Middle English papers would have remained mysteries! The Sports side might have been better, I was still immature as a cricketer and as a runner. That showed up during the summer following my Finals. I joined a tour of the Cricket Club to Devon and played in only one of the matches. Our openers put on 120 for the first wicket in two hours and then I went in during the over before lunch and was out third ball! But it was a lovely occasion at Linton-by-the-sea just a few miles from the beautiful Lee Abbey.

When I got home there was the official looking envelope from the Ministry of Defence requiring me to report to Winchester Barracks at the beginning of August. The sublime was about to become the ridiculous!

One more visit to Oxford was necessary. Everyone who had sat the final exam had to have an oral test by a panel of Examiners. At one time this had been necessary only for those who were border-line cases and whose 'Viva', as it was called, could put them up into a higher grade. However one or two students had become so over-wrought by this process they had committed suicide, so it was then decided that the process should apply to all students. On the required date I sat and waited in a big room in one of the Colleges with many others. The atmosphere was like a Doctor's waiting room! When my turn came I went into the inner sanctum to be confronted by six Fellows of the English Department all wearing academic uniform. I recognised Dr. Margaret Gardiner and Professor Tolkein at once. The others were new to me. The interview was straight forward enough until one of them asked me a question about a quotation I had used in one of the Literature papers. It was from one of John Donne's spiritual sonnets. I remembered it well and started confidently 'Batter my heart three-cornered God' only to be interrupted by the questioner, 'Surely Mr. Duffett even at Keble they don't teach you that God is a triangle?' I suddenly realised what I had done! The word 'cornered' comes from the last line of the poem and refers to the world which was at the time thought to be square. The correct words are 'Four-cornered world' and of course the word in the other line is 'person'd'! I was covered in embarrassment as the whole panel laughed at my expense. I had made the same mistake in my essay. It was Professor Tolkein who came to my rescue, 'Don't worry, you are in the middle of a Degree and what you say will make no difference.' When the results were published I got a 2/2 – slap in the middle!

CHAPTER 5

..... ON TO THE RIDICULOUS

In 1955 National Service was part of our culture. It had been prescribed by the Government as a way of keeping the military commitments which our nation had become involved in all over the world. It was a form of conscription which was also a form of compromise. Young men generally didn't feel too bad about it as long as they knew it would only last two years. It also offered a form of employment and training which many otherwise might not have got. However looking back on it after nearly fifty years one wonders how those in charge of the country got away with it! I suppose my expectations were much like anyone else's at that time. National Service was taken for granted and I don't remember asking any of my friends at Oxford what it was like, I just accepted that it was something that had to be done.

So dutifully I reported to the headquarters of the 1st Battalion of the Royal Hampshire Regiment at Winchester. Bishop Lancelot Fleming had asked me not to volunteer for the Education or the Medical Corps because, he said, it was important for me to get to know men who had not had the privilege of the education I had been given. He was right but nevertheless there was something of a shock in store! I certainly knew a little about the Army through my experience with the Cadet Corps at school but this had been pretty superficial – especially as I had only joined to support a proposal that I become headboy.

We were kitted up and shown to our barrack rooms. There must have been between 12 to 16 in ours, metal beds in two rows opposite each other. Each bed had on the mattress a pillow, two sheets and two blankets. The first job was to make our bed. Having achieved this in came a Corporal who with a loud voice introduced himself and told us that this ''orriblelot' were to be in his charge. He then went to the first bed and stripping it said 'and what do you think this is?' This was followed by a demonstration of how a bed ought to be made with corners at 90 degrees and the sheet folded back one foot from the pillow. Then he stripped it again and showed us how it was to look every morning with the blankets folded exactly in four and the sheets folded neatly between the two like a sandwich. The pillow was to be placed on top without a wrinkle in it and the whole lot pushed neatly against the head of the bed. He then commanded us to strip our beds and present them to him for inspection like that. We were placed in alphabetical order and the man next to me was Nicholas Chubb. After the inspection of the beds accompanied by a lot of shouting and stripping again in came an older man, stout and muscular who barked like a bull. He was the Company Sergeant Major and was to be immediately obeyed at all times unless we wanted to be boiled in oil! He went down each row asking us our names and making us shout them out, ending with 'Sir'! He then asked if any of us had some education meaning 'Ordinary levels' or beyond. Both Nicholas and I spoke up and to my surprise and the confusion of the CSM we both said we had finished degrees at Oxford. Afterwards I spoke to my new neighbour and was amazed to discover that like me he too was considering ordination. This, I concluded, was a miracle and God had put us together to help one another through what was fast turning out to be an ordeal.

Indeed it was to be three months of what was called 'Basic Training'. The daily programme went like this…..Reveille sounded at 6.30am and by the time for breakfast at 7.00am your bed had to be ready for inspection which took place at 7.45am with an order to 'Stand by your beds!' After this came the drill. The barrack square was about 200 metres long and 150 metres wide. Above us on another level was the square for the 'Green Jackets', a regiment which at that time was much involved in the Mau Mau troubles in Kenya. Drill meant marching up and down learning the maneuvers like 'right wheel' and saluting and so on. About once a week we would be inspected by the Captain or the Commanding Officer who was a Major. One morning he didn't like the way I had put on my beret so 'Name and number' he barked. Private Duffett, 284641, I shouted back as taught. 'You wear your beret like a bloody Frenchman' was his retort. This meant I had to sharply stand 'at ease' and take off the offending garment and replace it 'properly' whilst the Major waited impatiently. Such 'little things' were constantly happening. Moving about the camp had to be done at marching pace with the arms swinging 90 degrees to the ground. The evenings were often spent cleaning the brass bits of our uniform and 'bulling' our boots, which meant putting on layers of black boot polish with spittle to make them shine like a mirror. There were occasional route marches in full kit for between six and ten miles at top speed. Then there were the rifles which were constantly inspected in case specks of dust were to find a place on them! These guns were used entirely for ceremonial drill duties and were never fired in those first three months. Learning to present arms took hours to perfect to the Sergeant's satisfaction and bayonet drill took even longer. Supper was at 5.30pm and then theoretically one was free – apart from all the cleaning and polishing there was to do!

There never seemed to be much going on in Winchester apart from the pubs which didn't attract me much. There was the occasional film but as we had to be in by 10.30pm and we were usually very tired anyway I can't remember the title of any film I saw at that time. Home leave was forbidden during those first months but there was one solace. A local clergyman had set up a Toc.H in some rooms he acquired in the city and though they weren't very pretentious they were good enough for us soldiers. There one could find a room to read in with periodicals and books available, a room in which to play snooker and a cubby-hole where one could buy a cheap cup of tea or coffee. There was a nice garden as well and croquet was available there. He organised a weekend away for five of us but what we did eludes the memory! Another time away was organised by the Chaplain to his Headquarters at Bagshot Park where potential ordinands were given lectures and encouragement. It was heaven to be treated like a 'normal' human being!

As Christmas approached I was asked to take one of the readings at the Carol Service to represent the 'Other Ranks'. This meant sitting next to the Regimental Sergeant Major, R.S.M. Watton. He was an Irishman with a voice to rival that of the famous R.S.M. Brittain who made his reputation in one of the 'Carry On' films. He was much feared and not least by me. One morning he crashed into our billet and shouted was there anyone there who could play the piano? I was terrified because I was wearing socks in bed which was strictly forbidden! One poor chap was too sleepy to think ahead and replied that he could. He was ordered to get up at once and sweep up the leaves which had collected outside! Anyway on the occasion of the Carol Service the RSM was shaking with nervousness at the prospect of reading in public. I always felt differently about him after that!

There was two weeks leave in the middle of November and a short break over Christmas and almost immediately afterwards six of us were told that we were off to Exeter to train as Officers. It was my first visit there and I quickly became acquainted with the beautiful Cathedral which could be reached in a twenty minute walk from Topsham Barracks. This Officer training consisted of more doses of 'Square Bashing' but also included learning how to shoot the 3.3 rifles we were given. Our first visit to the range was a disaster for me! Our Sergeant was a pleasant man with a good sense of humour and after returning from the shooting exercise he came into our room with the results of our target practice. I had been third in the row as we lay on our bellies shooting. The scores were out of 50. He read them by numbers; one – 40, two – 70, three – 0......! I had shot on my neighbour's target! He asked if I had ever worn glasses and when I replied 'No' I was sent off to the Army Doctor for examination. I have worn glasses ever since!

Our Sergeant was particularly keen on bayonet drill and this meant charging at human shaped dummies and thrusting your bayonet into them and withdrawing immediately. All this had to be performed to the accompaniment of suitably bloodthirsty cries! One day as we started this drill I realised that I had left my bayonet behind. There was nothing else to do but pretend, so for fifteen minutes I went through all the movements until suddenly the Sergeant realised what was happening. He was so flabbergasted by the fact that he hadn't noticed before then that I was let off with a jolly good telling off delivered with a smile on his face!

Our other Drill Colour Sergeant was quite different. He appeared to loathe and despise us. One day he sent me to the guard-house for being persistently, and he thought deliberately, wrong. On another occasion we were doing gas mask drill in large masks with a plastic window in their face. First he got us to run in pairs around the parade square and laughed when we began to bump into each other because our windows had steamed up. He then went from one to the other of us 'testing' our masks which involved putting his hand over the air-pipe to see if we could breathe! Of course he kept his hand there until you started to panic because you couldn't breathe! He had fought in the Korean War and we decided that this experience had affected his mind.

The training included some 'Leadership Skills' training but not a great deal. We were required to drill our fellow trainees a few times and on one depressing occasion we had to lead a group of other soldiers on a night exercise. It was a foggy, cold February night on Dartmoor and not only did I lead the group in the wrong direction but I was hopelessly lost myself. I wandered alone in the dark until I heard the sound of firing and saw flares going up. At this point I decided that the exercise was over as far as it mattered so I threw the live ammunition away and slunk home feeling guilty and feeble! We had been told to fire the ammunition into the air rather than risk hitting anyone but I didn't and was also fearful that someone might stumble across the bullets and not know that they were still live!

Another exercise was to lead the others over a mythical river using two barrels and some rope. This was done under the watchful eye of the officers in charge. Again I failed miserably and during the exercise I looked round to see the officers laughing. I knew it was me that amused them.

Just before the Officer examination we were allowed a week's leave. I thought it would be a good way to save money by wearing my uniform and hitchhike home carrying my casual clothes in a hold-all. It worked extremely well taking only three lifts and three and a half hours for the 180 odd miles. There was a lot of sympathy at that time for National Service men. I treated myself on the return journey and took the National Express coach!

The test was a nightmare! One of the exercises was with the rest of the group, one was in front of the group and the rest had to be undertaken individually. The exercise with the rest of the group was by far the worst. It was one of those group tests where you had to work together to get some barrels over a space without touching certain given parameters and the ground. What the trainers were looking for of course was initiative and speed and to see who the group leaders were. Again I was completely lost and had no idea how to begin the exercise or even to understand the orders given by those who did! Then came the bit where you had to run to an officer who was hiding behind a hedge. He thrust a machine gun into my hand and said 'There is a terrorist over there. What are you going to do?' The reply we had been taught during training was 'Shoot to kill, Sir.' But by this time yours truly was becoming bolshie! Here were these nice young people, three years younger than me, being brain-washed into believing everything they were taught was right. This was not for me. I was quickly becoming far too big for my boots. So I answered 'Well Sir it all depends on who he is and what he has done.'

The exercise I enjoyed the most was one where I had to give a talk in front of the group and an examiner on a topic of your own choice. I had twenty minutes to prepare this talk and it was to last five minutes. I chose to talk on Dr. Johnson and his dictionary. Now I would show them!

When the tests were over we were seen individually by the head of the panel who was a Colonel. He asked me if I was a pacifist and I replied no, but that things were not always black and white and sometimes needed further thought and clarification. His reply was that there wasn't always a lot of time for that when you were in Turkey and under fire from the Cypriots! We then had to sit in a room and wait for our results which were handed to us as a folded piece of paper with just one word written on it – pass or fail. The papers were passed out in alphabetical order and all those before me passed. There was a much longer gap of time before mine was passed out and it said 'Fail.' It was in fact the only failure and I felt gutted. How I had thought I would pass given my demonstration is beyond me! The rest of the group were sympathetic but we soon had to part. The next day we were all sent home and they then went on to Eton Hall, the training ground for officers, and I returned to Winchester. My parents came to pick me up from the barracks. Father was dismissive saying, as I had thought he would, that the outcome was inevitable given my performance. How anyone could be so stupid was beyond his comprehension!

Back at the barracks after a week at home kicking my heels life became increasingly boring. I was allowed home every weekend and I found this very unsettling. My time in barracks was spent on morning parade and then doing some kind of menial task such as peeling potatoes or washing the officer's mess walls and floors. After a month or so of this I decided to see the Company Sergeant Major and ask for a transfer to the Education Corps. He was astounded! He asked if I would prefer to go abroad and this seemed an interesting prospect to me. I soon found myself on parade with the next draft for Malaya. The war there with 'terrorists' representing the Communist Party fighting a jungle gorilla war was nearly over, but not quite. The idea was that after jungle training I would work as a clerk in the Motor Transport office. I didn't know how to type but this didn't seem to matter! There was more embarkation leave – another two pleasant weeks at home. The day before we were due to go there was a big parade with the R.S.M. inspecting and he was furious with our turn out ordering us all back into the barracks for a lecture. We had to stay in and clean our gear all over again and he would be back to inspect us again first thing in the morning. This was disappointing for me as I had been invited out to dinner by some friends of the family and was really looking forward to going. It dawned on me that Mr. Watton's intentions were actually of a different nature. The reputation of the Hampshire Regiment would not be improved by 100 National Servicemen painting the town red on their last night before embarkation. I decided to call his bluff and quietly slipped out of the barracks for a very enjoyable dinner appointment. I did make the time to give my brass a quick polish before sleeping. Early the next day we turned out into the cold to be inspected again and as the tall Irishman stopped next to me I hoped he could not see me quaking in my boots! After a very brief inspection he said 'One hundred percent improvement' and passed onto his next victim!

After lunch we were off on the train to Southampton to join H.M.S. Fowey, a troop ship for about 1500 soldiers. Mother and Joy came to see me off and Mother cried. I couldn't think why when everything seemed so exciting to me. Now, as a parent myself, I know why, but in my naivete then I had no idea that over 200 men had been killed so far in the conflict in Malaya. This journey was my first outside Britain since I visited Austria for two weeks at the age of fourteen. It passed very smoothly and having slept in bunks on one of the lower decks we had parade at 8.30 every morning and were then left pretty much to our own devices. I met up with the Padre on the first Sunday. He was short and cheerful and seemed pleased to have an ordinand on board. He offered me his office for study if I should so wish. What more could I have asked for? Someone had given me a New Testament Greek grammar and so with an exercise book I started to look at a completely new language. I had also come across a copy of Tolstoy's 'War and Peace' in the excellent Petersfield book shop and decided to see if I could read it in the three weeks it took for the ship to reach Singapore. I once made the mistake of leaving my writing book on a toilet shelf and on my return it had of course gone. On asking the duty corporal if he had seen it he replied yes it had been taken as rubbish and so was now floating somewhere in the Red Sea. Hopefully the predators became Christians!

Another hiccup occurred in Aden. We had stopped there to drop off some off the Highland Regiment who were going to defend British interests there. I must have typically left my locker unlocked and when shaving time came in the morning the very nice kit which Daphne had given to me for Christmas had disappeared. The sergeant on duty said 'Let this be a lesson to you. In the Army someone will steal your lunch when you're not looking.' Fortunately there were cheap razors for sale in the Naafi!

We arrived in Singapore in full kit and carrying rifles. We traveled the three hundred miles north by train and there was always the chance that it could be ambushed. We were huddled into carriages with wooden seats and although it was night time there was little chance of sleeping. Once during the journey four of us had to sit in an open carriage and keep guard. The air was warm and humid and the stars a brilliant blaze. The night noises of different insects was both strange and haunting. The dawn arrived with a great rush of reds and yellows and a view of endless flat fields and dense jungle around. We had been travelling for eight hours. At last we were bundled out into three-ton lorries with tarpaulin sides. We had no idea where we were heading for but soon became aware of the road narrowing and our lorry climbing higher and higher with tall trees on each side of us. About 11am after over two hours of traveling like this we passed through a tiny village with people and animals all over the place.

Soon afterwards we arrived at a small camp in a clearing. The buildings were of bamboo with open sides and here we were to stay for six weeks. Hungry and tired we were fed on eggs and bacon which seemed strangely out of place somehow! Then onto the parade ground of brown dirt to meet our new commanding officer. He was tall, sunburnt, handsome and muscular. He told us we had ten minutes to change into vest and shorts for a five-mile run. Talk about 'mad dogs and Englishmen!' Our three weeks of travelling with a minimum of exercise had led to an increase in weight for us all. At least I had my experience of cross-country running to call on and came in second to the corporal who had been at that camp for some time. It was, I think, the first and the last time that the Major said 'Well done' to me!

Life in these open-sided rooms took on a new turn. Square-bashing was minimal and the camaraderie quickly developed. The main objective seemed to be for us to become as fit as possible so there was plenty of physical training. The arms drill was mostly held in a jungle clearing where one had to walk down a path in which some special targets had been placed. Directly one saw these the exercise was to fire at them as quickly as possible. One of the most frightening type was on a spring and suddenly rose up from the ground as you approached it. There was a certain amount of propaganda input as well. The Colonel of the Regiment came to lecture us and brought with him two captured terrorists. He seemed to think that the best way to get alongside his soldiers was to swear even more than they did! That was saying something, for what intrigued me about the swearing was that not only did it have to occur every two or three words but even words were split up into consonants with a swear word between them! Swearing was something that on the whole I had given up except for brief outbursts in bad temper. There was one occasion when all my kit fell off the top of my locker where one had to place it just so ready for morning inspection. There were only two of us in the room at the time and as it fell I swore. As I stood up having picked it up off the floor the other soldier in the room asked if I was feeling unwell. 'Fine' I replied, 'Why?' 'You don't swear' was his reply.

Colonel Mann gave a brief outline of the war going on at that time. The British had asked the Communists to help them get the Japanese out of Malaya during the war and afterwards these same people, armed by Britain then took to the jungle in order to get them the British out of the country as well! The two captured men confessed how badly they had been treated by the Communists – promised this and that but never getting anything. At the end we were invited to ask them questions. After a long silence I asked them why they had decided to get involved in the first place. One answered that he had become disillusioned with the Government and British administration which had promised him education and work but had not fulfilled these promises. So when these clever men came to his village and told them all that would change when the British were driven out he had joined them. I felt only sympathy for this man with such ambition who had been badly treated not only once but twice.

The most interesting part of the training were the 'patrols' in the jungle itself. The first was just for a part-day and we traveled in single file, fully armed with live ammunition

A typical Army Barrack Room in Malaya circa 1956

– one bullet up the spout! The main incident that day was a meeting with a hornets nest! Harrison who was in the front saw a great bag like thing in the path and put his rifle in to move it out of the way. The result was startling to say the least. The first I knew about it was when I saw Harrison running full-tilt past me with a look of sheer terror on his face. My first thought was that we had met up with the enemy but his shouted words 'Hornets' reassured me. Fortunately they didn't fly too far down the line and after a wait of about fifteen minutes we were able to move ahead circumventing the outraged insects.

The next incident was concerned with the order to keep strict silence at all times. The excitement of our first trip into this mysterious world was too much for most of us. The chatter wasn't loud but was fairly persistent. The next day we were summoned by the Company major and told that very sadly one of our number had been shot and killed whilst on patrol. It transpired that it wasn't that far from the route that we had taken. It was a real warning of the seriousness of our undertaking.

Another foray was by night to the edge of the jungle, firing mortar shells into the hillside opposite which was covered by thick trees. We were told this was 'psychological warfare' to make sure the enemy didn't sleep. The noise of the shells leaving and then exploding about a mile away was both deafening and eerie. Once we were placed in ambush and told to expect a group of terrorists to run into the clearing ahead of us, having been flushed out by soldiers from the other direction. I was scared, not so much by the appearance of the enemy, as of the soldier behind me! He had been placed almost directly at my rear and as I knew the quality of his shooting I feared for my life. After some three hours we gave up and my relief was enormous.

Our second patrol into the jungle was meant to be a full day but went wrong. Our guide got lost and as these local men seemed to know the jungle like you and I know our own village this must have been a great surprise to the officer in charge and perhaps also a matter of great concern! It was fast becoming dark and we were all worn out from the intense heat and humidity. We were told that we would have to camp for the night which at least made us feel that the tents we always had to carry around could be useful sometimes! Four of us were trying to put up a tent with groundsheet, etc. when it began to rain. 'Cats and dogs' hardly describes the vertical downpour which felt like buckets being emptied over our heads. We decided to strip off as we had quickly become soaked. Suddenly the ridiculousness of our situation became too much for us and we rolled around laughing. We dined on dried milk mixed with a dried porridge biscuit and fell fast asleep. Two hours later I was awoken and told it was my turn for guard duty. My companion on guard was Lance Corporal Dale who had done his National Service and then decided to stay on for a further three years. We sat in the thick darkness watching the fire-flies bobbing up and down like little lights. The Sergeant had told us that he didn't want anyone saying they had seen men on bicycles riding through the camp! There was also a strange luminosity from the bark of old trees lying all over the place. We were sitting on a rock whispering when suddenly there was an almighty crash – the sound of falling trees. We were shaken. What was out there? Corporal Dale decided to go and investigate. This was strictly against orders as there was always to be two soldiers on guard duty at all times. Time seemed to stand still when all of a sudden I felt a hand on my shoulder. If I had been a better soldier I would have shot whoever this was at once! As it was I froze with fright and then started to fumble with my rifle. A voice said 'It's okay.' It was one of the Malay guides who had crept up behind me without me hearing or seeing anything. He wanted to know what the noise was. When Corporal Dale returned we decided between us that nothing untoward had taken place, apart that is from my near heart attack! The dawn arrived soon afterwards sounding like some exotic zoo with all the bird song. To my utter amazement the rock on which we had been sitting was only about three feet from a thick thorn bush and we had been staring straight into it not even knowing it was there! After more dried milk and biscuit we set off arriving back at camp around 10am.

Some days later we had ambush training and this time it was we who were to be ambushed. We were told what to do. Divided into groups of six we were to be driven in a lorry along a dirt road and then the Sergeant and his mate would open fire on us from a hidden position, using blanks. If the sound came from the left the Leader was to shout 'Ambush left' and we were all to jump out to the right and take up a shooting position behind whatever cover there was and fire back. We were to take turns as the leader. My turn came and the shooting began. I shouted accordingly but with the opposite side to the correct one! We all jumped out on the same side as the ambush and took up whatever positions we could. The Sergeant advanced and I was sure I was for 'the hot house.' He looked at me somewhat bemused and said 'That was very clever. On the other side there is a bog and you would all have sunk up to your waists! We did that intentionally to show you that sometimes you have to use your initiative and intelligence'. What good fortune. I was too cowardly to admit it had all been a mistake on my part! This training lasted for three weeks and then another group arrived. It had been a good experience and I have never been so fit either before or since.

We were piled once more into the three-ton lorries with all our kit and off we went back down the hill to Kwalalumpur where I began my stint in the Motor Transport office. The camp was about two miles from the centre of the city and much bigger than the jungle camp but with the same sort of buildings. One of the main differences was the much larger parade ground and the presence of R.S.M. Watton. I learnt the routine of the office which didn't involve much. The main duty of the day was to ensure the 'detail' as it was called, was posted each day on the various notice boards and given to the officer in charge. Various officers would send in a request for transport and it was my job to put a driver's name on the detail beside each request. Other duties for the day were also included such as who was on guard during the night. After that there wasn't much to do. One day I was busy with my New Testament Greek again when the Sergeant in charge had some idea that I wasn't about Her Majesty's service and asked what it was that was occupying me so studiously. I told him and he nearly exploded 'You can't do that here. You're here to work.' When I explained that there wasn't any work to do he said 'Well pretend that there is!' On another occasion when I had made some mistake on parade he shouted at me 'You over-educated Greek idiot!'

He also failed me on my driving test. There was a Corporal Hunt who was in charge of lessons for new drivers and the first time he took me out we went to a town sixteen miles away where he had some mates in the camp there. I had negotiated all the new scary things fairly well and after we had parked he said he was off to the non-commissioned officers Mess for a break and we would start back after lunch which I would find available in the Naffi. Lunch taken I went to the parking place and waited. One, two, three hours passed and it began to get dark. Then out of the gloom staggered my Corporal – inebriated! We set off for home with him slouched in the passenger seat and when he started to instruct me in slurred tones I lost my cool and told him to 'Shut up!' He did but as I had never driven in the dark before it took us a longer time than usual to get back to camp. He fell out of the truck and said to me 'You won't tell anyone about this will you? It would be the end of my career.' I immediately felt sorry for him and promised that my lips were sealed. He gave me a few more lessons in absolute sobriety and then I was ready for my test. The lessons had all taken place on a one-ton lorry and the test was on a three-tonner which made me very nervous. It was another five years before I got my driving licence!

Sundays were fun! The nice Padre whom I had met on the ship asked me to go with him to the various services he would take during the day. These meant journeys up to twenty miles long and helping unload the hymn books, etc. Once we held a Communion Service using the back of his truck as an altar! It seemed so right to me and perhaps sowed the seeds for my future missionary work. The Queen's birthday was marked by a big parade when we would be woken at 5.30am to be on the square by 6.00am. Our big Irishman tried to teach us to present arms over and over again. Once, in desperation, he shouted 'God made the rifle before he made you and he made your arm to fit on the butt – so!' (he demonstrated). I was sure he looked straight at me when he said it and noticed the broad grin I gave afterwards.

The city was full of high-rise buildings even then and my main memory is of going into a café with its very American style service and adverts. It was also the first time I had come across air-conditioning and Knickerbocker Glories! Coming out of the café you were met by a wall of heat. Another memory is of the Chinese ladies in long trousers.

There was at least one big Anglican church in the city where the assistant priest was Indian and the rector named Chu Ban It. He later became Bishop of Singapore and made a name for himself in charismatic circles. There were bible study meetings at the church which I attended but all I can remember is making the lady leader cross because I disagreed with her about something in St. John's gospel!

I once went to a game of badminton in the big stadium with thousands of spectators present. It was a Finals game and the standard they played to left me breathless. There was also a little bit of cricket played in the camp and one of the officers asked me if I would be interested in a game. It was a little embarrassing to have to turn out in khaki rather that whites but I remember a pleasant afternoon and a short innings. The game was interrupted by a tropical storm and I found it amazing that play could be resumed only half-an-hour after the storm had ceased.

Before leaving I wanted to visit some caves which were a place of pilgrimage for Hindus and something of a tourist attraction. It was a ten-mile train journey from camp and they stood in rocks which suddenly appeared like a mountain out of the flat plain. There were many people there some festooned with flowers and some with sharp wires in their flesh. It was the first time I had seen Hindu pilgrims and at that time they seemed quite alien to my very English soul.

After five months it was time for the Regiment to return to England and the return journey to Singapore was memorable. The Colonel's driver was to take the car by himself as the Colonel was going on ahead some other way and I was asked if I would accompany the car as the ruling was always two soldiers with every car. It was very nice traveling in the Jaguar and to my astonishment some Ghurka troops that we passed on the way smartly saluted us!

Arriving in Singapore we were taken to Changhi Beach where we were to be under canvas until HMS Fowey arrived to take us home. We were told this would take a week but in the end we waited three. This city was amazing with little sign of the war still left. The cathedral had a thriving congregation with coffee served after the service. Life in the heat and the tents was extremely boring and I have a memory of a day when one of the NCO's came to our tent and said 'Hey Vicar ...(a nickname I was sometimes called)....the lads are having an argument about the Bible and wondered if you would help them.' What an extraordinary opportunity! I can't remember what this argument was about but the Prophet Isaiah comes to mind and I don't think I was a lot of help to them in the end.

At last we were mustered to march to the docks and on board the troop ship. This time the padre had apparently spoken to the officers about me because he asked if I would like to teach their children each day between 9 and 12 am. There were about twenty of them ranging in age from 6 to 12 years. It was fun and made a pleasant change to the boredom of just sitting around. I also gave some basic lessons to the troops on how to write letters amongst other things but this was stopped when some NCOs complained about being taught by a private! A very curious memory I have is that of crossing the line. There was the usual fun of people dressing up and being thrown into the small swimming pool that was available to the officers but what really struck in my mind was the laugh of the officer in charge. I knew that I had heard it somewhere before. I was still puzzling about it later that day when suddenly it came to me that I had heard it previously at our home in Horndean. It was the laugh of one of Daphne's boyfriends who visited her at home when

I was about eight years old. The next time I met the padre I asked the officer's name and he said it was Surgeon Commander Stride. The name came back to me at once and so I asked the padre if he could arrange for me to meet him. This he did and the only place we could meet on equal ground was the padre's office as it was forbidden for ordinary ranks to enter the officers' decks. We had a most pleasant hour together catching up on family news. I think one of the children I taught was a daughter of his.

The outstanding feature of this trip was the fact that we couldn't go through the Suez Canal which Nasser had closed to British ships. This meant we had to travel all the way around Africa. What fun! The padre told me one day that it was costing the British Government £400 a day per soldier! This was because when we had stopped off in Aden again and off-loaded more troops it left only about 500 of us on board. Our first call in Africa was Mombassa but we were only allowed four hours on shore. A friend and I headed for the market near the harbour and whilst we were looking around a man approached us showing interest in who we were, why we were there and where we came from. He was a Kenyan settler and before leaving us he said he had a good friend in Cape Town whom he felt sure would welcome us. He gave us the telephone number of this friend and said he would contact him to say we were on our way! The rest of our time there we spent looking at some of the old Colonial buildings, mostly Portuguese.

On our way again our next port of call was in fact Cape Town. As we approached the great city the ship began to roll precipitously and word went round that we were hitting the 'Cape rollers.' This was the first time I discovered that I had good sea-legs! Up to the top I went and witnessed the amazing sight of these enormous waves approaching the ship with about half-a-mile in between them. One could see six of these waves approaching at a time looking just like rolled up carpets. As they crashed against the ship water poured onto the deck everywhere. They must have been at least thirty feet high! We were given a great welcome with people on the dockside offering us their hospitality. The City Council had laid on several buses to take all those who wanted to go on a trip to the Constantia Vineyards. The scenery was breathtaking and the old Dutch farmsteads magnificent. We were given tea.

Back in the city my friend and I decided to phone the Mombassa contact. Yes he had heard about us and would be pleased to meet us at the Nelson Hotel but not for too long as he had just got married! To this day that connection is still not quite clear! However we had a very pleasant hour over a drink and he had kindly bought us some magazines to take away. In the evening we decided to go to a concert in the City Hall having bought the cheapest tickets available. We sat near the back and observed that the audience was of more or less equal racial proportions. I commented on this observation to my neighbour in the seats and she said 'Yes, but not for much longer.' Of course sadly she was right.

The next part of my journey was long and became increasingly uncomfortable. Eventually we put in at Dakar which was a genuinely African country. The heat was oppressive and everything in the shops massively expensive. My friend and I went into a roadside café and found all we could afford was a bowl of soup which at £2 was a large sum in those days especially for poorly paid soldiers. It's a pity that most of this last leg of the journey is lost to me in the mists of time. Surely there must have been something worth remembering about the trip around Italy and eventually home again. All that comes to mind is that I did complete 'War and Peace' which I had started on the outward journey.

We had been at sea exactly four weeks.

More leave followed before yet another journey across water – this time to the Hook of Holland, on a much smaller and more crowded ship than the last journey. Then we travelled on by train to the lovely city of Munster in North Germany where they say if the bells aren't ringing then it's raining! This city is a lake of Catholicism within a land of Lutheranism and yes it does have a pretty wet climate! The Hampshire Regiment were placed in the barracks built by Hitler for his Panzer Division. They were like a fortress but better appointed than the Winchester barracks. For example one room was shared by only two people and had its own washing facilities with double-glazed windows and excellent heating. Even the R.M.T. office was warm in the depth of winter with outside temperatures in minus degrees celsius. My job was much the same as before and equally mundane but there were a few surprises in store for me!

The first thing to happen was when a Corporal came to me and said he had been rostered to work over Christmas and as this would be his third Christmas of duty could I possibly find a replacement for him. Being a coward I agreed but was then left with the problem of who? In the end I rostered myself on duty to cover for him! How I thought I could do this without first checking what was involved is beyond my comprehension but the next step was to have Captain Alderman sign the 'detail'. He did this without demur. Everything would have been alright if some damn fool hadn't decided to steal a vehicle from the garages and drive it around in a drunken manner finally dumping it in a ditch several miles away. It was the duty N.C.O.'s job to lock the garages at 5pm each day and naturally this hadn't been done this day. The Captain returned to work the day after Boxing Day and in due course I was sent for. He listened to my story open-mouthed and was faced with the fact that he had personally signed the detail. I was perfunctorily dismissed. Of course the poor man had to accept responsibility and was probably in quite serious trouble. The following day he summoned me again and told me exactly what he thought of my deception ending with the words 'Well as a soldier I cannot punish you but between gentlemen it was a bloody poor show!' Later when I was at Ripon Hall undertaking Theological training I wrote him a letter care of the Hampshire Regiment apologising for my bad behaviour.

There was also a sort of personal battle between myself and the Army going on at this time. Every Christmas it was customary for the officers to entertain the troops at Christmas lunch by carving the turkey and serving at table. The prospect of sitting through this appalled me. It seemed hypocritical and pointless. In fact the truth of the matter was that I was actually suffering from anger and jealousy because I had failed to obtain my Commission! The problem I had always had with Authority was still plaguing me. I decided not to attend the lunch but to book myself out and have a meal at the Church of Scotland Hostel in the city. This had been set up to provide some help for soldiers in need of rest and relaxation away from Army life and was a kind of Toc.H – the famous organisation set up by Tubby Clayton a World War One padre in France which then spread all over the world. So I sat down to eggs, bacon and chips with christmas pudding to follow. I was alone in the dining room, it had snowed and was very cold and after lunch I wandered alone around the deserted city. I even followed a girl for a while but then took fright and headed back to the barracks cold and misreable. I had been to church in the morning at the little Lutheran church which allowed services in English for the sake of the Army. The Army padre was a nice man and before I left Germany he actually offered me a job as a curate in two years time when he would be working at a church in Kent. He became quite cross with me on one occasion when I suggested my room mate as a Sunday school teacher. He was a Lance Corporal and a friendly Welshman some years my senior. The padre called to see me the day after my request and asked if I was aware that my room mate was married with a family back in Wales but also had a girlfriend in the city! I said that he had spoken about a girl in the city but in my naivete I hadn't thought anything of it! All in all Christmas had been something of a disaster for me.

The Church of Scotland hostel was a good place to visit. There was a reading room with British newspapers, a music room for playing classical music and table tennis and snooker available in another room. It was at this hostel that I was asked for the only time in my life if I had been 'saved'! The question came from one of the staff. I had to ask what he meant and when he said it was about knowing Jesus as my personal Saviour and Lord. I told him about my invitation to Jesus to come into my life when I was at University and this seemed to be the answer he was looking for. At least I now understood that this was the meaning of the terminology 'saved'!

There was another visit worth making in Munster and this was to an organisation called 'The Bridge'. They met in a Library and the aim was to bring German and English nationals together so that the Germans could improve their English. This suited me well as it provided somewhere acceptable for me to go when off duty. We would read mainly plays one of which was 'The Admirable Crichton'. We were supposed to act these plays out but this never happened. On one occasion we had a debate and I was asked to oppose the motion that 'Democracy has within it the seeds of its own destruction', a notion close to the hearts of post-war young Germans. My main thesis was that democracy was the result of christian civilisation and Jesus' teaching about the leader's role as servant was the foundation of democratic ideals. The proposer of the motion criticised me for bringing religion into the argument but we won the debate!

Out of this pleasant gathering grew two new friendships. One was a Christian student at the university who also lived in the city and he invited me to the Cathedral for the Easter vigil. In those days it started at 11.30pm and lasted until 3am. It was my first experience of Catholic worship and I think I understood very little of it. But the atmosphere of the Cathedral re-built after the bombing of the war during which the Bishop had boldly preached against Nazism, was something I found quite wonderful. My friend then invited me back to his home where the rest of his family entertained me to a breakfast of painted eggs and other Easter specialties.

The other friend was a girl called Rosevita. She was very shy, had long blond hair and seemed keen on learning English. We went for long walks and she invited me back to a very grand house for tea one day. Her parents were most suspicious of me. She also came to the Lutheran church with me for an Evensong but next week told me that her priest was not pleased with her at confession and had forbidden her to attend again. We held hands but kissed only once after which she fled into her home. The next time we met she told me she could only kiss the man she was to marry! When I returned to England we wrote a few times and then the relationship fizzled out. I actually saw her once more about two years later but that story can wait. She was a committed catholic and was the first person to tell me she loved praying to the Holy Spirit, something that hadn't occurred to me before. I did write to Ben Forster - the curate in Sheet who had taught me to serve at the altar and had encouraged my vocation, to ask about marrying a Roman Catholic and he wrote back 'Can't be done! Yours Ben'. These were my only social activities outside of the camp apart from an infamous visit to a Night Club with a young officer who had been junior to me at Churchers and was now in the same barracks as me. He thought it would be great fun to treat his old Head Boy but unfortunately he was a bit over generous!

Guard duty sticks in my memory as this was on a rota basis and came round four or five times whilst I was there. It involved two hours on duty patrolling the camp perimeter and then four hours off for sleeping. The trouble was that the Duty Officer was expected to do an inspection at least once a night and if you happened to be sleeping at the time it was a rush to get out in line at the double. It was against the rules to remove ones belt whilst sleeping but it was also the rule that the belt had to be worn so tight the inspecting officer couldn't get his fingers between your belt and your body! Sleeping therefore could be very difficult. Most of us removed our belts anyway to get some rest. However on one particular night we were suddenly awakened and I just couldn't get my belt done up. The only thing I could do was to appear in line holding my belt in place with one hand. The young officer was so surprised that he couldn't refrain from smiling and let me off with a word of caution. Another memory of guard duty is of getting very cold walking around the perimeter fence and creeping into an old shed for a break only to wake up about twenty minutes later. The shock of what would have happened if I had been discovered or some emergency had occurred kept me well awake for the remainder of the time.

On another occasion I was put on a 'charge'. A certain officer had put in a request for transport and somehow I had omitted this on the rota. Suddenly there was this irate figure at the door shouting for his jeep. When he discovered the error he shouted again 'Corporal, put that man on a charge.' These 'trials' took place every Wednesday morning when the offender was marched in front of the Commanding Officer by the Company Sergeant major shouting 'Left, right, left, right, halt, left turn!' The culprit was then facing the Officer behind his desk. I had no idea what to expect when out of the blue help arrived. There was a tall, rather gormless-looking Lance Corporal who had been in the Army many years and the previous morning he had strolled into the office, sat on the table and said to me 'You know what to say don't you?' I looked puzzled. He went on 'On the charge you say 'Sir, the job I am doing is usually that of a Corporal and I am a Private. It is above my level of responsibility.' That's what you say.' I thanked him very much and he slouched out. Obviously there are some people in all walks of life who know the system and how to use it to their advantage! The following morning I repeated what he had said and it worked as if by magic. The Major said at once 'Quite right. Case dismissed'. About turn, left, right, left, right and I was out the door again in about thirty seconds. Before he dismissed me the C.S.M. said 'Some people have all the luck'.

A much happier memory is of a visit to have dinner in the home of a contact made through my friend Hugh Crawford in Sheet. Two brothers from Munster had visited Hugh at his home in the early 1950's and he had invited me along to his lovely home in an old mill to meet them. Karl was the elder and became a lawyer and was also the Mayor of Munster in the 1960's. Jurgan, the other brother was studying English at Munster University and I lent him my copy of 'Boewulf' and never saw it again! Sadly I heard several years later that Karl had committed suicide and Jurgan became an alcoholic. Anyway Hugh had written to the family to say I was in Munster and they kindly invited me to their home and to bring a friend if I so wished. There was a lovely bloke called Hibbs who was something of an academic and therefore viewed as a misfit in the Army and we had become friends. In fact there were four of us there who had all failed Commissions. The other three all came from Public Schools but as I had been to University I was allowed to join the 'ex-Public School Pupils Club.' On the day of the invitation Hibbs and I dressed in our best civvies and went along for a meal that was super and hospitality of the very best. The father had been an officer in the first world war and was a real monarchist and also a romantic. He entertained us with songs on the piano following dinner. I can't remember there being a Mrs. Gessau present so perhaps she had died. I heard later from Hugh that the family had said they really enjoyed the evening but the father had been unable to understand why we had dressed in our civvies. He had thought we would have been proud to wear the Queen's uniform!

Another happy occasion was a weekend in Amsterdam when a coach trip was organised. We were to stay in private homes and visit the bulb fields. Hibbs and I went together and we found our hostess (a widow lady) very sweet and anxious to please but with very little understanding of the English language. Still we managed well enough except for church on Sunday when we tried to explain to her that we were not Catholics and she just nodded her head agreeably enough. On the Sunday morning she indicated that we should go with her and we found ourselves in a Catholic Mass. Nothing daunted we decided to receive Communion. The bulbs were amazing, masses of colour for as far as the eye could see. I sent a colour postcard home. Of course we had to see the red light district as well.

Towards the end of our time there it was decided to have a mock attack on the camp. Those in charge must have decided that life was a little dull! When the siren went we were all to put our gas masks on and get on with our work as normally as possible. This wasn't too difficult for me as all I had to do was to sit at my desk and wait for the phone to ring. However when it did I realised how difficult it is answering the telephone with a gas mask on! Listening wasn't too bad as long as I could decipher what the caller, also wearing a gas mask, was saying but replying was well nigh impossible wearing the kind of mask I had been issued with. I lifted my mouthpiece up so I could talk more coherently. It was the R.S.M. wanting to know if the R.M.T. Captain was there as he couldn't raise him in his office. When I replied he interrupted me saying 'Have you got your gas mask on?' 'Just lifted it up to speak' I said. 'Then bloody well put it back on again you mut head.' It then took him several minutes to hear that the Captain was indeed not in my office!

So the time passed reasonably peacefully by and at the beginning of July I was sent for by the Commanding Officer. What now? Left, right, left, right, into the same office as before. He looked at me and I saw for the first time what a studious man he appeared with his glasses on and what a kind face he had. He said, 'Duffett, I understand that you are to start training at a Theological college when you leave here.' 'Yes Sir.' 'I believe there is a term which begins at the end of July?' 'Yes Sir.' It was the church's way of making use of the very long summer vacation which most other colleges have. 'Very well. I have decided that you can be de-mobbed a month early so that you can attend. Good luck. Dismiss.' I more or less flew out of his office. What thoughtful kindness. That meant I had less than two weeks left to serve! To this day I don't know who had furnished him with this information. Rosevita was thrilled. 'You have a very special vocation' she said and gave me a card with an icon of a Black Madonna on it and she had written the words 'With best wishes, Rosevita.' I still have this somewhere.

I can remember nothing about the journey home – I must have been on cloud nine. The two years had come suddenly and unexpectedly to an end. It had been a strange time but perhaps I had matured a little and had the corners rounded a little as they say. Maybe that is what the Bishop meant when he had advised me to join the Infantry. I have never regretted it anyway.

CHAPTER 6

BACK TO ALMA MATER

Boars Hill on the way to Abingdon from Oxford is a place of dales and woods. The strangely named Ripon Hall was on a site that was once the home of a Peer of the Realm. It had been bought for a handsome sum of money by the Reverend Dr. Henry Major, the founder of a theological college for Church of England ordinands which had begun in the early 1900's. A bequest enabled the good Doctor to fulfil a dream and move to Oxford in 1919. The site there was coveted by the Bodlein library who paid therefore a good price for it and enabled the move to Boars Hill to happen. Here there was room for expansion and the generous grounds including a small lake made the site ideal for a college of young gentlemen seeking Holy Orders. Across the roads was a large field used as a paddock for several horses. The village was sparsely spaced over a wide area and consisted mainly of large houses for the well-heeled and had one pub, 'The Fox'. Unfortunately the college had fallen on hard times. The dear Doctor was known for his liberal views and was in fact the last Church of England clergyman to be officially tried for 'heresy'. In the early 1920's he had written and preached that the resurrection of Jesus did not depend on the empty tomb. Before his trial was held the then Archbishop of Canterbury asked him to write an essay on the subject. After the Archbishop had read this essay he said he could find nothing wrong with it so the trial never took place. But the reputation of liberal theology stuck with the college. It was said that 'The Times' might be read in Chapel for the second lesson at Matins! Also the Principal had become aged but refused to give up so in 1955 the college had only some four or five students and something had to be done about the situation. The 'something' was that Colonel Nasser expelled the Anglican Bishop from Cairo and at the same time the national number of ordinands was growing every year. Dr. Geoffrey Fisher, the Archbishop of Canterbury at that time asked the exiled Bishop of Cairo, Geoffrey Allen, to take over Ripon Hall and 'pull it together'! Dear Dr. Henry Major had just turned eighty and was offered the living of Merton, a village a few miles away where he could end his days.

Geoffrey Allen set about the job with great enthusiasm and it was the new prospectus he had put together that had so attracted me before I joined the Army. Sometime after my finals I had been put forward by the Bishop of Portsmouth to attend a selection course for the ministry. This took place over a weekend at Farnham Castle the vast home of the Bishop of Guildford. It consisted of a number of interviews with the entire Board and also with individual board members. Their decision that I was acceptable was communicated by the Board before I left on the Sunday afternoon. That then gave me the freedom to look around for a place to undertake my training for the statutory two years which would be paid for by the Church. My vicar took it for granted that I would go to Cuddesdon where he had trained and I did visit there and was told by the Principal, Knapp Fisher that I could apply. But I felt the village was acceptable, rather remote and too cut off from my beloved Oxford nine miles away. When Ben found out about my application to Ripon Hall he was not at all pleased referring to it as 'hardly a Theological College at all!' My interview at Ripon Hall went well and it was suggested that I study for an Oxford Diploma in Theology, a suggestion that pleased me very much.

What I found there in July 1957 filled me with interest and hope. A good proportion of the members were mature men and most of them were already married. The Army and the Navy were giving men in their late forties 'a golden handshake' and this provided them with some financial freedom. New arrivals at Ripon Hall included a Colonel and two Naval Commanders one of whom had been in submarines and lived in Gosport. Oliver St. John became a good friend. Another new arrival had been a school inspector and was in his late fifties. Both he and his son were ordained on the same day. There were only three full-time staff and the chaplain was a young priest, an excellent preacher who was also full of fun and a real demon on the croquet pitch on the main lawn. The Vice Principal had served with the Church Missionary Society in Nigeria at a Theological College and as he was musical he helped with the practices we had each week for our chapel services.

In fact I had very little to do with the academic side of the college, as because my Diploma in Theology was offered through the University it meant I had a tutor in one of the Colleges there. The diploma was about half-way to a degree and allowed me to be exempted from certain of the subjects required by the ordinands' final exams. One other student, Mervyn Wilson was also taking this route to ordination and we would board the red bus which terminated just outside college for the four mile journey into Oxford. How wonderful to be back in the city of dreaming spires! The freedom was like champagne and almost as dangerous as drinking too much of it could be!

We had been directed to Oriel College to a Reverend Dennis Whiteley who I think was also the author of science fiction novels. When we met we found him to be a small man in a dirty cassock with a head larger than most – because his brain was! We sat full of nerves in his tiny book laden room on the second floor at the end of a narrow winding staircase. He didn't do much to alleviate these nerves, speaking to us as though we knew much more than we actually did. He made us work hard and expected a high standard from us which was no bad thing especially as I had lost the aptitude for studious work. It was like being back at Keble in some ways and I soon settled to the routine of attending a few lectures each week in the Theology faculty.

One lecturer was a young chaplain and fellow of Lincoln College by the name of Kemp. He recently retired in his eighties as the Bishop of Chichester. Another was in his 60's, a Professor Jenkins who arrived carrying a large alarm clock and when it went off one hour after the start of his lecture he would stop, even if in mid-sentence, and march out! It was said that he used pieces of toast as book-markers. Certainly one student who was curious about the pile of books this Professor always brought in was amused when he crept up to get a closer view to discover that most of them were on gardening! Another famous lecturer was Dr. Chadwick who taught on the Old Testament and ethics. Our teacher on doctrine was the Bishop of Oxford. He also marked the 'doctrine' paper and always had my admiration as you will see later. An outside member of staff at the Hall was a lovely retired classics teacher who came in three days a week and tried to teach us New Testament Greek. He was always affable as he sat smoking his hooker pipe. One set of lectures which were particularly noteworthy were given by the Principal of St. Stephen's House, the very High Church college in the city. They were all about Liturgy. This subject is largely of interest to the clergy but it has many historical, theological and pastoral aspects to it. What was illuminating was the way the church was always developing and experimenting in spite of its uniform appearance. It was amazing to learn that even as early as 1958 priests in France were pulling their altars away from the wall in order to stand behind them and experimenting with modern music, but putting them back whenever the Bishop came to visit!

Ripon Hall had a simple chapel full of light but very traditional. Nothing but the Book of Common Prayer was ever used and the hymns were all 'Ancient and Modern'. The setting for the Sunday Communion service was Merbeck written in the 17th century. It was here we had Morning Prayer every morning before breakfast and on Fridays a Holy Communion as well. Every evening there was Evening Prayer before supper. We were expected to attend all these services but students were always missing and no questions were ever asked. Just occasionally I missed a service because I had over-slept or made arrangements to go out somewhere in the evening. On Wednesday evenings we would have a visiting preacher and felt most spoiled by hearing some of the best in the land all eager to set us off on the right track. There are only two whom I can actually remember by name. One was the then Bishop of Hong Kong, a chap called Hall and the other was the rector of St. Aldates in Oxford, Keith de Berry who was at St. Aldates when I had been a regular attender there. Otherwise Evening Prayer would be led by a student and after the third collect someone else would lead more informal prayers. On one occasion the conductor had been especially slow – either that or the two hymns were exceptionally long – but the bell for supper rang just as the formal part of the service ended. When the student who was to lead the prayers said 'Let us pray' the Principal interrupted with 'I don't think we will. Supper is ready!' The Principal always sat in the same place, a corner seat, and he had a habit of quite often taking a little black notebook from his pocket and writing something down in it. This would happen even whilst prayers were being said and it annoyed some of us who found it difficult to understand how he could pray and write notes at the same time. Duncan Buchanan and I decided to speak to him about it. We asked him for an interview and he listened politely, if a bit stiffly, thanked us and we left. He never asked us what we were doing looking at him whilst we were supposed to be praying! That little book then stayed in his pocket during chapel services for about a week! He was a cheerful and almost expansive character at times, beaming away especially when visitors like the College Governors came to see us. He was quite rightly very proud of his achievement in turning a failing college around into a vibrant fellowship of committed and not unintelligent men.

Of course there were no ladies present at the college and in fact those men who were married had to leave their families at home and visit them just twice a term. Fiancees and girlfriends were allowed to visit for Saturday and Sunday tea only. This proved to be a problem when one fiancee from South Africa came to stay for some length of time to see her future husband. The only solution was for him to visit her where she was staying as often as he could. On the whole life was very pleasant – too pleasant really. There was a sort of feeling about the college that it was actually a 'Gentleman's Club' where work was done but at no great pressure. The Church in those days still saw its training as academic above anything else. The only training in preaching that I can remember receiving was to prepare a sermon for the two or three occasions when it was my turn to do Sunday duty out in a parish. The prepared sermon would be read through in advance by the chaplain and suggestions made on its style, etc. and was then available for delivery at the church which had asked for our help, or more precisely had offered to help us! If there was ever any follow-up with the vicar I never heard about it.

There were two occasions that I can't allow to be forgotten however. The first was at Merton where dear Henry Major had been put out to grass. He was practically blind and very doddery on his feet and insisted on saying the service from memory which meant that on this occasion we had part of the consecration prayer twice. He also prayed the collect from memory and announced the Epistle and Gospel which was then read by the student. He was very deaf and carried an old-fashioned hearing aid and when you began preaching he would hold it up in front of him in order to hear properly. I had been told to keep my eye on it as he had been known to switch it off and put it away. On this occasion the most extraordinary thing happened in the vestry. It was a very cold November day and he came in with his overcoat on and his 'man-servant' helped him into his cassock over his coat. Then followed his surplice and stole and after that he was turned around three or four times in a circle. I was wondering what this was all about when I realised he was standing over a heating grate and the 'man-servant' was warming him up! He always turned round at the words of consecration to face the congregation and this was the first time I had seen it as it was practically unknown at the time. He told me later that it had been a practice of Bishop King, the saintly bishop of Lincoln who had died many years before. Henry liked talking and at the meal in the Rectory after the service he talked so much his meal lay untouched. His wife who was a sprightly 83 year old and in charge of the Sunday School said 'Henry if you don't eat your food I'll take away your hearing aid!' He didn't and she did! We then ate in solemn silence. He asked me if I had met Bishop King obviously forgetting how many years he had been dead. He also told me that he had his wallet stolen when he went to Mass in St. Peter's, Rome with the Pope presiding. He insisted on calling all the students 'brother' but as he had a slight lisp it came out as 'bwuvver'. It was at Evensong that I had preached and when I left later that night I felt that heretic or not I had been in the presence of one of God's saints. The 'man-servant' was called 'Box' because he knelt at the end of the Holy Communion rail and Dr. Major gave him anything that was left over to prevent any mishap on the way back to the altar.

The other memory is of a terrible moment when I was preaching somewhere in quite a large church and an elderly lady sitting beneath me said in an audible whisper during my address 'It doesn't mean that at all.' Afterwards when I enquired who she was I was informed 'Oh that's Miss Ward. She is Professor of Hebrew at Oxford.'

Apart from that we didn't go out much at all apart from a very nice engagement once every two weeks when two of us would catch the bus on Sunday morning down to Abingdon to help with the Sunday School. What I especially remember is the lovely lunch we would be given afterwards at the Simmons' home. Mrs. Simmons kept in touch with me for several years afterwards.

As drama had always been an interest of mine and I had failed to get a part in one of Keble's plays I thought I would try and have a go at producing one myself at Ripon Hall. I chose a favourite of mine, Christopher Fry's 'Sleep of Prisoners.' It wasn't until my second year that the way seemed clear to put it on. The college had been invited to take part in a parish 'Mission' in the town of Leek and we were to be stationed in different churches but the mission would be for the whole town. This was to take place over Easter so the play could be performed at the end of the Lent term and then taken to Leek to be part of the mission. The great advantage of this play is that it only involves four men. They are prisoners of war locked up in a church and they dream of some of the great biblical stories – Cain & Abel, Abraham & Isaac, David & Absalom – and act these out in a composite dream. Finally they find themselves in the fiery furnace of Daniel and his friends and the whole experience is one of healing and spiritual growth. The four who volunteered to take part in the production included my South African friend, Duncan Buchanan who has recently retired as Bishop of Johannessberg, my colleague who was doing the diploma, a student whose name eludes me and a New Zealander, St. John Edwards. Of course others helped behind stage and it all proved to be a great success. When we took it on tour to Leek we were honoured to be offered the large Victorian church of All Saints with its enormous chancel and arches. On dress rehearsal night we had until 9pm when Compline was to take place. The last scene requires the production of a lot of smoke to simulate the fiery furnace and we had a chemistry graduate to help with this. We ran a bit late and unfortunately he got carried away with the size of the church and when the vicar arrived to prepare for the service he was met by clouds of smoke through which he could hardly find his way to the front. Like Queen Victoria 'he was not amused'!

In the first year our dramatic efforts had been confined to a performance on the old kind of tape recorder of a 'Goon Show' performed by Duncan, St. John and myself to be played at the end of term party.

At Christmas it was decided to invite the Sunday School from Abingdon for a party and I hit on the idea of doing a joint impromptu Nativity play in which all the children could take part. We had a lovely large dining hall with oak panelled walls and a vast fireplace. This was divided into stations and the story was read in parts with the children acting then out on the spot. The stable was the fireplace! It went down very well with the fifty or so children who were there.

The holidays were used for special courses or missions like the one to Leek. The first year we went to Didsbury, part of Manchester, to the parish church Holy Trinity and the pattern was much the same as my earlier visits with the Oxford Pastorate. We visited homes, attended coffee meetings with some talk given by a member of staff or student and went to larger gatherings in the evenings with films or longer talks. I stayed in the home of two good church people, the Butlers. They had a daughter Susan who was a photographic model. It was fairly inevitable that she and I should become firm friends, being the same age and it was agreed that she would come to Ripon Hall for a weekend. There after we were boy and girlfriend and she visited my home in Sheet on a couple of occasions. She was very sweet but rather quiet. Eventually we decided to visit Devon together as one of my fellow student's parents owned a Christian holiday home above Exeter and not far from Dawlish. In exchange for free board we were to help with the washing up and so on. Susan came down to Sheet first and it was worrying me that we had been together for a year and the relationship seemed to be 'stuck'. It wasn't moving forward and nor was I sure that it should but yet again felt guilty at the prospect of breaking a nice girl's heart. I decided that the best way out was to take a step forward and ask Susan to marry me. As I was almost penniless I had asked Mother if I could borrow her engagement ring until such time as I could afford to buy one. So we set off on the National Express coach to Exeter duly engaged! I think I regretted it almost at once and felt trapped and Susan also knew deep in her heart that things weren't quite as they should be. On the third day at the home where morning devotion was held after breakfast each day Psalm 112 had been used 'For the godly light arises in the darkness' and I asked Susan if we could break off the engagement. There were of course some tears but it was agreed and after that the relationship just more or less fizzled out.

Soon after returning to college we had a visit from a South African businessman. Douglas had lived in Natal all his life and struck me as an old-fashioned English gentleman, always immaculately dressed, carrying a rolled umbrella and wearing a trilby. He had joined the political Federal Party which campaigned for Natal to secede from the then Union of South Africa. He had been surprised, hurt and frightened at the hatred this had inspired and felt that he had to leave for fear of his life. His story touched me and as he lived near Exeter he invited me to visit him the next time I was working down at the Christian Home there. He had bought a little pig farm and seemed to be enjoying his life, when I heard that he was losing money and would need to sell up. He had a buyer but nowhere else to live and so I asked the owners of the Home if they could accommodate him pro-tem. They agreed and the next time I went there he was also there. Later he bought a 'castle' on the side of the river near Dartmouth. How he could afford it remains a mystery! I have always maintained that the reason he could afford this sort of property was because of something he later told me. He had received a telephone call from Buckingham Palace to say that the Queen wished to visit the castle and would come for coffee. It may not be true but that was his story. The student I was friendly with whose parents owned the Christian Holiday home became an Army chaplain, married a German girl and tragically died of a heart attack at the age of 47 years. I kept in touch with his mother until her Christmas cards stopped when she was 94 years old.

The two parish 'missions' weren't the only extra-mural activities and there was also an exciting week trailing the Industrial chaplain for the Manchester Diocese. This kind of chaplaincy was in its infancy in 1958 but Peter Brooks had established himself in a run-down church abandoned when the motor industry took over the site, and was deeply involved with the workers, unions and management. We had seminars about the aims and objectives of the work and visits to various factories and I also experienced my only journey underground at a Wigan coal-mine. The college paid for these activities as well.

Apart from these exceptions the so called training was rather laid back and theoretical. I think I was still under the illusion that I was going in to a fairly undemanding job with a most acceptable and pleasant social status attached to it. The middle class 'social climbing' had obviously rubbed off on me! I suspect at that stage in my life it was a sub-conscious attitude but even at that early age present in me. The other association with my future work was known as a 'calling', and I felt sure that God had made it clear to me that it was what He wanted me to do. This helped me a lot with the emerging academic theological questions at that time. There was one student who had been taught a very simple biblical faith and all questions about the bible seemd to threaten him. He left after just one term.

Going back to my visit to Leek there is one story that perhaps merits a telling. It was decided that three of us should do some open-air work and that one of us, David Chandler should mount the memorial in the town square and give a short 'word' to the local shoppers. The other two of us would stand and support him encouraging the shoppers to attend the mission meetings by giving out flyers. Of course 'muggins' had to come up with an idea of doubtful morality! I decided to borrow a flat cap and an old raincoat and masquerade as one of the locals. When David had finished his talk I got up onto the platform and said how well he had spoken and that we should all support the mission. I remember at the time that David had grave doubts about this idea.

There was one other mission type situation whilst I was at Ripon Hall. Duncan Buchanan the South African had to find somewhere to spend Christmas and the vicar in my sister Coral's parish had asked her if I would be willing to go and help him out in the week before Christmas. It was decided that both Duncan and myself should go. It was in the town of Stevenage, a fast growing area, and based on one of the old churches, St. Mary's. We had a lovely time wearing our cassocks visiting and I still remember the story I had made up to tell at the childrens' service.

Duncan was a useful cricketer and was made Captain of the college team. We played three or four matches in the summer usually against other colleges or local villages. There was one celebrated occasion when Duncan, who opened the bowling, started his run-up for first ball of the match and suddenly stopped in full flight. He had seen a cow patch right in his path and had to alter the direction of his run up which completely ruined his rhythm. In the same match another of our team was running for the ball in the field when he too suddenly stopped. The ball was nowhere to be seen. Eventually it was discovered down a rabbit hole! By this time the batsman had run five. In another match I wondered why some of the other team were staring at me. I discovered later that the reason was the sweater I was wearing. As it was chilly and I didn't possess a sweater I had borrowed one from a fellow student and it happened to be the one he was awarded when he had played for the Cambridge University hockey first team (a 'blue'!)

Towards the end of the summer term in 1959 we had exams. It was made clear to me that Dr. Whitely expected Mervyn to do well but he was far from sure about me! We also had to write the papers in the ordinands' exam which we had not been exempted from. This scared me because I had worked hard for the Diploma but couldn't put my heart into the others. The results came out in the vacation term we had in July/August. I had passed the Diploma and had in fact just missed a distinction in the 'Doctrine' paper. Dr. Whitely was profuse in his congratulations hardly able to conceal his enormous surprise. The 'Ordinands Exams' however were a flop and I only just scraped through. This called for a summons to the Principal who said he was disappointed with me as he was sure I could have done better and I obviously hadn't worked hard enough. On the whole he was right!

Before the end of the summer, dealing through the Principal, negotiations had to be made for a post as a curate in a Parish. It was expected that I would serve my 'title' somewhere in the Diocese of Portsmouth as they had sponsored me. A couple of years previously Ben Forster, who had been Priest in charge of Sheet, had taken up the offer of a larger Parish in the east of Portsmouth – St. Cuthbert's in Copner. I wrote to him and asked if it would be possible for me to join him. He already had two curates but as the Bishop looked on him as one of the 'trainers' in the Diocese and had once described him to me as a 'corker', it was agreed that I could join his staff. The accommodation was to be in a 'clergy-house' opposite a large pond and next door to a pub called 'The Baffins' after the name of the area. On the other side of us were a couple belonging to the Salvation Army. The church was about ¾ mile away and we were expected to travel by bicycle. I can't remember where I got mine from but it was to see a great deal of work in the next four years. There were just two of us in the house to begin with and we each had a bed-sit and shared a common sitting room. When Tom, a third member of the house joined us I was designated the sitting room as my bed-sit. The family rallied round to furnish me with the necessaries and I recall my new bed sheets were a present from sister Joy. There must have already been some furniture in there and probably a carpet and a bed. The desk was against the wall with a bookshelf close by. It was really much the same as I had at Ripon Hall. We had a house-keeper who 'did' for us, coming in each morning and cooking our lunch before leaving after the washing-up. For breakfast and supper we looked after ourselves.

The last day at Rupon Hall Oxford March 1959. Dont know about the moustache!

All these arrangements were in place before I went on Ordination Retreat at Catherington House, the Diocesan Retreat Centre. The ordination was set for Trinity Sunday, 1959 in Portsmouth Cathedral. We looked very fresh in our new cassocks and surplices and more than a little green in our new collars and bibs as was the fashion in those days! I felt very excited but quite nervous as the day approached. It was reassuring to have about twenty others waiting to become deacons at the same time. 1959 was the record year for the largest number of ordinations into the Church of England – 930!

CHAPTER 7

CITY PARISH – THE HALCYON YEARS

There is nothing that I can remember about the pre-ordination retreat except that the priest from Hayling Island, who was known for his popularity at Butlins, played skittles with the Bishop. I wondered at his familiarity with someone I stood in awe of. The same thing happened later when the 'junior' clergy were summoned to meet the Archdeacon of Portsmouth at the Cathedral. We all wore our cassocks with the exception of one slightly older man who even addressed the Archdeacon by his christian name! I was shocked out of my socks!

The morning of the ordination arrived and we were all up at the crack of dawn. It didn't occur to me at the time how blessed I was to be in the village where I had been baptised with my family just down the road. The cathedral was packed and many of my supporters were there. It was a transcendent occasion. I had received letters of encouragement from many people who couldn't be there for the service including Eric Abbott who was then warden of Keble and later became Dean of Westminster Abbey. He had taken a retreat at Ripon Hall and arranged for me to see a christian Psychiatrist because I was worried by the fact that I was constantly falling in love with girls and then running away. The Psychiatrist told me it would get better when I married – not very deep wisdom really! I still have those ordination letters received from priests, relatives and friends from all over the country. The Greek New Testament with Lancelot Fleming's signature in it still sits on my bookshelves although it does rather gather dust these days. The white stole which was draped over us, deacon-wise, stayed with me until it was stolen in Durban together with a white cassock and other books and stoles. I didn't know at that time that African 'Zionist' (a sect made up of a mixture of African indigenous religion and christianity) ministers stole these as they were unable to afford their own. After the ordination service we all had our photographs taken and went out to lunch. Later that day Mother and my sisters descended on Clergy-House to help me settle in.

St. Cuthbert's was a parish church of about 16,000 people and had been a 'plant' of St. James Milton just two miles down the road when Portsmouth dockyard took on thousands of new workers. It was a visionary building. A copy of the Roman Catholic cathedral in Westminster, it could easily hold 300 people with many more if necessary. The beautiful Byzantine apse had been blown off by a Nazi bomb and replaced by a flat end which spoilt its symmetry. This new piece in the building had only just been completed in 1959 and was still to be consecrated. It included the whole sanctuary and chancel with brand new organ and choir stalls and a beautiful Lady Chapel on the south side which held up to thirty people. On the north side there were new vestries and upstairs a parish room where the PCC could meet. The thirty Sunday School teachers also met in here every Tuesday evening for preparation. Next door was an ample church hall in which the parish 'breakfast' was held every Sunday after the 9.30 am sung Communion service. A hundred or so teenagers also met here on Friday evenings and a smaller number of 11–15 year olds on Wednesdays. The church hall was also the meeting place for the Womens Guild once

My first church
The consecration of the East End St Cuthberts Copnor 1959. The original was bombed 1941

a month and occasionally even hosted wedding receptions. It was an impressive 'plant'. The congregation would average about 25 for the 8.00 am said Communion service and about 200 – 250 at the later service. All the teenagers attended this service as it was compulsory for admission to the 'Red Door Club' as their Friday evening meetings were called. Sunday school began at 11 am and was for 7-11 year olds. The numbers attending Sunday school varied but there were usually at least 150. Older children had special classes as a pre-confirmation class and Evening Prayer at 6.30pm was usually attended by about 30 people. The choir was impressive with about 30 members ranging in age from 7 to 80 years! Baptisms took place at 3.00pm once a month and on one memorable occasion I baptised thirteen infants at one time. The noise was deafening but not because of the children squalling as much as because of their parents talking! There was always a parents' preparation meeting for baptism during the preceding week and attendance was obligatory.

Ben organised his staff like an extension of Cuddesdon Theological College! There was a Communion service every morning at 7.00am followed by Morning Prayer followed by twenty minutes of silent reading or meditation. Our departure was signaled by Ben rising from his knees and marching out of the Lady Chapel door. We left by the side door collecting our bikes and cycling back for an 8.30am breakfast. Seldom did Ben greet us! After breakfast came time for study, writing or preparation for a meeting or class. Once a month or so we had a sermon to prepare. We all bought the daily papers – Patrick took the Manchester Guardian, I had the Daily Mirror and Ted and Tom both had the Times. I think we took some time to read our paper before getting down to the work! On Wednesdays there was a 10am service and we would attend this with coffee afterwards.

Once a week on Fridays there was a staff meeting which would usually last from 10am until lunchtime. I enjoyed these staff meetings. First of all we reported back on our week's visiting. We had all been assigned to a district and given a black book in which we wrote down all the names of the people we had visited, their address and anything interesting of note about them. The book had to be kept tidily with neat lines across and up and down so that it could easily be consulted and understood. The details were filled in as soon as possible after the visit for the sake of accuracy. I was given streets called Dover, Folkestone, Chesterfield and Baffins Roads with St. Pirans Avenue – some 1200 houses in total. I was expected to visit every single one of them and indeed I did. We used abbreviations we made up in the columns of our black books and carried them with us in our cassock pocket. We always visited in our cassocks hitching up the back and fastening it inside our belt when cycling! Cnfd=confirmed, cmct=communicant, non-c=non-churchgoer, bapt=wanting baptism plus a few others I can't recall. It wasn't often necessary to mention the couple living together were not married as in those days very few weren't but dvcd=divorced was quite common. Some other note might be entered indicating whether they were interested in another visit and if they were friendly, or not, to the church. Most people were welcoming and on one day of almost constant visiting I drank seventeen cups of tea in seventeen visits! There were occasional mishaps like the lady who was registered blind. I had performed her wedding a few weeks previously to a man who was also registered as blind. They were both in their sixties. When I knocked on their door one day it was opened and a parcel wrapped in brown paper was thrust towards me. All I could do was to take it in my arms upon which another was placed on top with the words 'And that is for the lady next door.' On realising it was me on the doorstep she cried 'Dearie me! I thought you was the laundry man.' On another very hot summer's day in 1959 I called at a house and the front door was open. As I was about to knock on the open door a scantily clad young lady emerged from a side room. Seeing me she screamed and shot back into the room again. It seemed wise to move on to next door! Then there was the first time I saw a dead body. The news that someone had died was imparted by a neighbour and I arrived at the house before the undertakers, as they were then called. We had a good system of 'street-wardens' who kept an eye out for their neighbours and if something was amiss or they heard something they thought we could help with they would telephone us or drop a specially printed card through our door. Many of our hospital visits were triggered in this way and were most favourably accepted. Most people were kindly disposed towards the church and glad that we took the trouble to get to know them and offer friendship or whatever it was they were most in need of. However there was a general air of apathy about joining in with church activities or accepting that belief in God required some kind of commitment. I remember commenting that the church appeared to me as a kind of a Bank. Many people had invested a great deal of love and service in her over hundreds of years but the generation of the 1950's and early 1960's were living off the capital and that one day she would be bankrupt! Succeeding generations have proved that to be true with changing values and the growth of a pluralist society. The staff meetings were also opportunities to work out strategy and some kind of on-going programme of activities for the next few months.

During the second year of my curacy Ben gave me my head and allowed me to see if I could produce a passion play. Copies of this venture have been discarded over the years but I remember it included a couple of angels as well as the disciples, a large crowd and other gospel figures such as Mary Magdalene. I also clearly remember that there was a cast of nearly one hundred and that I took the part of the leading angel and chose to sit on a sort of a throne on the top of the baldichen over the altar. I'm quite sure this was never intended to be sat upon! Ben's face was a picture when he first saw me doing this but he didn't forbid it. Music was provided by the organ and fellow curate, Tom Devonshire-Jones, on his violin. Where people got changed I cannot imagine! It ran for three nights to a packed church and I think affected all of us in the cast as well as many in the audience. The crowd scenes were particularly realistic and moving. The figure of Jesus never actually appeared but the crucifixion and resurrection were depicted. Rehearsals took place between 2 and 5.00pm on Sundays and as they started before Lent they became a sort of Lent Course in progress. It amazes me today that so many people were willing to give so much of their time and effort.

The next play put on in the parish was less ambitious as I suspect I was becoming more and more involved in my work and had less time to spare. It was a charming Christmas play translated from French and called 'Christmas in the Market Place.' It was the story of a group of 'travellers' who find themselves in a town one Christmas Eve and decide to perform their own version of the nativity. This ran in the Church Hall for three nights and again was well received.

The news of these performances soon spread and I received a letter from the new Bishop, John Phillips, asking if I would take on the role of 'Advisor on Drama' for the Diocese. He envisaged this being a sort of 'Lord Chamberlain' role where I would vet plays which could be performed in our churches. There was a significant event when this role was challenged ! There was a play put on by the Youth Group of the next-door church, St. Alban's, and they had a very keen youth leader who encouraged them to write their own nativity play. It was a very short play, only about twenty minutes long, and consisted of Joseph driving a large motor bike down the aisle with Mary on the back and a discussion about how it would feel to be an unmarried teenage mother. The word had got around that this was suggesting that Jesus was illegitimate with the result that for the two nights it was being performed the church was packed to the doors and the Press were there in force! The Bishop appeared to panic and sent along his Adult Education Officer without prior warning just to check that nothing untoward was taking place. He was most charming and said how impressed he was by the actors' simple sincerity! Amazingly two months later one of my Parishioners showed me a press cutting from a French daily newspaper with a photograph of Joseph and Mary on the motorbike.

There was also a 'bit of a hoo-haa' when I wrote to the Portsmouth Evening News after a poorly attended performance in the Cathedral which had been given by two actors who dedicated their work to the Missionary Society, U.S.P.G. They would perform extracts from plays and their own sketches in a truly professional manner and are still active some forty or so years later. My letter provoked an Editorial to the effect that the people of Portsmouth were not as bad as I had painted them to be but could probably improve their cultural pursuits. I never did discover if the Editor responsible was the same man I had been sent to read to at the age of five years! Also at this time the Religious Drama Society was becoming more active and I attended one of their summer schools whilst on holiday, at Bangor University, North Wales. We did a lot of workshops and generally had a great time. One person I met there obviously had a need and she invited me to visit her in Balham for a few days. I did so at my next available break and fortunately all was well as there was a risk involved in the visit – she was divorced! However she wasn't very pleased when I seemed to want to spend more time sleeping and visiting museums than listening to her. The tensions between work and relaxation are never far apart in a priest's life.

Mentioning the new Bishop means that I have jumped again. He came to the Diocese in 1960 when Lancelot Fleming was 'translated' to Norwich. It was therefore John who ordained me as a priest in his first ordination service. It was again a splendid occasion remembered chiefly by Mother because I wore one black sock and one grey one! Perhaps the murky early morning light at Catherington House had something to do with this. We were on Retreat there again. Much more memorable for me was the celebration of Eucharist the following morning. It had to be at 7.00am of course as Ben would not budge on 'the usual time' but even so about twenty parishioners and friends turned up. These included Mother who was concerned about how she was going to get there at such an early hour. Not to be daunted she asked the young man who was boarding with her if he would take her on the back of his Lambretta. He was a friend of mine who had been introduced to me by Michael Hamilton-Jones, the chaplain at Ripon Hall. Michael had heard that Andrew had got a job at Churchers College on completion of his training at Oxford having met up after a church service somewhere. Andrew had been in 'digs' at Greatham about five miles from the school but had to leave these after a year. Michael must have mentioned this to me because Mother agreed to take him in in September 1959. So at about 6.00am they left Sheet and roared up to the church at 6.50am with Mother still holding on to her hat which she had nearly lost going over Butser Hill! After the service we were all invited to breakfast at the Rectory. Ben had been very punctilious about how to celebrate 'the Cuddesdon way' and explaining the reason why one did these things in a certain way, like (in those days) keeping the thumb and fore-finger together after the consecration of the bread, and which candle was lit first. The 'gospel candle' never shone alone.

The work went on apace. As a deacon I had become familiar with the local crematorium and cemetery. In those days services at the cemetery were far more common than these days when the practice has almost ceased. The cemetery chapels were depressing Victorian brown barns with just a few pews and a place for the coffin. It took a long time for the church to persuade the authorities that it understood peoples' pastoral needs, with suggestions about a more appropriate way of handling cremations. As a deacon I was also allotted most of the weddings. This entailed meeting with the couple beforehand for what was called 'preparation'. What could I as a 26 year old bachelor tell them about marriage! What I did in fact was to go through the service in some detail with them, a lesson learnt in Theological College. It must have sounded like another language to some young couples. Another of my responsibilities was to help with the running of the 11-14 years old Youth Club on a Wednesday evening between 7.30 and 9.00pm. This meant generally helping with discipline and becoming involved in playing their games with them. I well remember the noise generated by thirty youngsters letting off steam under one roof! It has to be heard to be believed. Unfortunately one Wednesday evening during Lent it really got to me. We always had a 6.00am service on Wednesdays during Lent to cater for those going to work. Usually only about two or three people would attend. On this particular Wednesday it had been my turn to officiate and so as 9.00pm approached I was feeling particularly worn out. I 'snapped' as the popular expression would explain it! The shout I let out could have woken the dead and was such a surprise to all present that total silence descended. Embarrassed I then tried to explain why I had been so annoyed.

Then there was the Sunday School already mentioned. Every year there was an outing and one year I foolishly suggested Guildford Cathedral. We invited the school to apply for places by name and had almost 100% return! When we counted up the numbers including the teachers it came to 300! I rang British Rail and they agreed to lay on a special train but then we had to work out how to transport everyone to the station. I can't remember how we accomplished that – perhaps the trauma of it all resulted in amnesia! Anyway we left in good time. You can imagine the stock of energy required to keep almost three hundred children from leaning out of the windows, running along the corridor, which in those days trains had, fighting and generally creating mayhem! We did however arrive in one piece at Guildford station and somehow managed the journey up the hill to the Cathedral without mishap. The tour guides were magnificent and after an hour looking around we all assembled for a short service taken by one of the Canons. After that it was all outside for a picnic. In those days before the University of Surrey was built there was plenty of grass for 300 to decamp themselves onto. Our train home left at 3.00pm and we arrived back exhausted but happy.

This outing gave me an idea for the junior Youth Club. During their summer holiday I organised a Holiday Club but along different lines from those that became popular in the 1980's. We had outings to various institutions in the city such as The Guildhall, The Fire Service, and not forgetting H.M.S.Nelson and the Metal Box Factory which I visited every week as a sort of chaplain. They each gave us a talk about their work and then back at the church once more we would discuss what we had seen and learnt. This went down very well even though only about twelve to fifteen youngsters were prepared to join. Another activity which became popular was the collection of newspapers every Saturday. Our next-door neighbours had a friend in the Salvation Army who was prepared to lend us his lorry free of charge and also drive it for us. A man whose daughter was a member of the Sunday School and who lived across the road from the church offered to help me. Together with about six youngsters we went round the entire parish collecting about one ton of paper every Saturday. This brought in quite a good income for the Youth Club as the selling price for paper then was much better than it is now. I can still see Archie Deacon with his pipe standing by the side of the lorry. He telephoned me a few years ago and I couldn't understand why the Archdeacon of Portsmouth would want to speak with me! He was much amused. He was at that time a very keen Socialist and suggested that I become chaplain to the 'Young Socialists' in Portsmouth and so I went to a few of their meetings.

Of course finance was always a problem along with how to increase the church income. It was decided that we should have a 'Stewardship Campaign'. In those days 'Wells' were the people to organise this for us. They had originated in America as fund-raisers for business and adapted their methods to suit church purposes. It was done through publicity and a big 'meal evening' with speeches encouraging people to fill in the forms beneath their plate. It worked but many people had serious reservations about their methods. The get-together was so successful however that it was decided to have an annual Christmas

Ball at the Pavilion in Southsea. These were very popular and one year Patrick Miller, who was the curate senior to me, got two of his friends to come along and perform a little Cabaret. They had all been on the edges of 'The Footlights', the well-known Cambridge University group. One of these friends became the Dean of Westminster Abbey and another the Archdeacon of Prisons, the highest chaplain in the service. A partner was a requirement for such occasions and one year I asked the secretary in the Diocesan office to accompany me. We remained friends for a further year until it became clear that she was looking for progress in our relationship and all I could think about was going to South Africa! Another year I asked a nurse from St. Mary's Hospital, to whom my good friend Brenda had introduced me, to partner me and we had a brief relationship. One day I was called into Ben's study and asked what I was dong kissing a girl goodnight outside the hospital gates at 11pm. One of the church members had seen me! It had been a Saturday night and it was expected that I would have gone to bed early to prepare for the Sunday. I apologised and was much relieved that the 'spy' in question had been kind to me as it was actually 1am when we kissed goodnight!

Another of the 'Fellowship Events' was the summer garden party in the Rectory garden, the only one in the area that was large enough for such an occasion. One year I suggested asking the Composer of the musical 'Salad Days' which was running for the summer season at the King's Theatre in Southsea to come and open the garden party for us. Much to our surprise he readily agreed and drew quite a large crowd.

We also had a 'Parish Mission' and for this Ben invited the Francicans. They had earned quite a reputation for themselves around parishes and schools. Two Brothers and a Nun came for Holy week, 1963 and held church services and house meetings around the parish, which they visited extensively. One of the Monks was a young Canadian who one day visited an elderly widow. She had taken out the best tea-service for his visit and he suggested that he pour the second cup for her. As he was about to do this she said 'Don't you want to use the slop basin?' He had never heard this expression before and couldn't think how to reply so he said 'Not just now thank you.'

Ben would also manage to get some interesting preachers to visit. One of them was his second cousin, Peter Harker who was on leave in England from South Africa. At that stage in my life I had no interest in going to South Africa but when I did finally arrive in Zululand he turned out to be one of the Archdeacons and was elected Bishop at the age of 65 years, nearly thirty years later. Another preacher was a missionary from New Guinea, Father Bodger. Ben had known a retired Bishop in Petersfield whose sons were missionaries there and we at St. Curthberts had sent money out to help support them. This visit was to inform us how our money had been spent and he was so enthusiastic his visit was a great success. After the service we were standing together in the porch and Ben, getting out his diary asked him if we could arrange another visit. Father Bodger's diary was full to over-flowing so Ben said 'Don't you ever have a day off?' 'Oh no' he replied 'I'm far too busy for that!' He then moved on to speak with one of the congregation and Ben turning to me said 'Silly Bugger'!

Another amusing incident took place when I went to visit a family as dusk was falling. When it was time to leave it was already dark and I was late for Evening Prayer. I was riding my bike carefully by the light of the street lamps when suddenly a torch was shone in my face and a policeman approached. 'What are you up to?' he enquired. I was just about to make my excuses for having no lights when he said 'Oh sorry Sir, I thought you was one of the boys! Please carry on.' And he disappeared into the darkness. Funny stories stay with me and tend to be remembered one after the other so I feel I must tell this one now as well. One afternoon all three of us curates had been visiting in the rain and I arrived at Evening Prayer looking very bedraggled. Soon after Tom arrived looking the same. It was obligatory for us to be there at 6.00pm each day and we had just begun when Patrick appeared soaked to the skin. He had been caught in a down-pour on his way to the church. Trying to stiffle our laughter we turned dutifully to the psalm for the day. Imagine our consternation when it turned out to be Psalm 69 which starts 'Save me, oh God, for the waters are come in even to my soul. I stick fast in the deep mire where no ground is : I am come into deep waters, so that the floods run over me.' We began to giggle and just couldn't stop with all our tension bubbling over. Ben wasn't too pleased repeatedly calling us to order!

But of course funny stories are just the outer edge of things. There were so many difficult and serious pastoral situations to deal with. One of these took me to London at 11pm one night. A parishioner's husband had been transferred from Portsmouth Hospital to St. George's which was situated then by Hyde Park. She was desperate to see him and as she was in her late seventies had no way of getting there. I decided to ask the Teacher who was boarding in the Rectory if I could borrow her Morris Minor, and bless her, she readily agreed. Although Ben was against the idea we set off for London. We arrived about 1.00am and I left again almost immediately. It was such a pleasure to do a 'U-turn' in the Mall as I drove back home arriving just after 3.00am. This wasn't long after I had passed my driving test – I had failed twice, the second time for driving too slowly. My third attempt was on a Wednesday after taking a Communion Service at which I had mentioned to a lady parishioner how nervous I was. She looked into her handbag and handed me a pill which she had broken in half. She told me it would help and it did! Truly I could have driven anyone anywhere. As the examiner got out he said 'Thank you for a nice drive.' The next time I saw this particular lady I asked her what the tablet was and was told 'Oh, it's a purple heart. I take them for my heart condition.' Some years later they were classified as a banned medicine!

The idea of going to South Africa happened in this way. Ever since I had been involved with St. Aldate's Church in Oxford I had understood that the church was a missionary body and in fact at one time I had thought of offering to teach abroad with a Missionary Society. The Portsmouth Deanery had a group of 'Friends of U.S.P.G.' one of the two biggest Missionary Societies in the Church of England, but they had no secretary. My interest in the Missionary field led me for this post. In 1962 the Society organised a rally in the Albert Hall and it was decided that we would take a coach trip to it. The hall was full and the main speaker was a Dr. Anthony Barker who was working in Zululand, South Africa. He inspired us all and on the coach going home I asked our Church Warden, Mr. Pepper, to remind me in six months time that I had decided to offer for service with U.S.P.G. He did and so in January 1963 I wrote to them. They replied inviting me to meet their Selection Secretary, an amiable man who smoked a hooker pipe. He asked me what motivated me and which part of the world I would like to go to, India or Africa. I had no idea and so his next question was whether I had any friends on either of those two continents. In fact there were two in Africa, Duncan Buchanan from Ripon Hall days and

Margaret Beer whom I had met at St. Aldate's and on the student missions. Duncan was now the Rector of Warner Beach a town on the south coast of Natal, and Margaret had become the Headmistress of the Diocesan School in Pietermaritzburg also in Natal. The Selection Secretary's response to this was 'Now we at least have a continent.' He then asked what my extra-parochial interests were and I replied Religious Drama. He then said that that made the answer clear because just that week he had received two letters, one from the Bishop of Zululand asking for a priest to replace the one who was returning to England after eighteen years and another from the Mothers Union worker in Zululand saying that she was interested in developing indigenous drama. It seemed to me that prayer had been answered in a very simple way. I told him that suited me fine and returned home to look where Zululand was on the map!

I must confess that I had only heard of the word Zulu as it had been my nick-name at school because of my curly black hair, but knew absolutely nothing about the place or people. About a month later a letter arrived for me from the Bishop of Zululand whose name was Tom Savage. He had amused the Bishops at the 1958 Lambeth Conference by introducing himself as 'Savage - Zululand'. In his letter he offered me the parish of Empangeni, a town almost on the east coast of South Africa not far from Richard's Bay which was about to be developed as a vast harbour and industrial centre. There was a congregation at that time of about one hundred people, almost 100% white as the Group Areas Act had been passed. This meant that ethnic groups had to live within their own prescribed areas. A large township had been built for blacks a few miles away which had its own church and priest. This offer was open for me to start as soon as possible. It was arranged for me to leave the following June, just four years after I had started my curacy. The U.S.P.G. expected nothing further from me apart from medical checks and a selection interview. This was conducted by the General Secretary and a few priests and lay people. The General Secretary had been the previous Bishop in Zululand but not, I think, very popular because the Diocese was almost bankrupt when he went there. However he was competent with finance and had made some hard decisions about property especially with the Diocesan farm on which he sowed wattle trees for paper production. I don't think he said much to me about Zululand except to encourage me to go there. Anyway the interview had gone well and I was formally accepted.

My farewell took place on a Sunday evening in June and was followed by a two weeks of leave. By this time I had acquired a car – a 1938 Morris which looked like a box. Father had bought it for me and it cost him £40. It had been in a garage unused for five years and had been very well looked after with an incredibly low mileage. This enabled me to drive out to Sheet on my day off and have more freedom generally for longer journeys. It also provided some 'fun' because of its age. Once I was driving up Portsdown Hill from the Havant direction, quite a high hill and the approach to the London - Portsmouth road is steep. At the bottom of this hill was a young policeman being taught point-duty and as I approached him he became confused. His Instructor approached me and asked 'Which way do you intend to turn Sir?' My right indicator is out Officer' I replied. 'Why then is your left indicator as well then?' he continued. The high wind had blown it out as they were of the kind that stuck out from the side of the car, flicking out with a switch. There was also the occasion when on a trip to Chichester a policeman approached the car which I had just parked. 'Where is your front number plate?' he asked. 'Well it was there when

I left home' I said. If one drove over fifty miles an hour the car rattled a great deal and it had obviously been rattled off! Despite a plea to the magistrate I had to pay a £2.00 fine. During my period of leave after I had left St. Cuthbert's the car and I toured around the country including a visit to my sister Daphne who lived near Lincoln.

Following this tour I returned to the Clergy House to collect my belongings and parked the car on the pub forecourt next door as usual. Suddenly a Police Officer appeared accompanied by a much younger Constable again. The older one kicked the mud-guard saying 'What, may I ask is this?' 'This' I said 'is my car and you shouldn't be kicking it.' 'Never-the-less' he continued 'I am asking this young Constable to examine it.' After forty-five minutes there was a knock at the Clergy House door and it was the young Constable by himself. He was rather nervous and as he sat down he said 'Here is the list of the nineteen faults I have found on your car.' I had to sign a piece of paper and I waited anxiously every day for the summons to appear. It never came. Not long afterwards I sold the car to a scrap merchant for £10.

The car was called 'Jezebel' and had often been used for visiting my new girl-friend called Hazel. I had met her through U.S.P.G. where she was working as a Telephonist. She was friendly with a couple whose surname was Badham and he was a priest who had worked in South Africa. He called on me one day in Copner and offered to tape record the Holy Communion service for me in the Zulu language. On this first visit Hazel was with them, she was twenty-eight and I was twenty-nine, and we were both without a close friend at that time. She had taken this job on temporarily in London as she was waiting to start her Teacher's Training at the Church of England College in Chichester. It was easy enough to meet her when she moved to Chichester and my days off were spent there. After she finished her Finals she took another temporary job with U.S.P.G. as Telephonist and also acted as a sort of Warden which came with a nice flat from which you could see Westminster Cathedral. This job of hers conveniently coincided with my leaving St. Cuthbert's but before she left her training we went together to the May Ball at her college. Driving home to Sheet we came over Harting Hill at 5.00am and the mist was hanging over the sparkling dew. Suddenly we came to a flock of sheep filling the road and there was nothing to do but follow them at their pace. All at once out of the mist behind us appeared a little man on a moped. He rounded up the sheep without getting off his moped or even turning it round and they simply went off into the field as though they did it every day! And then he was gone as quickly as he came. Another lovely outing was to the new Chichester Theatre to be opened by Sir Lawrence Olivier – the theatre was named after him – and it also took place in the May before I left. I wrote a letter to the Manager of the theatre explaining that I was about to leave for five years in South Africa and to attend the opening night would be a marvellous send-off. The opening play was St. Joan with Lady Olivier in the lead role – although I don't think she was actually 'Lady' at that time as Sir Lawrence wasn't knighted until 1963. The reply took some time but eventually an application form for two tickets arrived. It was a grand evening as we stood in the foyer, two of the few people not in evening dress, trying to identify the good and the great!

Just before my leaving date there was an urgent telephone call from U.S.P.G. to say the necessary visa for South Africa had been delayed. The Apartheid Authorities were highly suspicious of the Anglican Church! There was no telling when it would arrive so I was summoned to London. On arrival my fears were almost immediately relieved. As I would be officially on the dole from the end of June would I mind taking on some temporary work? The Treasurer's vicar was in hospital and likely to be there for some time and the Treasurer would arrange for me to live and work in the parish until such time as my visa arrived. My stipend would be resumed accordingly. What a fortunate break! The parish was St. Andrew's in the north end of Bromley, a fairly new and very Anglo-Catholic church. I was taken out there and introduced to my hostess who had offered a room for me. She and her husband were not church-goers but their daughter of ten years was in the choir and the Brownies. The church building was of modest size but full of light. There was a side altar where the daily Eucharist, attended by just two or three people was celebrated at 8.00am. Above the altar was a beautiful large crucifix with the face of Christ looking down. One morning I was kneeling in front of it after the service as I usually did for a thank-you prayer and looking up at the lovely wooden carving hanging there I watched and the eyes of Christ suddenly opened and looked directly at me. Shades of Don Camillo! This shock made me look momentarily away and when I looked back they were closed again. I remained staring at the face and suddenly they opened once more. This time they remained open but after a while they closed and then opened again. I could only think that either this was a miracle or the clever way in which the craftsman had shaped the eyes so they gave this impression. Some time later I visited the vicar whose job I was doing in the hospital and after a while I mentioned this occurrence to him. 'Yes I know' he replied in a whisper – his problem was a 'dicky' heart and as he was unmarried the Doctors had recommended he rest in hospital. I didn't like to ask him why this phenomenon occurred as somehow I felt his answer would spoil the mystery!

The Sunday services were well attended and there was a very good choir and organist. The Martin family had four members in the choir, parents and two sons both of whom were in their twenties. They were very good to me inviting me for Sunday lunch on more than one occasion. There were also very active Guides and Brownies groups to which I was expected to go for their prayers at the end. The Sunday School was small but enthusiastically led and there was a lively Youth Group which again I was expected to attend. When I eventually left this job at the beginning of September the Youth Group gave me a lovely 'Sick Communion Set' which stayed with me for the next twenty years. The Youth Leader, a Miss Johnson, sent me an invitation to her wedding when I was in South Africa and I also received one to their Silver Wedding Anniversary twenty-five years later. They were still living in Beaconsfield near Bromley. Although we were living in England by then we were unable to go.

So I was in Bromley for a full three months. I had done some visiting as usual and one day I met a man from the London City Mission and asked him what he was doing visiting in my parish! His name was Stanley, we became good friends and I heard from him now and then all the time I was in South Africa. One of his sons was ordained and was a curate at the Parish church of Bromley. Saturday was my day off and I would go into London to spend twenty-four hours at the flat in Tufton Street with Hazel. Somehow I had again acquired a car but I can't remember how it had come my way! I soon discovered that on a Sunday, if one exceeded the official speed limit by 5mph, one could reach St. Andrew's in forty minutes as the traffic was almost negligible! One particular Sunday morning we set off for the 8.00am service and after a few miles I noticed a Policeman sitting on a motor bike outside a shop. He immediately started to follow us and I knew that if I slowed down to 30mph I would be late for the service. I tried to keep my speed to about 33mph and then realising we were already running late I decided to take a short cut through a housing estate, without much success! I eventually arrived at the church at 7.50am allowing me just enough time if I rushed to change. The Policeman still trailing us pulled up on the passenger side of the car. He was not pleased! 'Do you know the speed limit in England?' he asked. I responded rather sheepishly 'About 30mph?' 'Yes, and you have been doing 35mph or at least the last ten miles. What's more you tried to lose me through that housing estate back there.' Hazel smiled at him. 'We are very sorry but we are late for the 8.00am service and were looking for a short cut.' He could see I was dressed in a cassock ready to leap into the church. 'Oh go on then. But just make sure you don't do it again.' Indeed we left twenty minutes earlier from then onwards! Thank God for a Policeman who knew about the blessing of mercy over judgement! The telephone call from U.S.P.G. to announce the arrival of my visa came on September 1st and it was decided that I should leave my temporary job on the following Monday and spend the remaining nine days at home.

In the 1960's I guess that most people travelling to South Africa went by boat and I sailed on 'The Windsor Castle' which left Southampton on Thursday September 10th. Mother and Joy came to see me off together with Hazel. It was the second time Mother had taken the same journey and it must have been difficult for her. Someone once asked her if she felt sad that I had gone so far away and she had answered 'What makes Paul happy makes me happy too.' There were other 'missionaries' on board including George wood who was returning after some leave. He had been in Pretoria but was now returning as Dean of the Cathedral in Zululand and rector of the parish of Eshowe. He had married a South African, Joan, and they had three little girls. U.S.P.G. had asked them to chaperone me and we became marvellous friends. The unmarried Dean of George Cathedral was also returning from leave and he organised a daily Eucharist in on eof the smaller lounges on board. There was also a Dr. Smit who was a Professor of Theology at Stellenbosch University returning from a visit to England. He and I had one or two chats and I remember his asking me what approach I would take in preaching to the Zulus. As I had never thought about this it was indeed a good question! Years later he became one of the Leaders of the Reform Movement to move away from Apartheid in the Dutch Reformed church.

The journey was full of fun. We had the usual games on board, horse racing with wooden horses and dice and a fancy dress competition. One dear elderly lady came up to me and asked if I would like to enter as King Farouk of Egypt. She had bought a pukha Arab outfit in a bazaar in Morocco and thought that with my beard, dark glasses and a cigar I would look the part. I borrowed a large cigar and duly paraded and to my surprise I received the largest number of votes from the audience.

Another surprise was when we reached Las Palmas. George Wood and I went to visit the Cathedral there and it turned out to be an Orthodox one. The bearded priests on the door wouldn't let us in because we were wearing shorts. We tried to explain that we were Anglican priests but the message didn't seem to be getting through when suddenly a look of recognition appeared on one of their faces. 'You like Fidel Castro, you go in.' I wasn't sure whether to be flattered or not but at least we had a pleasant visit!

It took the ship two weeks to reach Durban and we were met by Peter Harker, the

Archdeacon who had visited St. Cuthbert's and he immediately ferried us to Ehowe. George and his family were taken to their new home and I to the Bishop's house. Tom Savage was a kind but quite authoritarian Bishop supported by a strong wife who was even more so! Almost his first words to me were that a Diocese in the USA had sent out a priest to work as a Youth Officer and as he had small children they had sent him to Empangeni where I had been told I would be rector! However there was a priest working in the rural part of Zululand who had just left for another Diocese so would I be willing to go to the Retreat Centre for six months and teach myself Zulu? When one is thirty years old and in a new and completely strange place what does one say but 'Yes'! However I did have the courage to ask for a week's leave first so I could visit my mate Duncan Buchanan. The Bishop reluctantly agreed. After all, I had just had two weeks holiday on board the ship! My suitcases stayed at the Bishop's house and the next day I took the train for Durban having first telephoned Duncan to warn him of my impending visit. Little did I realise that this was to be the first day of the most amazing sixteen years of my life. It was also October 3rd, my birthday!

CHAPTER 8

'ABANTU BAZULA' (The People Of Heaven)

The first image to impact on visiting Warner Beach was that it seemed to me like Paradise! The warmth and the sea air together with the endless 'rollers' of the Indian Ocean mingled into such a glorious sense of well-being as we swam in the rock pools protected from the vast spaces and the surge like soft thunder.

Back to reality in Eshowe as the Bishop took me in his fast car up the hills and along the red-brown dirt road to the Diocesan Retreat and Conference Centre. Everything was so new to me. The steep sided hills were covered with bee shaped huts with small fields closely around them and cattle everywhere – sometimes even on the road. Along the sides of the road grew Eucalyptus and the occasional Palm Trees. Stones and rocks littered the countryside giving it a look of poverty. There seemed to be people everywhere and children trying to sell fruit such as pawpaws, oranges, pineapples, the sweet corn called 'mealie' and thousands of avocado pears along the roadside. The journey took about an hour the last part being through wattle trees where the men were cutting and large tractors did the collecting. Just before we arrived we passed St. Mary's, the Mission Hospital with its low wooden buildings and patients in white pyjamas sitting by the gates. Then around the corner a brick church building and down the slope and up again to the Centre named after the first Missionary, Robert Robertson who had lived and built the first church there. His name in Zulu, Nzimela, means 'the man who stands alone' because, especially after his first wife was killed in an accident with an ox wagon he would stand alone on the top of the rise outside the mission leaning on his walking stick and looking at the sunset. Kwa means 'the place of'.

This centre was the result of Tom Savage's vision and the building had at one time been a hostel for students and a Nurses' Home. For a number of years it lay abandoned but now rebuilt it stood, the first version of many revisions in design over the years. It is now thought of as a fine, well-appointed building used by organisations from all over South Africa for meetings. In 1963 there was no electricity and no water in the rooms. The toilet was about fifty yards across a lawn and down a rather slippery slope. The ablution block for men reminded me of the ones we had at school. At least it had a standing urinal! A few years later showers were added. Where the hot water came from I never did discover. The Centre had been up and running for a couple of years and the Warden was a priest in his fifties. Canon Wilmot Jali, a jolly fellow whose only obvious fault was a weakness for a drink – or three – of this or that! His wife was an excellent cook and ran the domestic side of the Centre. Rosalind was also the President of the Diocesan Mother's Union and a lovely, kind christian lady. She really 'mothered' me! Wilmot also had the job of running a Catechists' school. There were ten of these splendid chaps who were like Lay Readers but who in effect ran their own local congregations. I was able to join in their Morning and Evening Services in a chapel built in memory of Pamela Rhodes. Pamela had been a Mothers Union worker who died of cancer. It was a simple wooden building like an inverted ship on the side of a hill with windows all down one side overlooking a beautiful valley. It had an atmosphere unlike any chapel I have known before or since. The church down the road was called 'The Good Shepherd' and was in the charge of Leslie Gready. He had been a curate in the Diocese of Liverpool and like me had offered himself for work through U.S.P.G. He and his wife, Beryl had three boys under the age of ten and lived in the mission house on top of the hill behind the church. Leslie had become a good Zulu linguist and although he was too busy to give me formal lessons he was always a great encouragement. Later he followed his old Rector who had become Bishop in Matebeleland and trained non-stipendary and other ministers there. In the 1970's he returned to England and was made Rector of St. Cuthbert's in Darlington and later Rural Dean. In the early 1990's he was called back to Matebeleland to be the Dean of the Cathedral there but found a melanoma growing in his groin. He came back to Britain for treatment but sadly died after a couple of years. One of their sons is now a parish priest in the Chichester Diocese.

Everyone in the District was very welcoming in trying to make me feel at home and one of the local Farmers invited me to tea. They had a son who was training to be a priest in England and an unmarried daughter at University. Immediately I was invited to attend a twenty-first birthday party on the following Friday at a neighbouring farm. Leslie also invited me to accompany him to one of the Zulu congregations which also had a church on this same farm. It was a warm evening and most of the party was outside. There was the obligatory 'braivlais' – the South African barbecue, with plenty of meat. The beer and spirits flowed. About one hundred guests, all white, huddled in groups around the spacious lawns whilst black servants provided plates and carried food and drink. About 10pm we were invited into a large marquee for turkey sandwiches and champagne whilst the birthday boy's father made a speech. The son then responded thanking all and sundry for their presents and attendance at this splendid celebration. The father's speech was one of those bland, benign and banal ones in which the phrase 'keeping a straight bat' occurred more than once! It was a new experience and one that contrasted greatly for me with what followed on the Sunday.

Leslie picked me up at 8.30am and after driving over the dirt roads for thirty minutes we arrived at a cast-iron roofed wooden building which was the church for the workers on the farm whose owners had given the party on the Friday. It was already full when we arrived and became even fuller, to bursting point it seemed! Zulu time depends on the sun and not on the clock, on what needs to be done before-hand and on the necessary time for travelling. The children sat on the floor at the front on the left and to the right the church was full with women kneeling at wooden benches with the men sitting or kneeling behind the children on the left. The church was used as a school building during the week. There were far fewer men than women. The sun got hotter and hotter on the tin roof and it became clear to me that the burning of incense was to keep the flies at bay and sweeten the smell of many human bodies in a country where water was not readily available! The altar was kept behind a curtain which was pulled across whilst school was in progress. The floor of the sanctuary shone with the polished cow dung which was used to produce 'smart' floors! There were servers and acolytes galore all going reverently about their duties. The silence was profound and prayerful and the singing immediately brought tears to my eyes. It was unaccompanied but so harmonic in a very special way with everyone singing at the top of their voices. Worship was with the whole person – body, mind and soul. Although the service lasted two hours nobody seemed restless. Leslie did all the reading, preaching and administering of communion himself. Afterwards we were invited to lunch at the Church Warden's home. There seemed to be children and adults everywhere and during the course of the conversation, which I could neither understand or take part in, Leslie explained to me that the man looked after fifteen children! His brother had died and according to Zulu custom the Church Warden had taken his brother's eight children to add to his seven. He was the manager of the farm labourers and earned £5.00 per month plus a sack of 'mealie-meal' and free accommodation with a small field on which he kept six of his own cattle. The law meant that he and his family had to work for the Farmer as long as they stayed there or leave to live and work somewhere else. It was virtually slave labour and the stark contrast between these two sets of people I had met on the Friday and the Sunday struck me so forcefully it was never to leave me.

I was given two books and one exercise book with which to teach myself Zulu and I sat alone in my simple room each morning between breakfast at 9.30am and lunch at 12.30pm. Once or twice a week someone would come in and clean the room sometimes spreading more cow dung on the floor to make it shine even brighter! Strangely the dung didn't smell. At dusk every day one of the workers would come in and light the gas lamp hanging from the roof. In the afternoons I would walk or sometimes jog for an hour or so. The farm roads stretched for miles and I never came to the end of them. The evening would be taken up by Evening Prayer in the chapel, supper and then more study or reading of some kind. Bed was early because the chapel bell rang at 6.30am every day!

The chapel, as I have said, was one of the most beautiful I have ever seen and was Bishop Tom's pride and joy. The altar was of wood and simply dressed. The pleasant pews were made out of the same wood as the rest of the building and there was no ceiling only lovely beams reaching up to a narrow beam at the top. The steep sloping roof was thatched and the chapel could comfortably hold fifty people. There was a lectern but no pulpit and an aumbry in the corner for the Reserved Sacrament. It was a model of Retreat chapels. One other feature was a big dark wooden cross hanging over the altar. I spent many moments looking at that cross and the shadows it cast.

I found that the study of Zulu was made simpler by the fact that the writer of the grammar book wrote it in the style of the Latin grammar used in schools and it felt as though I had been there before. There was also the fact that I had spent many hours studying by myself since I was sixteen years old. It was like putting on an old and comfortable shoe! The kind Warden and his wife encouraged me to speak Zulu at the table and Leslie up the road spoke to me in the language as well. There were plenty of local people around who spoke little or no English so that also helped me. At the weekends I was sometimes asked to take services or preach, in English thank goodness! This meant I travelled around with other priests as I had no transport and wasn't allowed to travel by local bus as by law they were for blacks only.

On one of my first days off I asked the Warden if I could borrow his car to visit Durban some 120 miles south. He agreed and by 9.00am I was on my way. The sugar farms stretched for miles south of Eshowe over undulating hills towards the sea. Now and again the blue of the Indian Ocean appeared over the horizon. My first sighting of Durban came as I reached the crest of a hill about twenty miles north of the city and it was breathtaking as the sea crashed against the large rocks. Durban was full of light and different nationalities, especially Indians going about their day in noisy happiness, or so it seemed to me. It was marvellous walking along the wide beaches and into the sophisticated shops, sipping tea on the terrace outside one of the largest. My problems started when it was time to leave for home! The sea is on three sides of the city which disorientated me as all I could remember was parking the car 'by the sea'! It took me forty-five minutes to find it. The little Ford cruised home in the dark with hardly another car in sight. Dear Wilmot and Rosaline were so relieved to see me back home. I realised then that they were beginning to look upon me as a surrogate son.

The Diocese was blessed with a number of young priests who were keen to promote Youth work in the parishes. They arranged a conference at Kwanzimela and about one hundred people turned up. Where they all slept I never did discover! Youth in Zulu terms means anyone unmarried and so the age range was from fifteen to about twenty-five years. Some of the Leaders were also Teachers. This was my introduction to the Zulu way of doing things! Much time was taken up with singing and dancing in a rhythmical fashion all together. It was very catching! Singing grace for meals could take fifteen minutes! The talks were given in lecture fashion and at great length but no-one seemed to worry about that. Worship took the prescribed two hours which was not helped by the fact that the chalices were all so small in measure. There was that single-minded open enthusiasm which is such a mark of African spirituality. The Leaders were similarly warm in their welcome to me and immediately I was part of their movement. We laughed and danced the whole day through. There was also a 'white' Youth weekend but the numbers were small, about twenty, and the contrast with the previous one was amazing. Here we saw all the self-consciousness of the shy and withdrawn teenager. The theme was based on the popular song of that time 'Bridge over troubled waters' and had been well thought through with some good small-group work. Even the church here seemed to be ahead of its English Mother in its thinking and presentation. The Youth Officer for the Diocese was a dear man by the name of Bill Hardwick who after his retirement was murdered by burglars in his home to the south of Durban. He immediately invited me to join the Youth Committee. The other Zulu priests were on the committee as well.

Another memorable occasion was a visit to Cape Town which came out of the blue. The American priest who had gone to live at Empangeni was invited by the Provincial Synod to talk to them about something or another and was only given three days notice! Bishop Tom suggested that he take me along as his co-driver and naturally I wasn't opposed to the idea! Don was a cheerful, rather large American and a joke was never far away. The first day we drove five hundred miles each taking two-hourly turns at the wheel. We arrived in Grahamstown soon after dark and stayed at the Theological College there. The road through the Transkei had been spectacular with seemingly endless hills reaching as far as the eye could see. The road appeared as a little black line covering vast areas and surrounded by dry countryside set with houses, sheep and cattle sometimes even on the road. The next day following a service of Holy Communion in the cavernous Cathedral we set out early. It was another seven hundred miles to Cape Town and the temperature continued to rise as we traveled nearer to our destination literally 'sweating it out'! Again the scenery was amazing as we skirted what is now known as 'The Garden Route'. We arrived at our destination about 8.00pm having driven the last two and a half hours in the dark. We stayed in what was called 'District Six' in another smaller College for Teachers run by an Anglican Order. Not long after our visit the area was designated a 'white area' and the College had to close. The next day Don had to speak and it gave me the opportunity to look around the city which restored my earlier memories of my first visit seven years earlier. This visit I was able to spend time in the beautiful Cathedral, St George's – a monument to many years of British rule and Oxford Movement Anglican Missionary work. The botanical gardens were spectacular too. The journey back began early the next morning and was even more of a rush as Don had a meeting to attend. It was to be my only visit to Cape Town in the whole of my time in South Africa.

In November 1963 there were two events which remain strong in my memory. The first was the assassination of President Kennedy about which I felt so moved I wrote a letter to his widow. About three months later I received a printed card with a black border from The White House thanking me for my concern. The second was much more personal. It was a letter from my dear friend Brenda who had gone to Canada for reasons I cannot now remember. She wrote that she had gone to a party, become drunk, and woke the next morning to realise she had had sex with someone (rape was not mentioned). She had become pregnant and was writing to ask if I would consent to become God-Father to the resulting daughter. I was deeply touched by the request and wrote back saying how honoured I would be.

There were two further Youth Conferences during my six months of language learning. One was a weekend spent at a school out in the countryside. A lift must have been arranged for me. The planning for this conference had been done by the committee and there was room for one hundred people at the school sleeping on mattresses in the school hall and classrooms. We arrived in good time but by the evening of the Friday two hundred and fifty people had arrived to attend the conference! Nothing daunted the programme went ahead. I was asked to celebrate the Eucharist on the Saturday morning and it was very frustrating having to use two small chalices holding barely enough for twenty communicants each! There didn't however appear to be any alternative vessels and the service took at least two hours. Breakfast was most welcome!

The second conference took place at the Centre and remains clear in my memory for one thing. It was decided that a time of prayer should be held each day in the chapel. Leaders and the youngsters crowded together, about ten people in a pew which usually sat only six! One of the clergy started off with a Bible reading and a sermon and then we sang a hymn or two. This would be one of the popular choruses to which the congregation sways, hands up and bodies gyrating. Then the 'Open Praying' began. I was used to the idea of people praying in turn but here that happened to begin with and then someone started praying at the same time as someone else until after a while everyone was praying all at once! The noise was deafening as people became more and more emotional, some started crying and others were shouting at the top of their voices. I left the chapel shaking with shock! I thought about it for some days but didn't want to speak to any of the Leaders for fear of offending them. Then I was reading the Bible one morning and came across a passage in the Acts of the Apostles 'When they heard this they lifted up their voices with one heart to God'. There follows a longish prayer. Did this mean I wondered that they all prayed at once? They certainly didn't have books from which they could have read together. I wrote to Canon Somerset Ward to whom I had been sent for spiritual direction. Eventually a very kind reply came from him saying that he had asked his friend Professor Evans who was then teaching Theology at King's College, London. He had said that the author of the Acts, St. Luke, had probably summarised the prayers offered at the time and it was not therefore verbatim. Nor did he think that the christians of the time would pray all at the same time. However clearly different Nations had different customs and there was nothing to stop them praying as they liked as long as the church on the whole found it an acceptable method. Gradually I grew more comfortable with it. This method of praying came through the influence of the 'Iviyo' movement. It in turn had been influenced by the Pentecostal churches. The Charismatic Revival had been going in Zululand long before it hit the other churches of the Anglican communion.

There was another method of getting about without a car. If one could reach Melmouth, the little town about six miles away, there was a bus which went as far as Durban. This had a little compartment in the front next to but separate from the driver which was reserved for whites. I travelled both to Eshowe, to see the Woods, and to Durban by this method. Never was there anyone else travelling with me in this sealed little world. At least one could read a book or the paper. The bus travelled around the other towns and villages so one had a lovely tour of beautiful Natal. My six months language training passed very quickly. The question was what to do with me next!

The Bishop again summoned me. He wanted to do something which had never been done before and would I help him? It meant going to a remote place to polish up my Zulu and at the same time to be a curate to an African Rector. I couldn't see anything against this and considered it an honour to be part of a new venture although no great deal for me. I didn't mind who was in charge as long as we could work together. There was a snag however! The necessary 'pass' for me to work in what the Government called the 'Reserves' had not been granted. The Archdeacon of Swaziland, being the nearest in distance, was asked to go to Pretoria and try to persuade the Authorities to grant one. Apparently the man who had left the Diocese just before I arrived had had one and so there was a strong case for claiming it was a replacement and not a new or additional permit. In the meantime I was to be sent to Swaziland to the Mission where the Archdeacon himself was the Rector and there were already two other Assistant Priests and a Lay Missionary living. I was to take the place of one who just been appointed to a parish in Swaziland. I packed the big trunk I had bought at an auction for £3.00. It was called a 'Bachelor's Delight' and had drawers in one side and a compartment in the other side for suits, etc. There was a big drawer in the top for collars and all sorts. It took all my worldly goods in one packing!

I was given a lift to Swaziland by the Archdeacon as he returned from a Bishop's staff meeting in Eshowe. The mission was called St. Christopher' because there was a large Boys' High School on the site as well as the Mission House, a large Church, the Rectory and offices for the Archdeaconry covering the whole country. It was in a place called Usuthu and there was also a farm where they grew pineapples of which the Layman at the mission was also the farm Manager. We had someone to cook for us and we all had our own rooms – it was like being back at the Clergy House in Portsmouth!

We were assigned duties by the Archdeacon and as I was the least fluent in Zulu (Swazi is a sister language) I was given the work in Manzini, the local town about ten miles away. This meant helping with the services on Sunday and the unique job of Chaplain to the Lancashire Regiment. Swaziland had not long been independent and King Sobhuza was having trouble with some politicians who were inciting the Unions to strike for various reasons. The King had called on the British Government for help; hence the soldiers. I was invited to a drinks' party and the Company Commander was a very polite gentleman who welcomed me effusively. He soon introduced me to a lady who I discovered was a camp follower. The Major had quickly disappeared and it was soon apparent that she was also the Regimental 'bore'. She spoke non-stop for ten minutes about the woes of Britain and how it was going to the 'dogs' very fast! I had several times over the last six months been asked how I liked South Africa by white people eager to get approval for the way things were going there. Whenever I tried to be critical I was told that as I hadn't been in the country long I couldn't possibly understand their problems. End of conversation! This lady at the party was annoying me more and more with her wide sweeping criticisms of Britain. When she at last finished talking I asked her when she had last lived in Britain. She replied that she had moved to Swaziland in 1939 and hadn't been back since. I said as calmly as I could 'Don't you think you need to live in a country to understand its problems?' It was amazing how quickly she found an excuse to move to talk with someone else! I was asked to conduct 'Padre Hours' with the troops which could have been very enjoyable except that I found it harder to understand their Lancashire accents than I did the local Swazi people! There was also another opportunity offered to me through this contact.

The Company had a small Drama Group and had entered for the Mbabane One-Act Play Competition. The principal male actor had dropped out and the C.O. asked if I could help them. It seemed like good public relations to do so. The part involved me taking on the role of a blind man who was cuckold by his wife and their friend. It also meant I was directing the twenty-five minute drama. The part of the lover was played by a young Lieutenant not long commissioned. Fortunately there was a Volkswagen car, the old 'Beetle', which belonged to the Mission so I had the use of this to travel to rehearsals. My 'wife' was played by an Italian woman who was married to an Irishman, probably the richest man in Manzini because he owned the 'Swaziland Distributors' one of those big enterprises which sold everything from a pin to a piano! There was an invitation to dinner one night and I met their relatives. They had no children. The dinner was exceptionally splendid with the drink flowing freely and it was a good job that I had to drive the ten miles back to the Mission so I had the perfect excuse to refuse 'one for the road'! They were all Catholics and curious to meet this Protestant priest who liked acting. The night of the plays arrived. One good thing about the Army is that you are never short of stage hands who can build you any intricate set you want. There were eight plays in the competition and the little theatre housed a packed audience. The adjudicator was an actor from South Africa in his fifties. He had some pretty scathing things to say about most of the performances. My poor young Lieutenant came in for a hiding for a 'wooden' performance. 'Who' the adjudicator said, 'Ever proposed love with his feet tapping nervously on the floor?' I felt ashamed as the Director for not noticing this before-hand. There was little comment about my performance except that it was adequate. However when it came to the awards I was stunned to hear him call out my name for the best male actor. In fact he pronounced it in a French way saying 'Father Du-fet'! One of the audience was John Tibbs, the Anglican Rector of Mbabane and for ever after when we met it was 'Ah! Father Du-fet I presume!' I could only think that the little silver imitation cup was presented to me to prevent the local men from being overcome with jealousy of each other!

Rumours get around and it wasn't long before one of the Masters at St. Christopher's came to see me. The students had been learning Julius Caesar ever since it became the set book for the 'O' level exams and they really wanted to perform it but there was no-one around with experience of directing. 'And we were wondering whether……..?' Again it seemed like a good way to foster relations between the Mission and the School to say yes! The pupils were all male and so we needed a woman to play Caesar's wife. Quickly a lady from Manzini materialised and it was decided that I would take on the small part of the Emperor himself. I had never met such an enthusiastic set of performers and most of them were word perfect before we started. The 'crowd' were the most realistic I have ever seen. They were completely natural and needed no encouragement to shout out their adoration of or anger at Caesar. The man who took the part of Brutus was an outstanding actor. His name was Welcome Msomi and I tried to keep in touch with him after I left. He once wrote to me saying that he had decided he didn't want to be a Teacher (the soft option) but wanted instead to be an Actor and until he could realise this dream he would work as a Petrol Attendant! I heard later that he had made a breakthrough with Radio 'Bantu' in Johannesburg and when the black musical version of Macbeth, 'Mambatha' came out it was a great thrill for me to see that he was the author and producer. It had tours in New York and London with rave reviews.

We performed to packed audiences for two nights and the fact that a white Caesar was assassinated by a black Cassius was not lost on the onlookers or the cast!

Our dear Archdeacon made his visits to Pretoria and after three months a letter arrived from Eshowe to say that a permit had arrived in the office and was waiting for me. When I received it I was most surprised to see that it was just a scruffy piece of paper, rather badly typed and without any signature, saying that I was allowed to enter any 'Reserve' in Natal Province for the purposes of my work.

There were two things which were not revealed until later about Usuthu. One was that the Headmaster of the school was a bit too friendly with some of the pupils. This was discovered by Hugh Harker who went to the Mission after the Archdeacon had left. Hugh was a brother of Peter, the Zululand Archdeacon, and had been chaplain of one of the large South African public schools. Naturally he was interested in the school and it was his interest and his past experience of boys that provided his realisation that all was not as it should be! Tom Savage wouldn't believe Hugh at first but did promise to look further into the matter. The clever headmaster was able to persuade Tom that it was all a pack of lies put around by the boys who didn't like him, etc. etc. Hugh resigned and about six months later it was proved beyond doubt that something sadly had been amiss. It hit poor Bishop Tom very hard!

The other revelation was equally embarrassing. Archdeacon Arden had an irascible wife! Even I heard her speak to those who worked in their house very roughly indeed. It was said that she nagged the Archdeacon in the same manner. Quite what her problem was no-one ever said. However there was an excellent Diocesan Secretary called Margaret and it was decided that she should move to Swaziland as there was a greater amount of administration there especially with the church schools. Maybe it was felt that there was a more suitable candidate for the post in Eshowe. After a further year it was discovered that Margaret had been pregnant and the father turned out to be the sixty year old Archdeacon! One day they both disappeared and turned up in Durban but neither of them were seen again in the Diocese. Mrs. Arden together with her family of grown-up children moved back to England and some years later we were told that the Archdeacon had died in Durban.

So the time had come for me to move on and Mary Monroe, who was the Mothers' Union worker in Swaziland very kindly agreed to collect me and my luggage. She took me first to Eshowe to collect my permit and then on to Inhwathi where Father Ngema was the Rector. Mary was very kind and gave me her 'office book' as I didn't possess one at the time. I still have it with it's wafer-thin Indian paper. She returned to England and her last job was with the U.S.P.G. College in Birmingham where it was discovered she had cancer and she died shortly afterwards.

Inhlwathi means 'python' but why it was so called I never discovered. It is a district rather than a village with a lot of homes gathered over a wide area around the Church, School and Rectory of St. John the Baptist. Robertson, the first Anglican Missionary had arrived there in the 1850's. His idea had been to reach Swaziland but Inhlwathi was as far as he got! It is about twenty-five miles inland from Nongoma and just at the back of the Umfolozi and Hluhuwe Game Reserves. The name actually applies to the mountain over-looking the settlement. There is a bit of ancient forest there but otherwise the area is covered with smallholdings and 'mealie-mealie' fields in abundance with of course the inevitable cattle. Much of the area is unusable with large 'dongas', ravines, caused by soil erosion and the hilly dry land. There was a small number of 'coloured' people there including a descendant of the great John Dunn who arrived from England as a Merchant and ended up as an Honorary Zulu Chief with one hundred wives! I was sent to visit them as the dear Rector wasn't sure he would be welcome, and found them most friendly. In fact Mrs. Dunn sent a litre of milk and two avocado pears for me each day with one of the school children. Some of the milk was taken with the porridge and the avocado pears were eaten one at breakfast and one at supper. No wonder the weight crept up on me!

Robertson's house had been empty for a long time. It was made up of two simple rooms and had very thick stone walls. The locals said that he had built it himself and one of the stones measuring five feet in length by three feet high he had also put in place half-way up the wall himself! The church had kindly added a small kitchen with a stove and somewhere to prepare food and clear away. The day I arrived I was met by one of the Church Wardens wearing a straw hat which had split along the brim so that he looked at you through the hole. He was outside digging a privy for me! He looked up from the hole where he stood with his feet pressed either side on the walls so he could talk to me at the same time as he reached down to dig. He said 'Hello, Welcome! Do you think if I dig for long enough I will end up in Hell? Do you believe in Hell?' This was the first time I could recall having a theological discussion with someone half-way down a privy hole! At length he came up from the hole and we shook hands. The next five minutes were completely lost on me as he went off into a torrent of Zulu. I knew the trick by then to nod just my head and grunt saying 'yes' in the gaps! He seemed well satisfied! Mary and he helped me into the house with my big trunk. It was sparsely but adequately furnished and someone had put a colourful plastic cloth on the wooden table. The Rector and his wife soon arrived. She was a midwife and actually ran a clinic in the rondavel next door where she also delivered the babies. They couldn't have been more kind and at once took me to share a lovely meal in the old, original house which had seen better times. They also introduced me to a lady whom they said would look after me as my housekeeper, although she would only work in the mornings. She cooked porridge for my breakfast and had my lunch ready before she left at 1.00pm. I had to prepare my own supper but she washed, ironed and cleaned the house for me. The payment was the going rate at the time but seemed such a small amount each month. However my own stipend was only £50 per month.

What I was to do was not too clear! There was visiting and the Rector would take me to his other congregations of which there were four or five. But how was I to get there? There was no car but it was decided that the Church Warden would lend me his spare horse. As I had never been on a horse before lessons would begin the very next day! The white horse was very lazy and tame, quite tall and with a will of his own! The Church Warden gave me some basic lessons and I learnt to trot the Zulu way which is slightly different from the British way. He never taught me to gallop, just a gentle canter so galloping I discovered quite by chance! The horse was not inclined to go at all fast without a lot of encouragement, except when he so wished and then he would gallop away and there was no stopping him! The Rector took me around the churches mainly about four or five miles from the centre. The church at the Mission was quite large and had a congregation of between 150 - 200 each Sunday. I was to preach twice a month. The Rector would correct my written manuscript and I would then read it. Outside the Mission church I would sometimes find an Evangelist who would translate for me or I would try to do this myself. Each sermon would be used four or five times and then I would try out a new one. The Teachers were also most willing to help as they were keen to practice their English.

Visiting was fun. The church people feted me and there was always tea with buns! No visit would ever end without prayers and sometimes even a hymn or two with my hosts often spontaneously praying themselves. There was one special visit. It was to a lady who was reputed to be over one hundred years old, house-bound, and wanted communion once a month. She had been a cook for Robertson in her teens and had walked the hundred or so miles with him from Kwamagwaza to Inhlwathi. Another person whose company I enjoyed was the evangelist, Ngema. He was a fine christian man and was very helpful to me. Going out with the horse to congregations would take the whole day leaving after breakfast and arriving back home at about 4.00pm.

It got dark at 5.30pm in the winter and at 7.30pm in the summer and nothing much could ever take place after dark. I bought myself a little radio and listened a lot to the very biased South African Broadcasting Service as that was all that was available to me. One day I was overjoyed to hear the voice of John Arlott! The South African cricketers were touring England and the Test Matches were relayed through the radio several times a day.

The problem of long distance transport was settled in an interesting way! There was a bus which passed the store two miles away once a day. It would arrive any time between 8.30 and 9.30am and because it was an 'African' bus I wasn't legally allowed to travel on it. So I went to the Magistrate in Nongoma, about twenty-five miles away, and asked for permission to travel by this bus as there was nothing else available to me except the horse. He agreed but in a rather surly manner! I soon learned to take a book or writing material with me to pass the time as I waited for this bus. The driver was always the same man, a 'coloured' man who lived near the store, and one day he told me that he wasn't welcome anymore at his sister's house. Apparently she had 'passed' as a white person and was afraid that if her brother visited her at home she would be 'found out'! He said that I should sit at the front of the bus and my first journey was certainly a new experience! It took three hours to cover the twisting and sometimes very hilly road to Nongoma. Moreover as it was the only bus the driver tried to cram as many people as possible on to it. The bus legitimately held fifty passengers but I reckon that on more than one occasion it was crammed full of at least one hundred people. The stops took a long time as luggage such as beds and chickens had to be loaded on top! Progress up the hills in first gear on a dirt road and round precipitous corners was painfully slow. Once on the return journey from Nongoma one afternoon the clouds were beginning to look threatening and I decided to try and get home before the storm. No such luck! The storms in South Africa after a very hot day are severe with deafening thunder and frightening lightening. Being someone who doesn't like storms anyway I could only keep my courage together by singing hymns as I hurried through the teeth of the wind and the torrential rain which bent me almost double. Thank goodness these storms were soon over and the hot sun quickly dried me out again.

It was agreed that I would have four days off a month leaving with the Monday bus and returning on the 4.00pm bus Thursday. Michael and Amy Glover made me very welcome in the Nongoma rectory and asked me to be Godfather to their son Peter when he was born. I would arrive with them lunchtime on the Monday and catch the 'government' bus on Tuesday morning arriving in Durban at 1.00pm. My return journey would begin at 7.00am Thursday. Sometimes I stayed with Harold Terblanche, the Rector of St. Thomas's church for the Tuesday and Wednesday nights. At other times I would stop off at Eshowe and stay with the Woods. Once I called in on someone in Melmouth near Kwamagwaza and missed the connection to Nongoma! I had to catch the 'African' bus on this occasion. The driver was very reluctant but at last agreed with the proviso that I had to duck my head as we went through Mahlabathini where there were always police around. It was fun! On another occasion I decided that I wouldn't sit in the privileged front seat. The driver packed more and more people in and it became hotter and hotter. At the back of the bus were a number of men squashed in like sardines and at a stop towards the end of the journey the driver started to pack even more passengers on. The men at the back panicked and started to shout at the driver through the window. I got caught up in the atmosphere of this and joined in. I shall always remember the shocked look on the driver's face as he saw me shake my fist at him! We prevailed! I decided thereafter to accept the kind offer of the front seat.

There was one journey on horseback that remains with me. Alfred had asked me to make a special journey to a store between us and Hlabisa, the site of an American 'Lutheran' Mission Hospital. This store was about ten miles away and there was a charismatic female 'Minister' living there who had started a church. It was after the Pentecostal and Zionist model and she herself was dressed like a Bishop with all her followers wearing green or blue uniforms and white hats. She had made a special visit to Alfred and asked him if the new members could be baptised. He asked me to undertake an exploratory visit and report back to him. The service would be at 9.30am which would mean leaving at 7.30am as the church was fourteen miles away. At that time I still thought that I shouldn't eat more than a biscuit before the Holy Communion and the journey took one and a half hours. I had forgotten that Zulu time could run anything up to two hours late and on this occasion so it was! We began the service at 11am and finished about 1.00pm We ate lunch at 2.00pm and having already ridden so far I was tired out before I set off for the return journey home. The dear horse realised this and once he knew which way we were going he set off at a gallop and got me home in record time! I clung on for dear life and arrived home just before dark absolutely exhausted and not a little sore behind!

The dear lady Leader asked for twelve men to be baptised. But the problem was how? The local store had a large garage/store house built of steel with open sides. I decided to ask if we could use this for the service. The Store Keeper could not have been kinder. He offered the facilities and said he had a petrol drum which could serve as a font and invited me to stay with his family. After the previous horse ride this was an offer I couldn't refuse. It meant that I could use the bus! We fixed a date for about a month later on a Saturday and Alfred agreed that the service could proceed. The Baptism book for Inhlwathi would have to be used as there was no 'official' church in that place yet. The month passed quickly and on the Saturday the bus was on time. It arrived at the store about lunchtime and I was given a warm welcome by the Store Keeper and his wife busy in their shop. They closed for an hour at lunchtime. It transpired that the Store Keeper had been a former Policeman in the district and he had put the big drum in the garage and filled it with water. A bucket was supplied to douse the candidates! The service began about 3.00pm and the place was packed with well wishers many of whom were not christians. Never before or since have I had so many adult baptisms at one time! The bucket was used three times over each candidate, one for each of the Holy Trinity. They were soaking wet and the floor soon began to look like a small pond! There seemed to be great rejoicing.

My evening stay with the Store Keeper was interesting. After a real Afrikaaner supper with plenty of meat he and I sat on the stoep (veranda) and left to ourselves in true Afrikaaner tyle we had a drink. I had a beer and he drank a scotch and I noticed that it wasn't his first drink of the day! After a while he made a confession and told me that after he had left the police force he had let the freedom go to his head. After he had been some time in the store he had succumbed to the charms of one of the female workers there and had sex with her. His wife never knew but he couldn't forgive himself. We talked about repentance and forgiveness. I couldn't get over what an enormous privilege being a priest was when a complete stranger could open up his heart to me. What, I wondered would his minister make of it? Both he and his wife went to their nearest Dutch Reformed church every Sunday. He also had an eleven year old American car for sale for just over £100. I was interested to learn this but when I expressed my interest he was good enough to say that it actually had a hole in the petrol tank!

The store was not far from Hlabisa and Alfred asked me to go to the hospital there once a month and take the service for Anglican Nurses. The Church Warden was a charming and jolly Policeman who organised everything beautifully. We used the Lutheran chapel which was light and cool and I was given a guest room in the hospital in which to stay. It felt like a first class hotel after 'Annesdale' which was the name Robertson had given to the house after his deceased sister. When I left in May, 1965 the congregation of about fifteen gave me a lovely briefcase with my initials P.S.D. engraved in gold on it. It remained in use for papers and books, etc. until the family bought me a new one for my fiftieth birthday! Then I continued to use it for home and sick communions especially in Papworth where I used it every Sunday morning. After I retired it was taken by my son,

Christopher for use in his work! The Police Sergeant made an effusive speech in Zulu style after my last service there. He was such a good leader and committed christian I wondered how his beliefs fitted with his work. Perhaps he had been asked to keep an eye on me! I believe he would have seen his christian faith as priority in whatever he did.

There was a very bad drought in Zululand in 1964 and the 'mealies' in the field turned black. People were in tears about this and prayer meetings were arranged in the churches. It wasn't long after our first prayer meeting that it began to rain. It was about an hour after sunset and I felt such relief that I left the house and stood in the rain thanking God. Walking through the countryside over known paths was such a pleasure and often without seeing anyone else for hours at a time. One day the sheer beauty of the countryside overwhelmed me and I knelt by the path and said the Te Deum.

One day I heard the sound of voices and hammer against stone. I climbed the hill to see what was going on and in a small dip like a quarry were three men. One was white and he walked up to me and introduced himself as Kieron Rabbitt, priest of the Catholic Church Order of Missionaries and, of course with a name like that, from Ireland. That introduction began a friendship which lasted until he was posted to Nigeria after which we lost touch, although I heard some years later that he had left the priesthood and married. He was a very good Zulu linguist and had been to Rome to help write a 'Faith Formation' book in Zulu. He promised to come and visit me and we agreed the date. He came to tea and his eyes grew wider and wider as he saw where I lived and learnt about my methods of transport, etc. He said 'You are a proper missionary!' He offered me accommodation the next time I was in Hlabisa and also to lend me vestments and the bread and wine for the Eucharist. My next visit providentially was to be the day before Christmas Eve so I declined his offer of a room but was glad not to have to carry all the necessary requirements for the service on the bus. My evening meal was provided in the hospital canteen and after this I went up the hill overlooking the settlement to the Mission House. It was a massive Italian style building and in it lived just three priests. It reminded me of the joke about an Anglican priest who was invited by his Catholic counterpart to tea at the Presbytery. The visitor was surprised by the comparative luxury he saw. The Catholic priest said 'Well, you can have the better halves so we have better quarters!' Kieron and the priest in charge were sitting already drinking and I was invited to join them. It became obvious after an hour of small talk that Kieron had forgotten about his promise of vestments and the bread and wine. I didn't want to embarrass him in front of his superior in case he hadn't mentioned it to him and so in a lull I said as casually as I could 'Kieron have you got the parcel for me?' He hesitated for a moment and then said 'Oh yes, I'll fetch it.' He was gone for about ten minutes and when he returned he handed me a brown paper parcel neatly tied with string. When I opened it later everything I needed was there!

What Kieron had been doing at the quarry was helping with the building of a new church. There was a temporary one not far away and he told me with great enthusiasm about the Easter vigil he had led there. 'It was wonderful' he said. 'The readings were so exciting that I couldn't stop saying a few words about them and before I knew where we were it was five o'clock in the morning!'

The bus took me home in time to prepare for Christmas. Alfred asked me to go to a settlement where there were five 'coloured' families and they had built a little wooden church. It meant leaving by horse about 7.00am for the five mile journey as they liked to have the service early so they would then have plenty of time to prepare their lunch before it became too hot. I arrived to a polite welcome and after the horse was tethered I took out my bag with the church things in it. To my horror I had forgotten the bread and the wine! Bread was no problem but it appeared that in this small community no-one drank wine! After a while one of them produced a bottle of brandy and it was the one and only time that the chalice had brandy in it! I made sure there was also plenty of water.

I had one visitor whilst I was at Inhlwathi. She was a friend of Don Griswold, the American priest with whom I went to Cape Town, and came for six months to help him and the childrens' work in the Diocese. She was based at Kwanzimela and joined in the Youth week we held there. She asked me if she could visit Inhlwathi to get a glimpse of the 'real' Zululand. There may have been some ulterior motive but this didn't interest me. My only concern was where she would sleep and the idea came to me that one of us could use the clinic delivery bed! Mrs. Mkhize readily agreed and as it didn't seem appropriate to ask Liz Mulford to sleep on it it would have to be me. Liz was brought with the Childrens' Worker on the Saturday and would be picked up again on the Sunday evening. Everything went well for the visit as far as I can remember. It was certainly a revelation to me how hard delivery beds actually are!

It was at Inhlwathi that I discovered what my Zulu name was. It was customary for everyone to have a nickname and the one I was given means ' The one who waves like a branch in the wind.' It was probably so because I waved to everyone I saw some distance away and Zulu people never wave. They hold up their hand in a kind of salute. There was another name given to me but I think this was more out of deference than anything else. The Zulus are very good at deference! This name was 'Mountain of Heavens' and was the name also given to one of King Shaka's regiments.

Sometime around Easter 1965 a letter arrived from the Bishop asking me to become Rector of Isandlwana where Peter Harker had been for a number of years. It was to be my first appointment as the senior priest in a parish. There were already two assistant priests there, one in his sixties living at Isandlwana and the other about fifty years old living some fifteen miles away. The 'Parish' had twelve churches in it, the furthest being over thirty miles away. The idea was that I would travel by Landrover to the most distant or inaccessible and the other two Priests would use horses to get to the others. So the time came in the middle of May for me to move on. A farewell was arranged for the Sunday evening a couple of weeks before I was due to leave and at it I was presented with a goat. On enquiring what I should do with this I was told that it should be slaughtered and shared as a meal with the congregation. The evangelist who provided the goat kindly agreed to do the honours and on the last Sunday we all had a feast after the church service. It was my first and only time to eat goat and it was really nice! Before departing I went to see Robertson's grave. Stories about him were still circulating. One was about an evangelist who used to go hunting for him as well. One day he was at a place called 'The rocky hill' and came back home with some shiny metal-like substance which he had seen gleaming on the ground. Robertson told him to throw it away and never to tell anyone where he found it. It was gold! Another story was about a priest who was the first to be sent to England for training. When he returned he was quite incorrigible and in particular he was reported as having affairs with some of the local women. Robertson held a trial in front of the congregation at the edge of a pond which is no longer there. When a majority of the congregation found the priest guilty Robertson said to him 'You have behaved like a pig and your punishment should fit your crime.' He then lifted him bodily and threw him into the pond – not very edifying!

Robertson's grave is marked by a simple headstone made of granite in the local churchyard and is kept well tended by the local church people. Once a year on All Souls Day there is a procession to the grave with prayers said for him and all the departed. He had been a tough Scotsman who had been given some hard times but never abandoned his faith or his love for the Zulu people.

During my last few weeks at Inhlwathi I asked if I could join the Renewal movement called 'The Guild of Christ's Witnesses'. Their rules are based on the Franciscan ones for Tertiaries, namely Sunday communion, daily prayer, frequent Bible reading, sacrificial giving, simple life-style, moral integrity and witnessing to others about God's love for them. As these vows seemed to me to be what any priest would want to live his life by anyway, there seemed no reason why I should not apply. I was accepted and was privileged to be the first non Zulu member.

The day of moving arrived. I had been to Isandlwana once before when I was studying Zulu at Kwanzimela and dear Peter Harker and his lovely wife Rosemary had been kind enough to invite me for a weekend. There might have been something else on their mind as they had also invited the 23 year old daughter of Archdeacon Arden of Swaziland! Peter had himself helped to build the large house in which they lived near the Memorial Church of St. Vincent, so named because of the famous battle that had taken place there on January 28th which is St. Vincent day in the church calendar. Knowledge of this war of 1879 came thick and fast as Peter was an expert and took us both on a sight-seeing trip.

There is a memorial display at one end of the site full of artefacts from the battle and a model of the action. Having marvelled at all of this we then went half-way up the mountain where there is a marvellous view across the entire area, dotted about with white cairns which gave it a most unusual atmosphere. On the horizon to the left are the hills behind which the Zulu Army of 25,000 troops hid all night without being spotted. Not a fire was lit and no loud sounds were made! The British General, Lord Chelmsford, had not reckoned with the fact that these troops travelled forty miles a day jogging slowly, bare footed, across terrain very well known to them. He had not expected them for at least another two days and then possibly from an entirely different direction. In the early morning of the day of battle Lord Chelmsford had decided to move his troops forward and left base with a few hundred key troops to establish a new base camp. The Zulu troops could hardly believe their luck and about midday they rushed down the hill and overwhelmed the British forces. Very few escaped with their lives. It was the first defeat on the field of battle for a British Army for hundreds of years. One of the Zulu Regiments had not even been engaged in the fight and ran on to Rorkes Drift where the British contingent put up an amazing defence and inflicted terrible casualties on the Zulus. This was of course depicted as a glorious victory for the British helping to alleviate the fallout from the shocking disaster of Isandlwana! When Lord Chelmsford heard about the defeat he hurried back to the camp at Isandlwana but could see the devastation from afar and refused the troops accompanying him to enter the camp. This meant that the dead weren't buried until May when he returned with a much larger force to take revenge on the Zulu Kingdom. The King was finally defeated at his home and taken prisoner effectively ending Zulu National independence forever. So the bodies of foes were finally buried together in graves which were then marked with a pile of stones on the top of them. When the 'War Graves Commission' took on responsibility for these they painted the stones a bright white giving the entire area an atmosphere akin to some ghostly drama. The area is flat for some miles around and no-one can see in from the mountainsides so it is as if you are looking into an amphitheatre. Nowadays there are trained guides to take you around and I visited with one in 1999 and was given a graphic description of it all. It was an unforgettable experience, especially as I had lived in the area for two years.

I moved into the big house at the end of May and Archdeacon Dhladhla came to induct me soon after. The congregation must have been about two hundred as there were twelve churches and the other two Zulu priests as well as me. The fifty year old priest lived in a cottage above the big house about two hundred yards away with his family of five children, mostly grown-up by then. There were also several grand-children living there and his wife was fond of making very strong beer for which she could get a good price. She was also keen to drink it herself! This priest was renowned to be on the lazy side and as a result had grown rather large. However he and I got on fairly well together although I must confess the relationship remained a professional one throughout. The younger priest lived with his wife and children at a place called Magogo about fifteen miles away. He looked after the four congregations scattered about the mountainous terrain where he lived and I went to the places the Landrover could get me to. Father Similane would go by horse to the remainder and help at the home station when I was away.

There was a young woman of about twenty-five who was recommended to me as a housekeeper and I paid her out of my stipend of £50 per month. Her name was Betty Mazibuko and sometime after I left she married a Dhlamini.. Her cooking was mainly limited to porridge, mince and rice but she was very pleasant and looked after the house and me very well. As the house was so large it seemed only sensible to see if anyone would like to rent some of the rooms, I certainly didn't need them all. Two Teachers from the local school came to ask for them. They were both unmarried and living far from their homes. They looked after themselves and paid rent which helped me to pay for Betty. This arrangement was working well when I had a surprise visit from the Archdeacon of Swaziland on his way home from a meeting at the cathedral in Eshowe. He sat down looking very serious and told me that the Bishop had had a rumour reported to him that I was living with a woman in the Rectory! I showed him around and introduced him to my tenants including Betty who lived free at the Rectory and he went away quite satisfied! It wasn't too long however before I decided that it was stupid for me to be living in the big house when my colleague and his large family were cramped together in a much smaller one. We agreed to swap. It never occurred to me that I should let someone in authority know of the arrangement! Apparently the Bishop had told an Irish family that they could move into the Rectory with me until something was sorted out for them elsewhere. The priest, my good friend Bill, still teases me about this event! I was never told about it and only learned of it when I retired. When I moved up the hill to the smaller house the teachers of course stayed on in the Rectory but almost immediately I was approached by two male students from a school five miles away about staying with me. There seemed to be enough room so Jabulani and Michael moved in and replaced the rent I had lost from the teachers.

The little house was charming and had a wonderful view towards the river which curled in the distance marking the boundary of the Mission. I must have stayed in the big house for at least a year though because I can remember some events taking place whilst I was there. One was a visit from our dear Bishop, Tom Savage, who brought with him a priest who had worked as the Rector of Kendal in the Lake District for many years. He had now retired and was the chairman of a Diocesan support group in Britain called the 'Zululand and Swaziland Association'. They visited me on one of those July days which in South Africa can be very cold in the evenings and the house had the most wonderful fireplace on which Betty had put large logs. After a good supper we sat by this beautiful fire and talked about this and that. The Bishop was concerned that I might be finding it too lonely there on my own. Not long afterwards we learnt that he was sick but it was sometime before I learnt that he had inoperable stomach cancer. I saw him only once more and that was just shortly before he died. I remember his gaunt face and how he whispered the blessing I asked him to give me. He was well looked after by John Curry, one of the Doctors at St. Mary's, the church hospital. He was only 63 years old when he died. His funeral was a great example to everyone, a matchwood coffin, a beautifully sung Zulu Eucharist and a silent procession to a simple grave at Kwanzimela whilst a priest sang 'Tell my soul the glorious battle' next to the coffin as it was carried by four priests in cassocks. The grave is marked by a simple wooden cross.

So early in 1966 before he died the Diocesan Synod had to set about finding his successor to ensure a smooth handover. In the meantime whilst our dear Bishop was sick the Bishop of Natal helped out. I was told he would be coming to Isandlwana for a confirmation and although he was a kind man he was also a bit autocratic, therefore I was nervous! There were thirty candidates of varying ages. Father Simelane and I shared the preparation and there were also candidates from other congregations prepared by a dear Evangelist who took services and preached at Ngwebini five miles away by road. The service was attended by hundreds! Our new Evangelist, John Zulu, was very keen and had arranged the entire service. He was also to translate the sermon to be given by the Bishop so he was alongside us up at the front either side of the Bishop. John's enthusiasm was particularly noticeable in his singing which he did at full throttle and in harmony except that his version of it was to be honest not entirely orthodox or tuneful! The Bishop turned to him on one occasion with that kind of bemused look mixed with ecclesiastical authority that remains unforgettable! John took no notice. However the good Bishop remained affable throughout it all. He was given a splendid dinner prepared largely by Liz who had come to the Charles Johnson Hospital as a volunteer, and he then departed happily. At the meal I ventured rather foolishly to tell the story about a certain Bishop of London who was purported to have been at a restaurant when a waitress, after taking the order from the other guests, said to him 'And what would Robin Red-breast like?' The Bishop of Natal smiled and then said 'I wonder just how many different Bishops that story has been told about?'

On St. Vincent's Day the veterans association, called 'The Moths' (memorable order of the tin hat), held a service at the war memorial. It seemed rather odd to me that the descendants of the British should commemorate a glorious defeat whereas the Zulus never celebrated their amazing victory of the same day and so in 1967 I invited the Prime Minister of the Zulu Nation, Chief Gatsha Buthelezi to come for a celebration. 'The

Moths' politely declined my invitation to attend! We stood on top of the largest monument and after prayers the Chief addressed the assembled hundred or so people. Just below us right in front of the crowd was a security policeman with a tape recorder! After the service we went to the big house for a lunch. Things had to be done properly for the Chief and so a bull was brought forward and a local man produced a knife and slit its throat. It went down like a burst balloon! Then it was skinned and divided up for the big feast. The man who slaughtered it was speaking very softly whilst he performed the deed and I assumed he was talking to the ancestors.

One of the congregations I visited every month lived in the mountains about thirty miles away and I would drive the Landrover as far as the store in their area where a Norwegian couple and their son lived. They gave me a bed for the night and the following morning I rode a horse to the church situated on a plateau half-way down the mountain. The scenery was spectacular. On one occasion there was mist in the valley and for the first hour I was above the clouds in the hot sunshine. The horse travelled so slowly down the steep paths that after our first journey I decided to walk! There was always a lunch served in the vestry after the service and then I climbed back up the mountain for supper and another night at the store. Only once do I remember being caught by bad weather. There was a thunderstorm approaching and that always made me feel uneasy. It is probably subconscious memories of the war but thunder and lightening always scare me. On this particular occasion I decided to seek shelter in one of the homes and the owners were only too pleased to help. I was given the clean and smart guest hut to rest in. I was lying on the bed just about to drop off to sleep when I heard running footsteps approaching the door. Three small children appeared, their eyes popping out of their heads! I invited them in and asked them their names but they were very coy and replied in what was barely an audible whisper. Soon they ran out of the hut and as they skeltered down the path I heard them shouting 'The white man has red legs'!

But it was the first time I went to Qudeni, as it was called, that remains with me like a bad dream. I was looking forward to it so much like a young boy on his first outing to the seaside. The telephone rang and it was the priest at Magogo who was to accompany me on this trip and act as my escort. He lived about half-way and I was to pick him up on my journey there. His voice was solemn as he said we shouldn't go as the weather was on the change and he thought it might snow. Where I was the sun was shining bright and hot. I persuaded him to go anyway. Everything was going well until we were about five miles from our destination when it began to snow heavily! By the time we had travelled another three miles along the dirt mountain road it became clear we would be foolish to attempt the last and most difficult two miles of the journey. We came to a spot where there was a store owned again by a Norwegian couple, children of Missionaries, and I drove the Landrover into their yard. A large man came to the door and I asked him if we could possibly stay the night as it was already growing dark and the snow was still falling thickly. He said he would be delighted and invited me to step inside. My colleague hesitated on the doorstep and my host looked at him and said 'If you go to the stable block over there you will be given a bed.' I was staggered but could say nothing. The next day when we met up again to begin the return journey home I apologised profusely to my colleague. His response was simple – 'Don't mention it Father, I quite understand.' My only consolation that day was that we helped to pull a post-office van out of a ditch where it had slid in the three inches of snow whilst trying to reach some fallen telephone wires.

I did make some lovely visits to that region afterwards though. One was a confirmation. In early 1966 Bishop Tom died and the day he died he had asked for the newly elected Bishop to say the commital prayers and he in turn had given the new Bishop a blessing. Alpheus Zulu was the first Zulu to be elected as a Diocesan Bishop in the Anglican Church of South Africa. The manner of his election can be told later but about a year afterwards there was a confirmation for the congregations in the mountain area of the Isandlwana Benefice. To save the sixty-year old Bishop the steep ascent and subsequent climb back I took him the longer way round involving only a short but sharp climb. He was a stickler for time saying that Zulu time was merely an excuse to be lazy! The time set for the service was 8.30am, and so that was the time we must arrive. This meant leaving Isandlwana at 6.30am so the Bishop met me and we started our walk. He found the required speed rather hard going and eventually conceded that it wouldn't matter if we arrived at 8.40am! This we did. In the church were the candidates and the priest from Magogo with two church wardens. We started and by the time the Bishop had confirmed and preached the church was full. The service finished about 11.30am and we then had lunch beginning our return journey at 1.00pm. We were half-way to the car when we met an elderly man coming towards us with a walking stick. He leant back on his stick and said 'I thought there was a confirmation here today.' His sense of time was clearly very Zulu!

Another memorable service was the Patronal Festival at St. Andrew's, Qudeni. This was a little church opposite the store where I had stayed on my first visit in the snow. The congregation faithfully turned up on a weekday for the festival. At the start of my sermon I said that as St. Andrew was the Saint particularly connected with 'mission' we would proceed over to the store after the service, sing a hymn, and then mingle with the shoppers to evangelise as best as we could. So after the service I, the cross bearer and the Church Wardens started off to the store. When we reached the store I turned round to see only one other person had joined us! We stayed a little while and then returned to the church to find the rest of the congregation still there singing hymns! I asked them why and they told me it was to help them get the strength they would need to go and do as I had asked them! Unfortunately I wasn't able to pursue this conversation further as being rather tired and hungry it seemed better to just forget it and start the lunch.

One visit was rather frightening! I had agreed to stay the night with an evangelist and after the meal he was deciding which hut I should sleep in. The guest hut was clean and tidy but for some reason he decided on another as more suitable. During the night we were awakened by shouts and on going outside discovered the guest hut was on fire! I wondered if I had some enemies there. My overnight stays were usually very pleasant. On one occasion I visited the store itself and asked some of the workers if they were Anglicans. I found at least four or five who were and so asked my hostess if I could hold a service for them the next morning. She was surprised to learn that any of her staff were even Christians let alone Anglicans but readily agreed that we could use the kitchen at seven o'clock the following morning. Those who came all received communion. On another occasion the Dahls invited the Bishop for Dinner as we were visiting some of the neighbouring congregations together. We had a lovely evening and it was one of the rare occasions when Mr. Dahl was present. The reason for mentioning this is that when it was time for my next visit and I thanked Mrs. Dahl for her kindness she replied that she had enjoyed it and had found the Bishop 'so nice, just like a European really.' Not, I think, something he would have been glad to hear! I missed my visits to the mountain regions. I remember a lovely evangelist there who could walk across the rocks as though he were a mountain goat and regularly left me puffing behind! One day as I caught him up he was sitting on a rock by the side of the road looking at the clouds. It was one of those days when thunder threatened and the sky looked spectacular. I remarked about the fine cloud formations and he said 'Yes. I like looking when the clouds appear. You never know when the Lord might come riding in on them!'

Whilst staying at Isandlwana I visited the hospital at Nqutu rather more frequently than I should have done really. It was, I suppose, to help alleviate the loneliness that always seemed to be lurking in the background. The hospital there was always growing and at some stage someone, probably me, suggested that the uncompleted new Maternity Block would make an excellent place to perform a play. I had with me a copy of the York cycle of Mystery Plays and so I called a meeting for anyone interested in taking part in a performance. About twenty of the trainee nurses came along and we then had to find someone who could attempt a Zulu translation of the text. One of the nurses had a brother who was a Teacher and she felt sure that he could do what was needed. About a month later a large packet arrived with a typed script of the play. These were duplicated at the hospital and rehearsals began. The nurses were natural actors and worked very hard during the two months we had available. Some rehearsals went on past 10.00pm and the hospital 'Housekeeper', a beautiful Christian lady came every time to chaperone the girls and help with the refreshments and in all sorts of other useful ways. The performance was packed out! God dressed in chasuble and crown threw Satan out of heaven and she rolled down the stairs of the unfinished ward with a blood-curdling shriek. I have never been so proud before or since of a cast. Mind you that wasn't the last drama at the hospital!

In 1967 Alan Paton, the famous author of 'Cry the Beloved Country', came to give away the prizes. I discovered that he had also written a play about his experiences as a Warden of a 'Borstal' called 'Sponono'. It seemed like a good idea to put on a performance of this play for him. Again there was tremendous enthusiasm and the evening went off splendidly. He seemed very pleased with it. The nurse who took the part of the main character, the young man Sponono, caused great amusement amongst her friends with her abilities to act the part of a man!

It was about this time that Liz came to work as a volunteer at the hospital. She was twenty-one years old and very good looking. I am afraid that it didn't take long for us to become friends and we began to meet regularly. One or two of my friends voiced their doubts about the suitability of the relationship and there did seem to be something missing. For some time I had been to see the Vicar of Escourt in Natal as a Spiritual Director and so I discussed this with him. He simply said 'I think you know what you have to do.' So I told Liz. It was hard on her and I knew that in some ways I had spoilt her visit to the hospital because she found it difficult to continue there afterwards. I am glad to say that she married a couple of years later and I went to see her and her fiancée when I was on long leave in 1968.

Other aspects of my life were developing too. The American Priest who had 'displaced' me at Empangeni was encouraged by the Bishop to set up workshops called 'T Groups' at Kwanzimela. These were basically groups which were to work out for themselves how leadership functions and the dynamics of interaction within the group setting. It was all very new to us who were used to a leader up front telling us what to do. They were carefully planned. When we arrived we were told where our group was to meet and when we got there we all sat in a circle. The only clue available to us was a piece of newsprint up on the wall on which was written 'The object of the group is to form community.' There were two 'leaders' sitting in our circle. One was Richard Kraft, another American who had been given the role of Christian Education Officer for the Diocese. He was an irenic person whom everyone loved and admired. He stayed in the Diocese for about eight years and then was made the Provincial Director of Adult Education. He had this job for a few years and was then elected to be Bishop of Pretoria. Some years before he was due to retire he contracted Leukaemia with which he battled until a little time after his retirement when he died in 2000. His fellow leader of our T Groups at that time was Jean Poynton whose husband was a rector in Durban and Jean was one of the education staff for Natal Diocese. A number of years later David, her husband, was made the Provincial Education Officer and was tragically killed in a road accident when travelling home one night across the Transkei he hit some roaming cattle on the road. Jean went back to her home in England and I heard in the 1980's that she herself had died of Cancer whilst still in her sixties. That night at Kwanzimela they sat in our group and said not a word! After what seemed to be ages someone asked them the question 'What are we meant to be doing?' Their only answer was to direct us to the statement on the newsprint. 'What did this mean?' we asked and we were told that it was our job to find out. Some of us began to tell them that we thought the idea was stupid and a waste of time. Weren't they supposed to be leaders? They didn't answer us directly and one or two of the group began to show their disquiet as to what we were supposed to be doing. Someone also began to take over the leadership of the group suggesting for example that we introduce ourselves and say why we were attending the workshop. It began to grow dark and someone else suggested that we light the oil-lamp in the centre of the room. Others however said that they would prefer to be in the dark (as they were metaphorically) at least for some time yet. We couldn't make a decision and lapsed into silence when suddenly the door opened and a Zulu man came in with a big box of matches. He didn't say anything but simply took a chair and standing on it in the centre of the group lit the lamp. He must have wondered why we all burst out laughing! After supper we continued. Some people said that they thought it would be best to ignore our 'leaders' as they obviously didn't want to help us but we were still unsure how to proceed. After breakfast the next morning when we got to our room we noticed that our 'leaders' had removed their chairs from the circle and were sitting separately behind us. When asked why they said they had felt excluded from the group by our attitude of aggression towards them and some of the unkind things we had said about or to them. This then set us the problem of how to include them in the group again as we couldn't create community without them. We worked hard all morning to devise a strategy and eventually sent one of our members, Lawrence Zulu, to intercede for us. Lawrence was at that time a chaplain and tutor at the Anglican Theological College in the Cape and later he was to succeed Alpheus as Bishop of the Zululand Diocese. As he presented our petition, our sadness at what we had done and our desire for forgiveness, Jean Poynton burst into tears. It was a moment of truth for all of us. After that we were able to be even more open and honest with each other and a lot of 'bonding' took place.

We also had plenary sessions about some of the theory behind the group work and its relationship to the Christian faith and the church.

I went on a second course and what I remember most about that one was the Bishop of Swaziland sitting next to a young Roman Catholic woman. In an interval she took his hand and said 'I have been looking at your ring. Where did you get it?' He simply replied 'Oh, I was given that when I became a Bishop.' I have never seen a hand dropped so quickly! She was covered with embarrassment but it said a good bit about 'role and person'. Another moment of truth came when we had been deeply involved about some issue and one of the group, a white priest, said 'I have always had a prejudice against Indians and now I realise that it has suddenly left me.' There was an Indian in our group and the priest had found that as they worked together he had forgotten about the racial difference between us all. After this course I was asked if I would be an observer working with a group leader. This workshop was to prove to be explosive in a number of ways!

By this time I had moved to St. Augustine to look after it whilst the priest-in-charge was on long leave. Bishop Alpheus had asked me to do this and work in the Isandlwana Benefice at the same time. There were three residents in the Mission House already and an assistant priest, Jacob Dhlamini who was later to become the Bishop of St. John's Diocese in the Transkei. The other three residents were a student from Radley School on a gap year, a young Book Keeper, Tim Marks, who later became a Baptist Minister in England and then joined the Anglican Priesthood. He is presently the Director of a network of Christian Counsellors in the Bristol area. The third was a retired School Master who wore a false nose which fell off from time to time! St. Augustine's had a very large church building which was capable of holding over one thousand people. Most of the ordinations and other large events took place there. Then there was a Boarding School of some two hundred boys and an equal number of girls. This was the reason they needed a priest all the time as the priest was also the 'Warden' of the Hostels where the students slept. At 8.30am every day there was a Holy Communion service in the church at which the singing was superb. Some of the teachers at the school were Missionaries and the Head Master was an American whilst another teacher was Norwegian. The latter was very friendly to me and one day he invited me to meet with a visiting American Pentecostal missionary and his wife. We had coffee and then the missionary spoke about his work in Kenya with some amazing stories about conversions to Christianity and how the Holy Spirit was bringing about miracles there. As we left I asked if I could join him for a time of prayer and it was fixed for 6.00pm. At the appointed time I went to their guest house and after a time spent chatting we prayed together. Then he said he would bless me by placing his hands on my head and pray in a language I wouldn't understand. This he did very calmly and quietly. Then he stopped and said to me 'Now you pray in whatever language the Holy Spirit gives you.' I didn't know how to start and so kept silent. He then said 'Just begin, all the words are there.' More silence. So then I decided to say 'I don't think that the Holy Spirit intends to bless me in this way tonight.' I had got as far as the words 'Holy Spirit' when without any warning I broke into a language completely unknown to me. I couldn't stop praying and he said to me 'Stand Up' which I did. I continued for about another three minutes like a flowing fountain with words and sentences just forming themselves. At one point his wife who was praying with us burst into tears and ran out of the room. Suddenly the torrent stopped and I sat down feeling totally overwhelmed. I couldn't tell you what I had said but I knew that I had been praising God. My first question to him was 'How can I tell that it came from God?' He referred me to Luke 11 where Jesus says 'If your son asks for a stone will you give him a scorpion?' He also referred me to the gifts of the Spirit in St. Paul's letter to the Corinthians where the gift of 'tongues' is mentioned. I had always read this as some sort of special phenomenon of the time but had never heard of it being repeated in the history of the church. My next question was 'What is it for?' He said it was a gift of prayer to be used at any time but especially when facing a crisis or temptation. We shook hands and I left but not before inviting them to the Eucharist in the church on the following morning as I said it was the only way I could think to say thank you. It was lovely to see them there and receiving communion from my hands. One thing that did happen following this event was that all barriers between myself and other Christian bodies broke down and since then I have never been simply able to label people as 'catholic' or 'charismatic' or 'evangelical'. I suppose I lived on cloud nine for a few days. The next morning for example I went into the church early to see if I could 'do it' again! As I knelt there asking the Holy Spirit to bless me quite unexpectedly a shaft of light came through a side window and quite literally hit my tongue and I started again, although this time I stopped after a minute or so and found that I could start again by myself. That is how it has been ever since! Not that I pray in this way as much as I should being lazy and careless about it. However my life was immediately placed on a different path.

The following Sunday I had been asked to officiate at the Morning Service at St. James in Dundee. Of course I felt I had to say something about the experience and many years later a member of the congregation who began to attend a lunchtime Bible Study in Vryheid when I was the vicar there mentioned the sermon of that day. 'We wondered then what on earth you were on about' he said. At the time of this conversation he knew very well, as a renewal of the Holy Spirit had swept the church in South Africa during the early 1970's. Then there was this workshop at Kwanzimela I have already written about. It took place not long after these events and as I said I had been asked to be an assistant leader of a group. Two things happened which were great challenges at the time. One occurred during a plenary session when my good friend Michael was giving a talk on how this mode of learning was mirrored in the Acts of the Apostles especially in the close fellowship there was between the believers at that time. There were mental bells ringing for many of the listeners. All of a sudden a woman stood up and asked if she could leave and go to the chapel. Her arms, she said, were tingling like hot needles. Of course she was allowed to go. After a while Lawrence Zulu who was also a leader in the workshop whispered to me 'Perhaps you should go and see if she is alright.' So I left. She was kneeling on the communion step in the Chapel and I knelt a little distance away. She said something about the Lord wanting to give her a gift of healing so I approached her and said that I would place my hands upon her head and pray in a language she wouldn't recognise for her to be blessed in whatever way the Lord saw fit. As I did this she said 'You are to go to the rest and tell them what has happened.' It came to me that she was interpreting the words that I had said. It was terrifying and I began to shake all over. Lawrence had come into the Chapel too. I asked him what I should do and he simply said 'Obey the Lord.' At the end of the lecture I asked to speak and shared the experiences up to that moment in time. This had an immediate effect. The group was full of different Christian denominations.

The lady in question was a Methodist and there were Roman Catholic nuns also present. Two Methodist ladies came up and thanked me and said they had been praying in tongues themselves whilst it was all going on. The nuns announced that they would consider leaving if events got any further out of hand! The leaders decided to play it cool and the rest of the workshop went as planned.

Except for the second thing to happen and this was to do with the group themselves. As I look back now and reflect it seems that it might have been the devil trying to upset the apple cart! There was a clergy wife in the group from Pinetown in the Natal Diocese and she seemed to enjoy the growing awareness within the group of the importance of relationships and how each one could contribute to the corporate life of the group. After one session she asked to see me privately and as we talked in a small room she poured out her heart about her unhappy marriage. Her husband was a tyrant and a bully yet preached such nice sermons on marriage. They had four children all under ten years of age and she herself could only have been in her early thirties. At the end of our meeting she said 'I have fallen in love with you.' She must have noticed me turn white with fear! I said that we would have to stop the interview and that I would tell her the next day my thoughts on the whole matter. At the evening staff meeting I confided in the others what she had said. They thought it unwise for me to see her alone again but I felt I had to keep my promise to her. The next day I told her that I wouldn't consider breaking up her marriage even if it were difficult and advised her to seek help elsewhere. She asked if she could write to me and I stupidly agreed. Soon after getting back to St. Augustines long letters began arriving every day. They were protestations of undying love! I tried to reply in a friendly but uncommitted way about once every fortnight. Then one day the phone rang and she told me she had spoken to her husband and he had agreed she could visit me! Again I was silly and agreed on the condition that she stayed at the Hospital and we only met to talk things over there. Her conversation was the same old circle about how she would leave her husband for me. I played for time and asked her to see my Spiritual Director, the vicar of Estcourt. A week or so later I had a phone call from him asking me to meet her and her husband at their home with him present. We sat on their lawn in the sun and the vicar was very wise and good. Wasn't this obsession a way of escape for her from a stressful life? Their marriage could be improved but the way to solve such a problem was to work things out between them, etc.etc. She said not a word the whole time and the only thing I remember her husband saying was that it would be difficult for her to leave now as she was pregnant with their fifth child! I had one last sad letter from her saying she still loved me and always would. I didn't reply. Years later I heard that the marriage had indeed broken up. How sad but perhaps she found some freedom and fulfilment at last.

Before properly leaving Isandlwana I must mention the vehicles which the church supplied. I inherited an old Landrover which had given sterling service for my predecessor. The journeys were tough and visiting one place meant crossing a dried-up river-bed made up simply of rocks and without fail the old four-wheeled drive worked like a dream. One day I was taking Holy Communion to an elderly lady whom I was told was too disabled to get to church. Across the grass fields I went when suddenly the car went down a hole about four feet deep! I must have been travelling quite fast because it bounced out the other side immediately. My head bumped painfully against the roof but that was the only casualty. It turned out to be a trap for wild animals. Actually the journey turned out to be a bit of a con because the next month I was back in that area and saw the old lady striding out with the help of a staff. 'How come?' I asked. The answer was that today was the monthly pension day and if she didn't go in person she would miss it! However I decided rightly or wrongly not to risk life and limb by travelling to her house again.

Another occasion was when I was going to church on a rainy day. The track was rather muddy and suddenly I felt the car slip sideways. As there was a drop of forty feet to my right I slammed on the brakes and leapt out. The car stopped about a foot from the drop. What to do now? I called in at the next krall and without any hesitation the owner got out his six oxen and with a rope pulled the car to safety. I wasn't quite so lucky on another day when I went over a blind rise and suddenly hit a flock of sheep crossing the road. Four of them were killed. I called to tell the owner who was very understanding and after getting home I asked for advice as to what I should do. I was told that the polite thing would be to return to the owner and offer to buy two of the sheep. This I did and was able to dine on mutton for weeks afterwards.

Yes, I had a fridge and the story of how that arrived is worth telling. There was an old one there when I first arrived but it soon packed up and I was told of a shop in Vryheid where I would be able to get spare parts. When I got there they didn't have the part as the model was too old so they gave me the address of the makers. I wrote and after a month or so I returned from my visits to be met by Betty who told me that a worker had called and installed the new part. In fact within two hours the room was full of smoke so I wrote again asking if they could notify me when the repair man would call and I would arrange to be there. Again I returned one day to be told he had called and this time there was a note on the table saying he was sorry but the model was too old to be repaired. In the meantime a bill arrived for about £5.00 for the original spare part! I ignored it. This bill then arrived every month until finally it was accompanied by a red notice saying I would be taken to court if I didn't pay up. That made me sit down and write a letter to the Managing Director in Johannesburg. Nothing happened until two months later when once more returning from work I saw a gigantic fridge standing in the living room! With it was a letter from the Assistant Managing Director thanking me for my letter and expressing their apologies for their negligence. Please would I receive the fridge as a gift from the firm. Father Simelane was full of it! It had taken the men two hours to struggle up the hill to the house with it. They had said to him that they thought 'the old man' was about to die and the fridge was really a present for the Almighty! They had never had to do anything like that before. The fridge moved with me to the Charles Johnson Hospital where they gave me £50 for it. It was still there in the kitchen when we moved to Vryheid in 1971.

The dear old Landrover died eventually. I was in Ladysmith on my way home and going down a gentle hill when suddenly the steering came loose. Fortunately there was no traffic around as I veered across the road and came to a halt with the front up against a brick wall. The axle had snapped. My next vehicle was a Peugeot pick-up van and ignorantly I continued to drive it as I had the Landrover. One day up in the mountains I went over a rock and broke the oil sump! Still, it was mended and I learned to treat it a bit more gently. It had its moments mind you! Once on my way to a church I had to cross a river up a steep bank and at the top collided with a donkey who refused to move. This broke the left-hand headlight! That was also the occasion I saw the result of a suicide. The evangelist took me to a home where a crowd had gathered. Hanging from the rafters in the hut next door was a young woman in full Zulu dress. Prayers were said in the main hut and as I mentioned the name of God one of the men who had been crouching Zulu style for prayer keeled over backwards in a faint. Afterwards it was whispered to me that he was the husband of the dead woman but was also an Isangoma, usually translated as 'witchdoctor', and the name of God had struck him down. One was quickly out of one's depth in Zululand!

The truck was marooned once. I had gone to Kwaisa where I had to cross the dried-up river bed on a very misty morning and had parked the van to go off visiting for the day. When I returned about 3.00pm I realised that I had left the lights on all day. I had to walk the four miles back home and phone the hospital for help. The young Engineer arrived after his supper about 8.30pm, bless him, and we went off in the dark to the van. He couldn't believe how difficult it was to get there. We started the van with jump leads and arrived back at Isandlwana at about 10.30pm for a very welcome cup of coffee. Another time I drove over a python! It was about 10.00pm in the corridor between two Game Reserves and I saw what I thought was a pipe lying across the road. However after I had bumped over it I decided to go back and take a closer look. The 'pipe' had disappeared! When I got back home I jumped quickly out of the van. I had heard stories of snakes curling up in the warmth from the engine. There weren't any really dangerous encounters with wild life. Once Tom Zulu, the evangelist, and I were travelling somewhere when a snake crossed our path. 'Mamba' he said, and was after it like lightening. All I saw was the swing of his knobkerry and a thudding sound. He proudly picked it up and swung it in the air! People had told me to look out for scorpions and every day I shook my shoes. Imagine the shock when one day a large one fell out and scampered away quickly under the skirting board! He never appeared again.

It was during my time at St. Augustine's that Alpheus Zulu was elected Bishop. Bishops are elected in the Church of the Province of Southern Africa. All the clergy are involved plus a lay representative from each parish together with representatives from the wider Province. The election took place at Kwamagwaza in the church there. At that time the 'Vicar General', someone who stood as Bishop during an interregnum, was in the chair. There were three candidates. Two were priests from England and the other was Alpheus who for some years had been an Assistant Bishop in the Transkei. One of the English candidates was the priest whom I had replaced, Norman Gilmore, who had been an Archdeacon in Zululand. His daughter Margaret is at present one of the reporters for BBC News. The other priest later became Bishop in Swaziland. The discussion and debate went on all day about the suitability of the various candidates in turn and it was obviously going to be a close contest. It was nearly 5.00pm when a vote was taken. The elected candidate required two-thirds of the votes cast. I had been asked to be the clergy counter. The lay man and I retired to the vestry to count. When we finished it transpired that Alpheus had obtained just one vote less than the required two-thirds! It was getting dark and the church had no lighting and as the Chairman was announcing the result something made me put my hand into the voting box and there lay one missed vote – for Alpheus! I shouted 'stop', and announced what I had found. The chairman said that as he had already announced the result he couldn't alter the outcome so we would all have to reconvene the next morning. Besides it was getting too dark to continue that night. Chaos broke out! The Zulu clergy said that they would not vote again as they knew that some of the Zulu laymen were not able to return the next morning to re-cast their vote. I said that I would return to England as it would be my fault that Alpheus had not been elected. The Lawyers of the Diocese stayed up until midnight and as they had by then checked the number of votes cast against the number of those voting and found them equal they decided that the Chairman should declare Alpheus elected as soon as we re-convened the next morning. Of course none of us knew this that night and a lot of sleep was lost! It was the best possible decision and everyone except a few conservative whites was happy. The Zulus had wanted Alpheus at the last election when Tom Savage had been appointed and so had waited a long time for this moment.

It is difficult to believe that my stay at St. Augustine's lasted less than six months, such a lot had happened. Indeed the most important event in my life happened there too! One Sunday morning I was just finishing the 8.30am service for the school when three young ladies crept in at the back and sat down. As I went out I spoke to them and the Zulu lady explained that they had walked from Rorke's Drift about four miles away across the river in order to come to a service in English. Her two friends, she said, were Swedish missionaries who were studying Zulu but had wanted a break for just one Sunday. I explained that the next service was in Zulu but I would be glad to preach in English with an interpreter and would they like to come to the Mission House for a cup of tea and a piece of toast. They seemed quite reluctant but agreed under pressure as they had travelled so far. The Swedish ladies seemed very shy and conversation was difficult. One worked as a Domestic Sciences Teacher and the other was an Occupational Therapist. The Zulu lady was a Teacher at the Arts and Crafts centre at Rorke's Drift, and had befriended the Swedish ladies whose names were Ingrid and Anita. So along we went to the service and I preached about opening our lives to Jesus because he was The Way, The Truth and The Life, and was standing at the door of our lives knocking, and wanting to come in to be our Lord and Saviour. They sped off at the end for their long walk back. I thought the Occupational Therapist seemed very shy but sweet with a pretty, strong-looking face. I thought it would be a good idea to make contact with her again. As I didn't know her surname I wrote a letter addressed to 'Anita, Occupational Therapist, Rorke's Drift'. Fortunately it arrived and a return letter written in good English arrived some days later. She had been helped by my sermon she said as it had made the connection between God and Jesus for her. She had been searching for a long time but now, at last, things seemed to add up. She would be at a meeting where Beyers Naudee, the Afrikaans Minister who had left the Dutch Reformed Church over the issue of Apartheid was to speak in the Anglican Church at Dundee. So I decided to go this meeting also! He spoke wonderfully and Anita was there but she was with a man of about my age and I wondered if this was her boyfriend. That night some local lads put sand in my colleague's truck petrol tank. He had returned from long leave to take up his post again at St. Augustine's and came to listen to Beyers Naudee with some of the students from the school. I had returned to Isandlwana to live.

Anyway I established that Anita was studying Zulu at a place called Elandskraal which according to the map was out in the middle of nowhere! My next day off saw me heading in this direction. It was an old Mission Station with scattered farms in the area. The Apartheid Government had moved all the Africans from the farms and so the church and mission were largely deserted except for the farm workers and a few others. There was a large house there so I parked outside and went to seek help in locating Anita. A cheerful welcome awaited me. Pastor Wolf was a German missionary who had been there for many years. His Zulu was perfectly fluent and so he was teaching the young missionaries over in the old school. They were mainly Norwegian missionaries, one Pastor with his wife and four spinsters of whom Anita was the only Swede. Pastor Wolf was so glad to see another missionary that an invitation to lunch was immediately issued. It was already about midday and as I had no idea where I was to eat that day his invitation was welcome. The only thing was that he talked so much about everything! His wife was very sweet but I can't remember her saying anything at all! After about two hours I ventured to enquire if it would be alright for me to go across to the school and see if I could make contact with one of the students. He took me across and I was introduced to a very nice man who was in charge of the 'family' there. Yes, he would send for Anita and would I like a cup of tea? Eventually ALL of the group turned up with Anita the last to appear and then sitting silently and looking pale. The leader, a Norwegian priest was interested to hear about the Anglican Church and what we were up to so he dominated most of the conversation. At last I had to accept that there was not going to be a chance to see Anita alone and I made my farewells. I don't think we even shook hands as one should for at that time I knew nothing about Scandinavian culture. If I had at least I would have had the chance to say something! I reached the van, slammed the door and drove off saying 'That's that then!' Later Anita told me that she had been rooted to the floor even though she knew she wanted to accompany me to the door. The next time I made sure Anita was at Rorke's Drift and arranged to see her there. By this time I was living at the Mission Hospital at Nqutu and the only way there was by bus and then walking the eleven miles from where the bus turned off the main road! I left at 7.30am on a cold and foggy morning and arrived there at 11am still in my old overcoat with the sun streaming down. Anita wondered what she was meeting! She took me back to Nqutu about 10.30pm in her Volkswagen 'Beetle'. We had had a good day! The next sequence of events are lost in the mists of time but eventually we started meeting up on every day off we shared, usually going for picnics in the country. Gradually we became Boy and Girlfriend writing letters to each other as well as meeting. Sometimes we would have a meal in her little house at Rorke's Drift. She was an imaginative and capable cook.

Back to 1967! In the September of that year, soon after returning to live at Isandlwana a letter arrived from Bishop Alpheus asking if I would consider going to a place in the north of the Diocese called Ingwavuma. There was a Baptist Hospital there and also a Catholic Mission but he was interested in a small group of Anglicans who had their own Chapel in the little village as well as a large church for Zulus there. It sounded exciting so I took a trip up there. The Store owner who was also the warden of the 'chapel' was very welcoming. There was a service in the Baptist Hospital chapel on the Saturday evening and so I decided to go to it. There was an opportunity to introduce myself and I spoke about my charismatic experience which went down like a lead balloon! My meeting with the Catholics was more friendly. Kieron Rabbitt had moved there and so I was meeting up with an old friend. He showed me the little church which had a lovely plain new nave altar. I asked when that had been put in there and he told me just recently. 'When I came here it was against the east wall but one night I just took a hammer and knocked it down.' I thought of the Anglican church down the road where the altar was an enormous stone affair stuck against the wall and what would be likely to happen if I did the same thing there! It seemed to me that it would be rather lonely living out there but worth a try. However about two weeks later I received another letter from the Bishop. He had had a request from Charles Johnson Hospital for a full-time chaplain and my name had been included in the request. Perhaps after all I should move there and look after the Zulu congregation which used the Chapel as their parish church. Had God shown his hand again? I trusted so. My answer to the Bishop was positive.

It was arranged that I should leave Isandlwana just before Christmas. In the meantime my relationship with Anita moved along smoothly so why she never visited Isandlwana remains a mystery. Maybe her work was too much for time to be found. For some months she was posted to a hospital called Thulasizwe –'Quiet so that we can hear'- named after one of the Swedish Doctors. It was a long way away. Once I stayed the night there where the missionary staff were Norwegian, Swedish, German and South African. All I can remember is singing hymns around the piano. We also made a visit to another hospital a long way into Natal called Applesbosch. This was also overnight and Anita's 'Beetle' was much better to travel in than my clumsy old van. On my last visit to Qudeni I clearly remember that whilst climbing down the mountain I was given a very clear idea of what my Christmas sermon would be at Nqutu. It was to be on the subject of 'Religion' and the proposition that Jesus had come to destroy religion if by that we meant laws, rules, rites and institutions. Instead he had taught a way of relating to God that was direct and simple but absolutely committed to his will. I was looking forward to the move!

Isandlwana was a typical 'mission' of the old type where there were a number of girls who became pregnant by their boyfriends and were expected to sit at the back of the church for six months after the baby was born as a sign of their penitence. One such young lady had three children. Her first baby was born before I arrived so when she came to see me after her second baby was born I suggested that she actually needed God's strength to face up to the temptation of repeating the cycle and that rather than sitting at the back of the church she should sit at the very front and receive communion every Sunday. Such ideas were most strange and even repugnant to the church leaders. Sometime later her mother came to see me to say that the boyfriend had abducted the baby because he no longer wanted to marry her daughter. I tried to help by going to remonstrate with him and suggesting that he should give the baby back. After a time the Zulu priest came to see me and informed me that there was a rumour going round that the reason I had asked him to return the baby was because I wanted to marry the girl myself! This had come about because it was viewed that I had treated her differently from the other girls who had become pregnant before marriage! Clearly I was culturally out of my depth!

Another time which found me floundering was during a visit from one of the Zulu 'Princes'. He was an unpopular member of the Royal family always scrounging off one of his extended family members and using his position to do so. He came to visit one of his 'cousins' at Isandlwana and prevailed on me to give him a lift to the cousin's house. Clearly they were not charmed to see him and what followed was like a scene from Gilbert and Sullivan! They were not allowed to express their feelings because of the custom of 'respect' but needed to convey what these feelings were. In the end I left totally bewildered by this masquerade. I think the 'Prince' stayed on for a further two days. However much of a time warp this place seemed to be in one Sunday at sunset I was given what I can only describe as a strong premonition that God was going to do something big there. A few years later the Sisters of the Holy Name took over the house I had lived in as a convent and began a lovely work of God in the area and beyond.

It wouldn't be possible to leave Isandlwana without a reference to the night I saw ball lightening. The owners of the store at Ngwebini just opposite the track I took to the church there once invited me to dinner. They were kind people who in their small way tried to make the lives of their workers more worth-while. They put on a lovely meal and as it came near to 11pm Mr Dummer looked out of the window and said he thought there was a storm brewing and perhaps it was time I got home. I had travelled less than two miles in the old Landrover when the most extraordinary thing began to happen. The sky was an inky black colour, visible even in the dark night of no street lamps or electric lights from homes, when suddenly lantern-like fireballs appeared floating downwards and bursting on the ground around me and as far as the eye could see. The night sky was like a silent firework display! It unnerved me. What's more it suddenly began to rain with a ferocity I have never experienced before or since. I nearly drove into a ditch so mesmerised was I but managed just in time to reverse out. The river a mile from home was already in flood and the car just made it across. By this time my nerves were shattered and I drove hectically into the store at the bottom of the hill from my home. The owner was not exactly a friend of mine. He had complained to the police when I had encouraged the Mother's Union to make buns and sell them for the church! He was a German of the old-fashioned school. He opened the door to me in his dressing gown and the surprise on his face cannot be described. After all it was 11.30 at night. But he was kind and gave me a cup of cocoa whilst we waited for the storm to subside. It was raining quite gently when I left at just after midnight. It is the only time I have seen this kind of lightening and have met only a few other people who have also witnessed it.

Sometimes on my day off I would motor to Dundee about fifty miles away. The very first time I did so I went into the Anglican church and looked at the visitor's book. To my enormous surprise the name last entered was someone from Liphook about five miles from where I had lived since I turned eighteen! The next day I wrote to Mother to ask if she knew a Mrs. Story. She didn't but she looked her up in the phone book and rang her. It transpired that her nephew was a priest whom she and I had met before. Her sister, a Mrs. Robertson, lived in Dundee. It was my turn to ring! Marjorie Robertson was delighted to hear me and immediately invited me for dinner and to spend the night on my next day off. How good God was being to me providing friends like her. She was a widow of about sixty-five years at the time and her husband had been the M.P. for Dundee and District representing the party of which Jan Smuts had been the most famous leader. In 1948 this 'United Party' was defeated badly in the polls by the Nationalist Party which had brought in the draconian laws of Apartheid. Mr. Robertson had in fact been born in Scotland and Margaret in Cheshire. They had moved to South Africa about 1930 and Mr. Robertson became a successful business man. Margaret lived in a pleasant four-bedroomed house in a quiet area of Dundee. We got on very well and she spoilt me. In a way she became my surrogate mother and I know that my real mother was pleased that I had someone to keep an eye on me. There weren't that many opportunities to see her but when I did she always made me feel at home. On one occasion before going to see her I attended the Evening Service in the church there. I dressed incognito and went over to the hall for coffee afterwards to see if anyone would dare to speak to this strange newcomer. It took a little time but eventually one of the older ladies approached me. The church passed the test!

One last and sad story remains to be told. It concerns a Roman Catholic priest I met by chance one day. It was while I was filling up with petrol at a garage and he spoke to me thinking that I was perhaps a Catholic priest. He said he would be glad for me to visit the Mission where he was working. I thanked him and suggested that on my next day off I could make the journey to Pomeroy where he lived. 'Great, arrive in time for lunch.' he said. So the next Friday I set off on the fifty mile journey there. It was quite remote. The Housekeeper made us a nice lunch and he showed me round his patch. It became dark and he suggested that I stay the night and I thought this a good idea. We shared a glass of wine over Supper and talked until about 10pm. There was a nice Guest Room and about 11.00pm I was woken by the sound of the door opening. He stood there in his underpants and said 'Can I get into bed with you?' I said in a hurry that I wasn't that kind of a bloke! He departed as quickly as he had come but I made sure the door was locked before returning to sleep! The next morning he was full of apologies. What would I think of him? 'Please don't report me to the Bishop'. I said that I felt sorry for him and maybe he could get some counselling. He ignored this suggestion but told me that he had got into the habit when attending seminary in Rome. There it was rife, he said. He also hinted that he was involved with a lady in his congregation. On the way home I called in at the Hospital. I was in a state of shock and felt the need to speak to someone. Peter was the nearest one to the road and had a flexible job on the administration side. He was a good listener. Afterwards I wondered if I had chosen the right person to talk to or not as I knew he had been involved in the 'Gay Scene' in Johannesburg before his dramatic conversion since which he had married a lovely girl from Pretoria. They had come to work at the hospital in response to an advert and were happily settled into a new house built by the hospital for them. At any rate it was an experience I could well have done without except that it did help me to understand better the difficulties and temptations of priests, Catholic or not.

So the time came to leave. The local people were very kind and wished me well. I had enjoyed my stay at Isandlwana but it really needed a Zulu priest to do pastoral work in any depth. Bishop Alpheus's desire to move on the indiginization of the Ministry was timely. The week before Christmas I moved the old blue trunk to the hospital at Nqutu. The Engineer who had helped me before, Tony Reynoldson, sent out a truck to take the fridge and the odd piece of furniture that I had managed to acquire. It had been an exciting and unusual three years!

CHAPTER 9

CHARLES JOHNSON'S HOSPITAL AND LUKAS MEYER

Being a Hospital Chaplain was a complete mystery to me. What made me feel I was suitable for it is also a mystery! The only confidence I felt came from the fact that Jon the Doctor had asked for me and the Bishop had agreed. It was certainly a less lonely place to live in. Up until then my only experience of hospital visiting had been such as is common to all priests. During my four years in Portsmouth it was usual to visit the hospitals in the area on at least one afternoon a week. This was done according to a list the Rector drew up and we always wore our cassocks. The Sisters in charge of the wards wore blue and kept a vigilant eye on us. We had to report to them before visiting anyone in their domain but I once fell foul of one of them! She accused me of telling someone that they had terminal cancer, something only the Doctors could decide upon. I denied the charge and was let off with a caution! I never did find out how the poor man discovered the truth. There was of course the usual visiting of the sick in their homes sometimes taking Holy Communion with me. There was one dear lady who told me that she was dying of cancer but please would I not tell her only son. The following week the son also told me that his mother had cancer but under no circumstances was she to be told this! Whether they ever spoke to each other about it I don't know but her funeral was memorable. She had asked to be cremated and her ashes to be carried into the church for the funeral service. There was something special about the small box standing there, no-one could possibly identify with it as the tall lady they had known. I don't think either St. Mary's or Queen Alexandra Hospitals had full-time chaplains in the early 1960's. If they did I never knew about it.

So a week before the Christmas of 1967 I moved with all my worldly belongings to the little flat adjacent to the chapel in Charles Johnson Hospital. This bed-sit had a toilet and a basin in a smaller room in the corner of the main room and was to be my home for the next two and a bit years. There must also have been a cupboard of some sort. There was a 'coke' stove too, which glowed red on the chilly winter nights! It had actually been built as a Bishop's room for the occasions when he might visit or need a room in transit somewhere. It led straight into a vestry where I could hang my cassock and surplice. There was a desk, something I hadn't had since leaving England, and so it became my small office. The hospital kindly supplied all my meals. I began to work out a weekly programme of Bible Study and Prayer meetings at once. I soon discovered that here as with anywhere else the nurses were not really interested in such things and that most of my work would be through personal relationships. The Prayer Group did take off a bit and kept going all the time I was there. The most regular supporters were Anthony and Maggie Barker together with the Domestic Bursar, Maam Hlatshwayo, a lovely christian lady who supported everything she could that had anything to do with the chapel. It was also agreed that I would look after the local congregation which numbered easily one hundred adults and scores of children! They crammed into the chapel every Sunday for a Sung Eucharist at which we usually had incense and a longish sermon. There were lovely gentle Church Wardens and the congregation were always supportive. The Sunday worship began at 8.00am with a service in English and ended at lunchtime after the Zulu service. There was an Evangelist called Moloi who served and was sacristan as well as helping with the chalice and preaching about once a month. He would also translate for me although his English was far from perfect! Being chaplain also meant leading the Morning Prayers for the nurses in the chapel although these too were shared a certain amount. The day began at 6.00am with a service of Holy Communion and this was followed by the prayers at 6.40am finishing around 7.00am when ward rounds were due to begin.

Anthony Barker invited me to join in on the rounds which gave me some invaluable information about the patients' physical conditions. By far the majority had T.B. but there were also a number of other diseases and a goodly group of children. The bed numbers were 330 but there always seemed to be far more patients than that. The new Maternity Block was nearly always full and caesarian sections common. In fact Anthony had perfected a technique of performing them under local anaesthetic. A cooked breakfast with toast followed about 8.15am and was available in the Staff room. After that I worked out my own time schedules for the rest of the day. Often I would be visiting on the wards but sometimes there was reading to catch up on or a sermon to prepare, letters to write or a visit out in the community to someone who was sick. Lunch was at 1.00 in the main dining room with the rest of the hospital staff and this was a good time to get to know people better. It was like a canteen. I usually managed a break afterwards with a snooze for half-an-hour before beginning more visits. The 'missionaries' took up some of my time. There were big relationship problems and I would listen and try to counsel. One such problem was a long standing one between Anthony and the Administrator and for ages they didn't speak to one another. There was also an occasional wedding or a funeral, a few confirmation candidates and one or two confessions. One having to do with some Lesbian longings I seem to remember. One of the confirmation candidates was a delightful new nurse from the Transkei who had been a Presbyterian and came to ask for instruction. It wasn't until much later that I learned the reason for her change of heart! She was to marry Lawrence Zulu who later became Bishop of Zululand.

On one occasion I was asked to exorcise a 'Togolosh'! This is a little demon who appears in the form of a man rather like the elves, usually to frighten women. On this occasion the patient was screaming and staring wildly at the foot of the bed. She could see him sitting there grinning at her. Nothing the nurses or other patients could do would pacify her terror. I came and stood at the end of her bed and told him in prayer to go away. I then prayed for peace in our hearts and in the ward and for the protection of God against evil. It seemed to have the desired effect and we all went to sleep! There was another occasion when I was asked to exorcise. There was a 'ghost' in the village which kept appearing as fire both in and outside a home. Again prayer seemed to work as I was never called back. Maybe I was just never told whether it had gone away or not!

The first time I was called out at night I donned my cassock over my pyjamas and as I entered through the door there was a nurse coming down the corridor towards me. She screamed and fled! After praying with the patient, who was dying, I went to find her. She smiled rather coyly and explained she had thought I was the ghost of Charles Johnson! Mentioning his name here makes me think this may be the appropriate stage at which to mention the little I know of him although even that is by hearsay. He came out from England in the middle of the 19th Century and settled at what is now known as St. Augustine's. He started a peripatetic mission around the northern part of Zululand reaching up into the mountainous area. He developed a reputation for extracting teeth and when he had been successful and was asked what payment he required he always said 'A site please on which to build a church.' In this way he eventually built some thirty-five churches over a district about forty miles long and not much smaller in breadth either. His greatest achievement was St. Augustine's where he and two or three builders put up this enormous edifice which can accommodate easily over a thousand people if necessary. He stayed in Natal for the rest of his life and had sons who became clergymen. One of them was still alive during my time there and I was once sent to him for an oral exam in Zulu. It was said about him that he could walk on one side of the road in Durban after dark and hold a conversation with a Zulu man on the other side and the man would never know he was not talking to another Zulu. He began my exam with an idiom which means 'Where were you born?' I hadn't come across this expression before but I never forgot it and sometimes I could tell that people thought I knew more Zulu than I actually did because of this! He was kind and understanding and must have sent in a favourable report.

Anyway I didn't often get called out at night and neither did I get deeply enough into the language to be of much use to the patients in their personal lives. When it did happen I never forgot it because it was a little breakthrough as on the occasion I was asked by the Doctors to speak with a gentleman who was very agitated. He was being sent home because his cancer was inoperable and this was something he couldn't understand. I had recently learnt a phrase which meant something like 'So now the time had come to put your house in order' meaning death is coming soon or is inevitable. I used this as we spoke about his concern as to why the Doctors wouldn't operate on him. It was like giving him a tranquiliser which worked instantly. He sat very still with his face relaxed and he smiled saying 'Oh thankyou, now I see. I will go home at once as that's all right then.' It was very moving. On another occasion I was asked to accompany a man who was to have an operation to his home as he had insisted that that he must first go home and make peace with the ancestors. The Doctors were of the opinion that it would cause him psychological damage if they refused his request. As his illness was severe and he badly needed the surgery they felt it would be useful to have someone accompany him and so prevent him getting 'cold feet'! I contacted the Catholic Mission near his home and they kindly offered me a room with my meals for as much time as was needed. The hospital ambulance took us to the district and I went home with him to meet his family and explain the arrangements before going on to the Mission. It was three days before he had completed his business at home and was ready to go back to the hospital so the ambulance returned to collect us. His operation was a success and he returned home again a few weeks later. There was also a patient with the unusual name of 'Telephone'! He was convinced that the nurses were poisoning him. I was quite sure that he would not get better until he could be persuaded differently so I suggested that he be allowed home for a period. He may have been too ill by then because my request was refused and he died a few weeks later. Incidentally some years later when I was working at Papworth Hospital a similar situation arose. This time it was a clergyman who was hallucinating because of the drugs he was taking. This could also have been the case with Telephone.

Not everything went happily! Once I was invited to a wedding about sixty miles away so I asked the Engineer who was in charge of transport if I could borrow the courtesy car which the hospital maintained for 'private' trips. He readily agreed but as usual with my luck with cars it broke down on the way home! I had to be rescued by the Engineer and towed home behind his four-wheel drive vehicle. Of course Anthony Barker heard of it and was of the opinion that he should have been consulted in the first place. The next morning I was 'on the mat'! Afterwards a fellow priest asked me what it was like having a layman as a Rector! This of course was the true nature of things at the hospital but I hadn't realised so until that incident. This knowledge helped me settle into the job rather better I think. There was also a need to find out what special skills and knowledge I had to acquire to become a better Chaplain. Somehow I heard about a conference the Lutheran church were running at one of their Mission hospitals and I managed to secure a place at it. It was organised by a lovely christian man called Vivian Masondo. We had lectures and discussions about pastoral care and staff from the hospital explained their expectations of a hospital chaplain. One talk was by a senior Cleric about his experience of a Mission hospital when he had been sick and admitted to one. He had given a false name so that he could observe unknown what went on! He was treated abominably and eventually discharged himself. The lesson he wanted to hand on to us was that if the ethos of the hospital was seemingly unchristian it mattered little what the chaplain said in the chapel or on the wards. The patients would perceive the dichotomy between words and deeds and the gospel would not become the kingdom. It was a lesson I was never to forget and tried to communicate this whenever I could within the hospital.

In October 1968 I was due for 'furlough' and it was five years since I had first set foot in Zululand. During my first nine months at the hospital Anita and I went on seeing each other and she often recalls the day I took the bus on a foggy morning at 8am and got off at the turning to Rorke's Drift on the main road to Dundee. The walk there was about eleven miles! By the time I arrived it was 11am and the sun was pouring down at 75% Fahrenheit. I was still wearing my old overcoat and sweating profusely. As the months wore on it became clear that some sort of step needed to be taken in our relationship and as usual I just couldn't do this. We decided that as Anita was due for a long leave in the August, just before me, we would call off our relationship until further notice, so to speak! It was hard for both of us and a kind of 'deja veux' for me. I felt depressed and puzzled. I saw her off on the train at Glencoe.

The weeks soon passed and my first ever plane trip arrived. U.S.P.G. had carefully arranged the cheapest route and KLM took me to Amsterdam on a comfortable flight via somewhere in North Africa for refueling. I remember only that it was so hot it was almost unbearable. Amsterdam was not and on a blowy October day my most vivid memory is of going into the toilets and wanting to turn the continuously running water off. We had experienced a terrible drought in Zululand! Water was so short that we had to reduce the consumption in the hospital from over 100,000 gallons a day to just 23,000. Like everyone else I had been restricted to a basin full of reddish water a day for the last three months. One morning Dr. Barker's Secretary had met the lorry driver who brought a tanker full of water from the Tukela River each day and said 'Thank you for this nectar.' 'What?' he asked. 'Nectar' she repeated. 'Ach man' he said, 'It's only water!'

Arriving at Heathrow I immediately phoned home. Mother laughed. 'You have such a South African accent' she said. I hadn't noticed! Being at home was lovely – but strange! U.S.P.G. had arranged a number of 'preachments' for me and these really helped to deal with the great number of experiences that needed to be absorbed and re-evaluated. I travelled as far west as Devon and north into Yorkshire. There I preached at an Evensong with only six people in the congregation. One of them was a lady in the choir who screached like a banshee and a tenor who was standing behind her and kept disappearing from sight. After a while I realised that he was also pumping the organ! There was a visit to Welwyn Garden City where the vicar held prayers for healing after the Communion and asked me to join in. As I went along the row of people kneeling I heard him praying in tongues. This was the first time I had heard it in the Church of England. It was a large congregation there and obviously God was doing a good work. These visits kept me occupied for most weekends. At one church in Devon I received a rebuke, I had preached for too long! When he came in for lunch the vicar said I had delayed the start of the post-Matins Holy Communion by at least ten minutes. Something in me snapped and I sharply replied that I hadn't come 6,000 miles to preach for ten minutes! The atmosphere was a bit frosty after that but he remained courteous for the rest of my visit. It was on the same day as I went on a Deanery visit I seem to remember. After lunch there was a meeting to speak to followed by an enormous tea and the Evensong somewhere else. This was followed by Dinner and the Vicar's wife had done her best to see that the 'starving Missionary' would be well and truly fed! It was embarrassing as I felt that she had put out the best silver and done her best cooking! It was a not uncommon occurrence I'm afraid and after six months I had put on nearly two stones in weight!

Apart from these visits and a few to U.S.P.G. House where medical checks had to be carried out most of the time was my own. I say most because the Doctors had found that I needed a check on my behind and as I had previously had a kidney stone I needed to also have that area looked at. That meant a couple of hospital visits with one overnight stay and then a third visit to check out an allergy problem which caused me to sneeze every morning for a few minutes and clogged my nose a lot. The Surgeon suggested an operation on my nose with what he called a 50% success rate but I turned that offer down! One idea the U.S.P.G. had was an excellent one. It was to send me on a course for Hospital Chaplains led by Norman Autton who was the pioneer of this type of training in Britain. About twenty of us met at St. George's Hospital in London which was then still at Hyde Park corner. We had discussions with the Leader and lectures from staff in the hospital about their work and their expectations of our role. We also visited the wards and shared our experiences amongst groups. One visit to an Orthopaedic Clinic was instructive. The Consultant was seeing a boy of nine years old and whenever he asked the boy a question the mother replied for him. Afterwards he turned to us and said 'Not much wrong with the boy but I'm not so sure about the mother!' We also visited the first Hospice in Britain, St. Christopher's and met its founder Cecily, now Dame Cecily, Saunders. She spoke to us of her vision for living with terminal illness rather than dying of it. The whole place radiated a quiet faith in resurrection with beautiful art on the walls and flowers everywhere. The first patient I visited in Kings College Hospital where I was staying was memorable! The patient had a big bandage around his head and when I enquired he explained that he was a butcher and someone had attacked him in his own shop with one of his own choppers! It was strange for me to feel a sense of relief because this was quite a common occurrence in Nqutu particularly around Christmas time. The local white people would shrug their shoulders and say 'Well that's the sort of people these blacks are!' It was a relief to find that white people sometimes behaved in this way also! It was a memorable course and hopefully helped me to become wiser and more confident in my ministry.

Otherwise it was a time for meeting up with old friends again one of whom was Hazel of course. She was teaching in North London now and had a little flat in Muswell Hill. I spent at least one weekend there and once again we stayed in the same flat in separate bedrooms. It was touch and go at times but we managed it! I went with her to church on the Sunday morning. Still I couldn't make a decision and although we saw one another on a few occasions I think she realised that in the end that was all it was going to be. I also went to see Liz Lewis who was then engaged to a young Army Officer also by the name of Lewis. All I can really remember of the visit is that I sat on a chair which collapsed much to the amusement of them both as I had already put on a lot of weight! I wrote one letter to Anita asking if she would meet me off the plane in Johannesburg to take me back to the hospital. She, quite rightly, didn't reply! Before the time came for my return to South Africa I went to see a priest I knew slightly to seek advice about Hazel. 'Will she go with you to South Africa?' he asked. 'Yes' I replied. 'Can she cook?' 'Yes' I replied. 'Are you mutually attracted sexually?' 'Yes' I replied. 'Then what the hell more do you want?' I wished I knew but I just couldn't bring myself to pop the question. However she was staying with Mother and me the day I was due to fly at 8.00pm from Heathrow. As I was packing after breakfast she casually looked at my passport. It had expired the day before! A panic phone call resulted in the promise that if I presented myself at Pimlico Lane central passport office as soon as possible they would let me have one straight away. I was there by 12.30pm having said my goodbyes to Mother and Hazel at Petersfield Station. It was the last time I saw her.

I was in good time for the flight for which U.S.P.G. had supplied the ticket well in advance. There was only one stop for refuelling in North Africa and I was back in Johannesburg early the next day. Before leaving I had written to Hugh Harper who was a priest and brother to Peter, the Zululand Archdeacon. He had a parish in Johannesburg and had agreed to put me up for the night before I caught the train on to Zululand. He was very kind and saw me off at the station. Just before the train departed a Station Porter saw me through the window sitting in a carriage on my own. They sat six people and he asked his strong Afrikaans accent, which I would expect, if I would 'take care' of a man due to get off about four hours into the journey. I didn't ask why which was rather foolish of me and into the carriage came a small, pale-looking individual about the same age as me. As the train left we began to speak but I wasn't any the wiser why I had to keep an eye on him! After a while he said that he needed the toilet and when he returned he sat down and began to shake violently. He noticed my frightened face and said not to worry and that it would settle eventually. He lay down flat on the seat his whole body still shaking. Something in my mind produced the words 'Delirium Tremens' and I realised what was happening to him. Eventually he sat back up again and told me that he had been in a clinic in Johannesburg and was on his way home. Obviously he had concealed some liquor on his person. I have never encountered this condition at quite such close quarters again.

Back at the hospital the nurses greeted me with mirth! 'You have eyes like a pig' they said, because of the weight I had put on! It was already April 1969 and not long after my return, I was outside in the hospital grounds whistling, when I heard a car draw up behind me and stop. It was Anita, on her way back to Rorkes Drift from a visit to a Lutheran Mission Hospital! We drank coffee and caught up on each other's news. I'm not sure whether we arranged another date this time or on the next occasion when circumstances brought her to the hospital once more. A talented artist called John Mafengayo had come from Namibia to the Art School at Rorke's Drift and had been hit by home sickness and culture shock. His behaviour had become disorientated and a decision was taken to send him to the Charlie J. for observation. One night I was awoken by the sound of the chapel bell ringing. Quickly throwing on my cassock I entered the chapel to find the lights on, the candles all lit and John ringing the bell! Somehow I managed to persuade him that this was not the right time to be doing such things. The outcome of his observation was for him to be transferred to a hospital for the treatment of mental illness at Newcastle about fifty miles away. Anita was asked to take him there and I was asked to escort her! What she remembers about the journey was the fact that I took two bananas and two mars bars for our sustenance! After that we began meeting most weeks on my day off or on Sunday afternoons. Each time Anita would bring me home from her little house to Nqutu. Mostly we would take a picnic down to the Buffalo River and enjoy the silence and the beauty of the landscape. John the painter got better and completed his course at the Art School. He later became internationally famous with exhibitions in America and Europe. He returned to Namibia and was a Teacher there until suddenly at the age of forty years he died. He was a great christian artist and we have some of his original lino-cut prints and one oil painting which he sold to Anita. There is one carving of his which I treasure very much. Whilst at Nqutu he attended the Sunday services and sometimes the preacher would be a retired priest of nearly ninety, Father Ndlamlenzi, who had the most heavenly smile. John made a carving of him about nine inches high which now stands in our sitting room. The smile is captured perfectly and the whole carving seems to be alive with the dear priest's character.

The winter passed and the summer brought it's usual dry heat. It was then that the Security Police decided that this anti-Apartheid hospital should be investigated! It was pathetic really. First they tried to discredit Anthony Barker. An Officer appeared with some nude photos which he said they had found in the x-ray room. Anthony recognised one of the local Farmer's wives and suggested the Officer interrogate those who used the room for developing photos. He heard nothing more and told me that he suspected someone who himself was an Afrikaaner and a good friend of the local police. At the same time the police found a red-covered book in our Social Worker's room and because it was red the Officer suspected it to be Chairman Mao's little book on Communism. It was in fact a novel by Jane Austin about whom the Officer had never heard. Their next ludicrous attempt affected me. About 9.00 one night there was a knock at my door and a nurse and her mother were standing there in a very agitated state. They said that the police had had them down at the station trying to get the nurse to sign a statement to the effect that the baby she was carrying in her arms was mine! On inspection the baby did appear to be rather 'white'. I took them over to the Barker's flat and fortunately Anthony was at home. His response was a very calm and straight one. If you like I can sign an affidavit to the effect that this child is an albino. The two ladies were so relieved and again we heard no more about the matter. I did ask the nurse later if she knew who the father was and she told me the name of the son of the priest at Inhlwathi where I had been curate. It was not a nice few days and I wondered what my response should be. In the end I decided that doing nothing was the best proof of my innocence.

As Christmas approached it was clear that a decision about my future was also looming. Dr. Barker was of the opinion that Anita and I should spend a few days together and sort ourselves out once and for all! We therefore decided to go to the Drakensberg Mountains where one could hire a rondavel hut in a National Park of outstanding beauty. Before going I was in the chapel vestry one day when a Doctor came in for something. He was a Methodist minister as well as being trained in Psychiatry. I found myself talking to him about this problem I had with getting married and after listening to me talking about my childhood and so on he replied that he wasn't surprised at my difficulty and suggested that in fact for me the more difficult it seemed was probably an indication of how right it was. In that one conversation I felt I had received more wisdom than ever before on this subject! I had visited a Psychiatrist in Pietermaritzburg who had told me I was perfectly normal and not to waste his time. I had also been to another Psychiatrist in my student days who had simply told me that once I was married the problem would go away! He couldn't seem to understand that the problem WAS taking the step of actually getting married.

Anyway Anita drove us to the location and it was truly beautiful thousands of feet above sea level, warm but not too hot. Our meals were cooked for us by an African chef and it was the most ideal and romantic spot for a courting couple. We went for some long walks up beautiful river valleys where the water was clear and cool and took the car into the surrounding countryside where long grass swept like the sea across sloping downland. The day before we were due to return I decided to ask Anita if she would marry me. It was clear to me that she would make the most wonderful christian partner who would share with me all her many gifts including her love for children. She had opened my eyes in so many ways. She adored nature and was very knowledgeable about trees and flowers and delighted in decorating her little house with them. She also loved the sea and was never happier than when walking along the beach collecting sea-shells. She was skilled in crafts and had trained in Sweden in wood and bark as well as weaving. Being fond of painting in water colours she was also very gifted at this. She was excited about the skill of cooking and loved experimenting with different dishes. With her great love of walking Anita had done plenty of this in the Swedish mountains. Generally she had a lively interest in life and all its aspects. I remembered what Keith de Berry, the vicar of St. Aldates had told me all those years ago 'Try to marry a better christian than you are. That's what I did!' Anita, I felt sure would always be able to support me in the ministry by her prayer, kindness and her moral courage. She also loved a good laugh! So we climbed the highest of the hills and right on the top, after I had taken a photograph of her picking the wild flowers, I knelt in prayer silently to commit all of our future together into God's hands. Then it was the moment and she whispered 'Yes please.' We almost ran down the hill to pack and leave in time to call in at Ladysmith and buy a ring! I had 100 rand in the bank and the ring which Anita liked cost 95 rand (about £50 then but recently valued at £500!) She recalls that I looked very worried and didn't look at her when I put it on her finger. I was hit by a wave of panic as I had been many years before but, remembering the Doctor's words and knowing that I had done the right thing, it quickly passed. The hospital staff were overjoyed and Anthony said that they must put up the flag! This is a custom in the homes of Zulus when one of the sons becomes engaged.

Christmas that year was my first introduction into the Swedish way of celebrating it on the evening before with special food, lots of candles and a live decorated tree. We decided that we should get married at Easter in the church at Rorke's Drift and asked the Lutheran bishop, Helge Fosseus, to marry us with Alpheus Zulu leading the Nuptial Mass. For our preacher we asked our kind friend Erik Hallendorf and he agreed to preach in English, Swedish and Zulu! Of course it was unlikely that any of our relatives would be there. Anita's were not that well off and as they had at one time belonged to the Communist Party wouldn't have been allowed into South Africa anyway. Mine would, I think, have found it difficult to find the time as well as the money. There was also in those days a very different culture about travelling such long distances. We therefore asked friends, a Lutheran Deacon and his wife – Kjell and Bertha Lofroth, who had been very kind to Anita at Rorke's Drift to be 'in locus parentis'. Then came the task of getting the invitations printed and a guest list drawn up. We found it came to about seventy people! It was decided therefore that I would buy a sheep and we would have mutton stew with rice. We knew of the Zulu custom for the local populace to attend the feast after the service! The guests who were invited to the service would sit at long trestle tables under the gum trees and would be served with a drink and fruit salad as well. The remainder would sit on the ground as was their custom.

Just after Christmas the hospital organised their own 'Olympics' which made me determined to get really fit and run the three mile race. It was amazing that I managed to reduce my weight from over 13 stone to 10 stone 5 pounds in time! When the day came there were only a couple of other competitors in this race and I persuaded Jabulani who had stayed with me at Isandlwana to take part as well. He casually took off his coat and rolled up his trousers! In the end I only just managed to beat him and felt flabergasted that he could run so well without any practice or training at all!

The time passed very quickly. It had been originally arranged that the wedding would be on the Saturday before Easter Day but it soon became apparent that there was just too much work for me over Holy Week anyway. It was impractical and so we changed to the Monday. Just as well too as the invitations had to be sent out in good time. One couple were caught out unfortunately though because as soon as they heard we were to be married they ordered a pair of very nice pewter mugs and had them engraved with our names and the original date of 28th of March, the Saturday! It was decided that I would spend the night before the wedding at Rorkes Drift as the guest of the Lofroths. I had managed to get a smart black suit 'off the peg' in Durban and Anita had decided to be married in her provincial costume and was able to get the matching hat sent from Sweden with beautiful embroidery on it. The church was decorated with Cosmos which grows wild in South Africa and I went out early in the morning to pick the wild flowers Anita had chosen for her bouquet. Dear Kjell brought me a cup of coffee at 8.00am and I was still fast asleep! Anita had as matron-of-honour the Bishop's daughter in law, Barbro, who was accompanied by a page-boy and a flower girl. I had asked Anthony Barker to be my best man and to keep the Zulu tradition of having more than one I also invited the Zulu Chief, Gatsha Buthelezi to accompany and he kindly agreed. We had met at several church gatherings as he was a Lay Minister and had represented the Church of the Province of Southern Africa at the Anglican Conference in Canada in 1963. There was a young Doctor at the hospital, David Fielding, who was a Violinist and he offered to play a Bach piece for solo violin as we entered and left the church. There was no need for an organ, indeed there was none anyway, as the Zulus sing so loudly and in perfect harmony at the drop of a hat it would have been entirely unnecessary!

The service went beautifully with our friend Ulf Carlson doing what I have never allowed a cameraman to do at any wedding I have ever taken! He popped up at regular intervals in the most unexpected of places with his expensive Swedish camera. His job was Communications Officer for the Lutheran Diocese which made him ideal for this occasion. As a result we have an outstanding photographic record of the day – a gift to us from him. We had many other lovely gifts as well of which a number still remain including an Arabic breakfast cup in blue and white. There were a pair but one got broken and this one is cracked but it's still the largest breakfast cup we own! It was the Barkers' gift to us and so is very special. We spent over an hour unwrapping presents and it was nearly 4.00pm before we left for our Honeymoon destination.

I had reserved a room in a motel about fifty miles away on the road to Durban where we had been lent a flat for two nights by our dear friend Helga. I had thought that two hundred miles would be too far to travel after such a busy and emotional day. However there was a problem with the name of the motel! It was opposite a small fort which the British had built on a hill during the Boer War and then realised they couldn't get water to it. It had become known as Fort Mistake and the motel was named after it! I hadn't told Anita its name under the pretext that it was all a surprise for her. When we arrived I was disappointed to find that a Gloxinia I had ordered for her wasn't in the room. On enquiry it transpired that the room originally allocated for us had drainage problems so we had been moved but no-one had thought to transfer the Gloxinia! That wasn't the only mistake either! I had arranged for us to have our meal in our room and the chicken and vegetables arrived alright but when I took the jug to pour on the gravy Anita said 'No, that's the chocolate sauce for the ice-cream afterwards!' Sure enough when the ice-cream arrived there was no accompanying sauce. But when she poured from the jug onto her ice-cream she discovered it was in fact gravy! The motel had a good name!

The next morning when I paid the bill I couldn't help saying that it had been the first night of our honeymoon to which the Manager replied ' Congratulations. Don't overdo it will you!' I wonder what he would have said if I had been wearing my dog collar! Helga's flat was so peaceful and she had prepared it for us so nicely. We phoned my mother in England who was overjoyed. Ulf had prepared a tape for us of the service and we sent it off to Mother who proudly played it to the family. They must have found it a bit unusual to say the least as the sermon was in three languages. We still sometimes play it on our wedding anniversary.

The problem was where to go after Durban? I had left it far too late to book anywhere but knew of a place along the coast which had self catering chalets. That too was full when we arrived. After all it was peak holiday time! We continued up the coast and came to Stanger, a town with quite a large Indian population where we found a room at the Victoria Hotel and stayed for a week. Stanger is not a very pretty town and I have always maintained that we were probably the only couple to spend their honeymoon there. Mind you the beach was lovely and we spent a lot of time just walking and enjoying the Autumn sun. One morning I dropped and lost the car key! We hunted and hunted and eventually found a car key but it wasn't the one for our car. The only thing we could do was seek help so I walked to a garage but as it was Saturday the workshop wasn't open.

However a very nice Indian man took mercy on us and walked back to the beach with me. He opened up the bonnet and fiddled about and managed to get the engine going leaving us with the instruction that in order to start the engine we simply had to line up two wires and touch them together! No doubt a highly dangerous exercise but we had no option so we continued to do this until the following Thursday when we returned to the hospital. I guess the spare set of car keys were there.

At the hospital we moved into a delightful thatched cottage which had originally been built for Doreen Playne, a Sunday School worker for the whole Diocese who had arrived in the early 1950's when the hospital was still quite small. It stood close to the Staff Room where meals were served morning and evening for the senior staff and consisted of a largish bed-sitting room, a tiny bathroom and an even smaller dining room with a teeny weeny kitchen. But at least it was ours and we were grateful for this. It had been decided that Anita would work as the unpaid Occupational Therapist for the hospital and she was given a uniform and a very small budget with which to buy her materials. It wasn't easy for her as Zulu men don't take orders from women and couldn't understand why they should 'work' if they were sick! Much easier to sit under the trees with the local policemen and drink home-made beer. Gradually however things changed after Anita was told that if she discovered who the 'chief' in the ward was and won him over on to her side he would order the other men to work and they would. She also hit on the idea that they could sell the goods they made in a little hospital shop and once they saw someone get a little money they didn't need any more persuading! They made leather belts and bags, shoes out of old car tyres and wooden articles. The ladies decorated the carvings with their handwork as well as weaving their own baskets. One day one of the senior staff, a missionary nurse, told me that the culture in her male T.B. ward had completely changed for the better due to the work with which they could occupy their time. Anita also taught literacy and the delight for some of the men to learn how to read the bible or write their own name was wonderful to see. It wasn't easy for her to settle into the way of community life. I was used to it from school and the Army but for Anita it was new and English wasn't her first language. Life in the hospital was tense too, led by the frenetic Barkers who worked themselves and us hard and expected everyone to join in all the community activities as well! We ate in the Staff House and felt really guilty when we decided to have breakfast by ourselves. After six months Anita expressed her anxiety to one of the Doctors that she hadn't yet become pregnant. She told her not to worry and a month later she was! The Doctor was as well and so they had a jolly good laugh together when they confided in each other.

Towards the end of September we had a visit from Bishop Alpheus who asked us if we would consider going to Matubatuba or Vryheid. These were smallish market towns to the east with the former in fact being actually on the coast and very hot. Forty degrees in the summer wasn't uncommon! The problem was this. There were only a few white priests in the Diocese naturally and the laws of apartheid were such that they stated certain areas were 'white' and only white people were allowed to live in them. The priest at Matubatuba had been there for about twenty years and had started with a small congregation in a hall but ended up building a most beautiful church, Italianate in style with a cloister as well. The congregation had grown to about one hundred people. He had also designed a purpose built rectory. We went to see it and although it was tempting we thought it much too hot. Vryheid seemed to be the better option.

The rectory was modest but comfortable and next door to the church hall and the church. This had been built at the turn of the century in a pleasant neo-gothic style and able to seat about eighty people. The young priest there was a very popular South African who had been invited to become chaplain to the University of the Wittwatersrand in Johannesburg. What we weren't told was that his marriage was on the rocks as his wife had fallen for the local Chemist and amongst other things would turn up at his swimming pool early in the morning. Bishop Alpheus had advised them to move away and start again. Unfortunately this didn't work and they later divorced. Anyway we told the Bishop that if the Church Wardens were happy we would start there on January 1st the following year. The ladies of the church invited Anita to meet with them in the rectory to discuss furniture and so on. In the Church of the Province of Southern Africa the congregations look after the clergy houses. Anita remembers that they asked her if she would like a dressing table. In Sweden these are not known and she felt a bit embarrassed having to ask what a dressing table was!

Christmas at the hospital was full of fun with Anthony Barker dressing up as Santa Claus and cutting into enormous turkeys for all the staff as well as going around the wards dispensing gifts right, left and centre. The time came for our departure and the customary party. We both cried as staff and patients gave gifts and made speeches together with the singing and dancing which always accompanies such occasions.

We were both nervous about Vryheid as although we didn't know a lot about it we had heard about the steamy race relations there. Sometimes ignorance can be bliss! There was a ridiculous situation in as much as there were at one time two church buildings about fifty yards apart. One for the English speaking people, namely whites and 'coloureds' as the people of mixed descent were called, and one for the Zulu speakers. One of my predecessors had tried to bring them together making a choir of mixed races. This had caused a revolution amongst the 'white' congregation and he had eventually retired back to England in disgust. His successor stayed six months and then resigned going to the Cape where he later became a Bishop. The Zulu church had long disappeared because the Group Areas Act had driven the black people out of the district to live in a township about three miles away. There was a Zulu service on Sunday afternoons attended by Gardeners and Servants who lived on premises in the town. In the early 1950's a rather traditional missionary came who organised the building of the new rectory. He had a study round the back so that black people could come into the house round that way. White people came in through the front door. After him there was a lovely bachelor priest who tried hard to improve things but he was a bit bad tempered at times as well as rather naïve. He allowed some of his 'servants' to take advantage of him including borrowing the parish car as well as some other things which didn't go down well with the PCC. Vryheid also had a distinctive history. It was said that the Afrikaaners called it 'The Promised Land' because it was the only piece of Natal where they were able to assert any influence! It was also green unlike most of the Transvaal. One of the original Boer generals, Lukas Meyer, turned the little old market town into an Independent Republic. It only lasted nine months but long enough to make some oppressive laws, like the one preventing Indians living within its borders. It also gave the Afrikaaners a sense of power and they had worked hard to build up a majority on the town council. Since the National Party had come into Government in 1948 they had achieved this goal. It was therefore a town with a racist reputation. Indeed one of my first phone calls was to remind me of this fact! I had met the 'Moths' – memorable order of the tin hats – at Isandlwana where they held a service on the Sunday nearest to the anniversary of the battle every year. It was my privilege to lead that service. One of the members, an Alf Wade, was also very interested in all the battles of the Zulu war and would lecture on them. I had therefore met him at Khambula doing just that. He lived in Vryheid and came to the church fairly often as did his wife and children. On arrival he was amongst the first I phoned to see if I could make a pastoral visit. There was a distinct pause on the phone and then he said 'I'm not sure'. 'What was the reason?' I enquired. He replied that he was in two minds as to whether he wanted someone known for his friendship with blacks in his home. It was quite a shock! Of course being acquainted with Zulu did mean that I could offer my services to help in the Deanery and it was quickly decided that I would go to the coal mines north of the town for services in the Zulu congregations as well as those for the 'English speaking' people. I took on the Sunday afternoon Zulu service in the town as well. When Bill Johnston, the priest at Khambula, was on long leave I was able to minister at all the congregations in his area too. Later I was appointed the regional Dean which meant quite a lot of meetings with Zulu priests and their people as well.

Nevertheless the welcome we received was very warm. There were about fifty regulars at a Sunday service at 8.30am (it became rather hot after that) and two men had become Lay Ministers, one who liked preaching and the other who preferred taking services. They made a good team! The organist was young and enthusiastic but the choir had long ceased to exist. Soon we had a number of people who were willing to lead prayers of intercession and readers were plentiful. I started a small group of Servers and the 'sides-people' were welcoming and efficient. Of the regulars fifteen or so were of mixed race, called 'coloureds in South Africa at the time. They all sat at or near the back because, I was told, that was where they were expected to sit! It was difficult to persuade them differently. One was the Headmaster of the little school, a single building for about thirty children. It was on a site about a mile from the township for Africans where there were also shack-like dwellings for the residents. There was no official road in or out, just dirt tracks either dusty or muddy. The residents lived in a sort of no-mans land as nothing official had ever been decided about their presence. They were in fact an embarrassment. Everybody knew that the 'coloureds' used to live in the centre of the town and own shops or garages but they had gradually been 'unofficially' pushed away! There were one or two exceptions. Diana was an elderly lady with a family history as her grandmother had been Lucas Meyer's cook and so no-one dared to ask Diana to leave her rambling old house near the town centre. She was often ill and I would take communion to her home where she would regale me with stories of times past. The Headmaster was actually on the Church Council but he told me he didn't enjoy it as he would meet other members in the town and they would cut him dead. Still the church was officially 'non-racial' and we worked hard to try and turn this theory into fact. There was a window glazier, Claude by name, who came more and more regularly to the church and began to serve at the altar. After a time I suggested he study to become a Lay Minister and he agreed. It took him a long time to get through the training but eventually he made it and then joined the Church Council as well. There was never any objection to the fact that he was 'coloured' and therefore shouldn't take any lead in the church. The ecumenical relationships in the town were good but without anything out of the ordinary happening as a result. In fact the monthly meeting of the ministers was rather boring! Then we were joined by an independent evangelist, a Pentecostal, who had set up a congregation in the town. He suggested that we scrap the constitution that we had, and simply leave it to the ministers in turn to arrange the monthly meetings and set their own agenda. This worked well for three months until it was the turn of the Methodist minister. For some reason he didn't call a meeting and when asked he said he was sorry but he had been very busy and would do so soon. However he never did and the Council 'died the death'!

Sometime later I went to a meeting for the clergy called by Bishop Alpheus at Kwanzimela. He had been to Lausanne for the world conference on evangelism and had been very impressed by a Pentecostal minister from South America, Mr. Ortiz, and so had invited him to come and lead us in a series of workshops. He preached very powerfully on the Lordship of Christ now, and in one of his talks spoke about ecumenism. He told how once he had been invited by a group of ministers in Beunes Aries to speak to them on the subject of the Holy Spirit. He said that he went armed with his big bible to tell them a thing or two! When he came away however he was much humbled because, he said, he had never seen or felt such love at work as it was amongst these christian brothers. It changed his attitude towards other churches and as a result if he found someone coming to his church who been baptised as a baby he would not baptise them again by immersion because he believed they had already been baptised. This was too much for his own denomination and he was expelled. So his advice to us was not to start a formal meeting of ministers but to go to the individuals and try to get to know them and ask if they would perhaps share in prayer regularly. This is how he put it. 'You should go to your brother minister and sit down (if he asks you to!) and wait to see how long it takes for him to ask "What can I do for you?" And then you say "Well nothing really but I have come to get to know you better." And if it seems appropriate suggest that you meet regularly for prayer.' So when I returned home I went to see the Methodist minister. He had taken the place of the one who didn't call the meeting and we had met before as my predecessor had suggested that the services at the Coronation coalmine became united. This meant that the ministers traveled out together taking turns to provide the transport and then also turns to lead the worship and preach. True to prediction he did ask what he could do for me and the end result was very gratifying. He agreed to meet for prayer weekly and would also ask others to join us. I approached the Catholic priest and the Presbyterian minister also. The Dutch Reformed declined to join us but nearly every other church did and we ended up with about twelve regulars for a prayer meeting at 8.30am every Monday. It took time to get through! After a couple of meetings the Catholic priest said he wouldn't be coming any more as it wasn't really his cup of tea. Incidentally we ended with a cup of tea which Anita supplied and it was usually about 10'o clock before we broke up. The side-effects were considerable. I was asked to take services and preach at the Methodist, Presbyterian and Assemblies of God churches. We also shared services with them along with the Weslyan church which was a union of two churches in Canada. We joined in with their Holiday Club as well. The Catholics and us started sharing the Easter vigil and one year when the priest was on long leave in Germany I was asked to sing the Exultat, which is quite long and complicated, as well as read the epistle and do the intercessions. His stand-in wasn't a singer! Whilst kneeling in my place I heard the priest in a stage whisper say 'Move the candle.' As it was the Easter one it weighed what felt like half-a-ton! Afterwards I felt that being cantor, lector, intercessor and server was unity the hard way! Especially of course as we were not permitted to take communion.

It was the Nun who was the music teacher at the convent school who taught me the Exultat. We had a lovely relationship with the Nuns and when the children were four years old they were allowed to go there and they were made so welcome. We started inviting the Nuns for lunch occasionally and they so enjoyed coming. Father Alfred also came for lunch once or twice and he loved meeting the children. He usually had to eat alone apart from the Nuns with one of them serving him at table. The bill for the children's schooling never arrived and eventually I went to ask the Mother Superior about it. She said 'Father the children of priests attend free.' I had to cover up my smile as I thought to myself 'I wonder how many children of the Catholic priests attended the school!' Father Alfred was responsible for one of the most moving, and amusing, remarks in my life! Hanna, our eldest, was born at the end of May 1971. The week of prayer for church unity takes place between Ascension and Pentecost in South Africa and Hanna chose to be born during a meeting of all the churches which I was chairing. The call came from the hospital that 'it wouldn't be long' and I rushed up for what turned out to be the last half-hour. After a while I returned to the meeting which had ended but people were still there having tea and biscuits. Alfred came up to me and said 'Congratulations and now I can really call you Father!'

Not everything was straight forward. The churches formed a combined choir of about forty members and we sang during Advent around the different churches. It proved to be a great success until one year when I invited a coloured man to join us. He was something of an alcoholic but had taken part in his younger days in Gilbert and Sullivan operas. It seemed a way of helping him to offer his talents within a good christian fellowship. Unfortunately this invitation coincided with an offer from the Dutch Reformed church to sing in their church for the first time. This was considered a great step forward until someone 'informed' the minister that the choir had a coloured member. The truth was that he had yet to appear at a practice! To my complete surprise a knock at the door one night announced a visit from the Chairman of the D.R.C. Council and his deputy. He apologised for the absence of the minister whom he said was too ashamed to come. The Council had decided, so they told me, that the choir could not sing in their church if it had a coloured member. When I explained that he had yet to put in an appearance and it was most unlikely now that he would, it was to no avail. I had invited him and that was enough for them! What made matters worse was that the next day the Methodist minister phoned and angrily accused me of scuppering the choir's chances of singing a first performance ever in a D.R.C. church! Fortunately someone else must have thought this scandalous behaviour also because a couple of days later the choir received an invitation to sing in the D.R.C. church at Hlobane, the nearest one to Vryheid. Some face was saved! The man in question was most understanding simply saying that it was to be expected. There was another brush with the D.R.C. They kept a week of prayer for renewal and revival every year between Ascension and Pentecost. One year they invited the other churches to join in a big Pentecost service in the afternoon of that day. There were eight hundred in the church, it was packed to the doors. The Methodist minister had been asked to lead and preach so imagine my shock when he suddenly said 'And now our Anglican minister will lead in prayer.' He had not told me beforehand that he intended to do this. However he preached a good sermon but 'blew it' (in the eyes of his hosts) by saying at the end 'Who knows, perhaps next year our black brothers and sisters will be here too.' We never received another invitation.

Our first week in the town almost ended in a disaster of another kind. The 'Round Table' was very popular and someone kindly invited me to their weekly meeting held in a room above the local cinema. As was not unusual I arrived a few minutes late for the start of the meeting and parked my car hurriedly in a space across the road. It was 6.00pm. About 7.00pm a Policeman appeared at the door asking for the owner of the car with my number. The Editor of the Vryheid Gazette had been working late and then found it impossible to get home as his car was blocked in by my car parked across the entrance! I had to report to the Police Station. There I found a most irate gentleman red with frustration and anger. The Policeman began to take my particulars and I saw in my accuser's eyes the light beginning to dawn. He had replied to my apology with words like 'You'll be really sorry when you have to pay the fine' but now in calmer tones he inquired 'Who are you anyway?' When I explained he humphed and continued 'What were you doing there?' At my mention of the 'Round Table' meeting he said 'Oh that's a good organisation. Drop the charge.......but just you be more careful in the future!' What a relief. Later we were to become good friends and the incident was never mentioned again.

There were other difficult moments. Soon after Hanna was born a lady came to the door to see her. I was out at the time and when I returned home Anita said it had been a strange visit as she had cried such a lot. A day or two later the same lady stopped me in the street and introduced herself. She was French and a catholic but her husband was an Anglican. She explained that she felt very embarrassed for crying so much but she was sad because at a reception the previous evening the Chief of the Police Special Branch had told her husband that I had better watch my step because they would be monitoring everything I did. In fact we did have a couple of visits from them, once when I was out and once when I was at home. It was a black Constable in plain clothes who told Anita that he heard she was an artist and would she give his son a few lessons. He came twice with his son and spent his time looking at my books and generally snooping, trying I suppose to find something subversive. There were one or two 'funny' phone calls as well.

Anyway we enjoyed our times with the 'Round Table' and a few pastoral opportunities came from knowing the members. One in particular turned out in a wonderful way. I usually visited in the evenings and on this particular evening I had already tried two homes. At the first one they were out and at the second I could hear the rattle of dinner plates and voices. It was by then 8.30pm and not wanting to give up I decided to visit a couple from Round Table who had just moved into town from one of the mines. The wife was at home already, being visited by some friends and I was given a glass of whisky and we talked about this and that when the man visiting told me that he had just become a catholic and was very happy in the church. This didn't lead to much but suddenly he said to his wife 'Well my dear the priest hasn't come here for nothing you know. We'd better be going.' When they had left I said to Beverly 'So what have I come for?' To my surprise she said 'A month ago somebody said to me that it didn't matter what a mess my life was in, God still loved me. Is that true?' I usually carried a small New Testament with me when I did pastoral visiting and so I used it to explain that indeed He did. I employed the method that we were taught by David Steele at Kwanzimela in his workshop on personal evangelism. It was nearly 9.30pm by then and time to go home but before leaving I said that if she wanted to believe in God she could pray asking Jesus to forgive her her sins and to come into her life as Lord and Saviour and he would do that. I then left saying that if she did this I wouldn't have to ask her to come to church the next Sunday because she would want to anyway. Accordingly the following Sunday she appeared and told me later that after I had left she had knelt by her bed and cried and cried saying to God how she longed to be close to him. She had experienced such peace that she knew that He had answered. Tragically a couple of months later her husband died in a terrible car accident but her faith held and grew and she took more and more part in the life of the church. After we left South Africa she and her new husband, a Lutheran christian, moved and in their new home joined the Methodist church. Soon after she took up studies and became a minister. There was another person who joined the church in Vryheid and also later became an Anglican priest as also did his wife. He told me years later that I had arranged for him to go on a course at Kwanzimela without his permission first. I had then called on him and said that if he wanted to be a priest he had better attend! So he did.

We went to the annual meeting of 'Round Table' one year in Pretoria and another time I went with three others on a 'Wilderness Walk' which involved sleeping rough and digging for water from the river bed. My companions were two Methodists and one 'Bush Baptist'. All three of them seemed unaware that they frequently used the word 'Christ' as a swear word. At length it got to me so I said that if they didn't object whenever they said Christ I would say Amen. This seemed to get through and I never needed to use it.

Our church grew. We organised two missions. One was with other churches in the town and carried out by an organisation called Africa Enterprise which was run by Michael Cassidy who had become a christian at Cambridge University. He had wanted to be a politician but was moved by all the need he saw in South Africa and as an act of faith started up this mission which had become better and better known. Their purpose was to assist local churches to carry out their own mission in their own situation. They sent two men for ten days to help us and we held meetings in houses as well as the churches and went to visit people in their homes. One of the missioners, an Indian called David, stayed with us, I suppose illegally but no-one seemed to notice. He was a lovely christian and together he and I visited the houses of other 'coloured' people where he was given a great welcome. On our way to visit these homes one day a car pulled up behind us and out jumped the Assemblies of God minister. He wanted to know what we were up to! In the course of our conversation he told us that he had been diagnosed with a 'dicky' heart. David immediately produced a bottle of oil and there and then on the side of the road with cars throwing dust in our faces we prayed for him and David annointed him in the name of the Lord. David was very like that – spontaneous and went straight to the heart of the matter.

Our Bishop also stayed with us 'illegally'. The local law stated that all Blacks should be off the road by 9.00pm and apparently some time before we arrived there used to be a curfew siren. After that time no black person should be out on the streets or in the home of another person unless they were employees of the house-holder. Our Bishop simply tucked his car round the back of the house when he stayed with us. How could he come for confirmations or other occasions and not stay? He lived 130 miles away! He came once to baptise our son Christopher Inkosinathi (the Lord is with us) and on two other special occasions. One was to bring the then Archbishop of Canterbury, Michael Ramsey, as the Diocese celebrated 100 years in 1970. Part of the festivities was an ox wagon trek called '100 miles for 100 years'. It was organised by our friend Bill the Irishman from the next door parish of Khambula. I was invited to join in and it was to start from Vryheid with the Archbishop's blessing. He was a very shy man with virtually no small talk. After both I and the Bishop had tried and failed to start a conversation with him we all sat in solemn silence in the sitting room waiting for Bill and the oxen to arrive. The trek was duly blessed and the journey started. The oxen were not experienced in pulling a caravan as well as seven or eight people and we fell more and more behind in terms of time. One day we stopped at dusk and then decided to set off again about 11.00pm to try and make up some lost time. When 11.00pm came and went, I sought out the expedition leader and asked why we were not leaving. He said that if I wanted to move on I would have to go and fetch the oxen resting in a near-by field. This annoyed me, so I decided I would fetch them! To my astonishment when I went into the field calling out to them as the herdsman with us did they all rose sweetly from their knees and came mildly to the gate. We travelled until 3.00am when the lead ox suddenly sat down in the middle of the road and refused to budge. Bill put out lanterns 100 metres either side of the caravan and we slept where we could, I in a ditch for a few hours. Nothing disturbed us and we set off again about 6.00am. We arrived in time for the great Eucharist to be held in a special amphitheatre built at our Diocesan centre. The Bishop had asked me to write and produce a pageant of the history of the Diocese and we had tremendous fun with this. One of the first laughs was Mrs. Robertson falling off the wagon and dying! Others including Bishops being ambushed by Afrikaaner rebels and the Zulu War, etc. All this was performed in front of a crowd of about 3000 who had travelled far and wide for the service. What a great day!

The other occasion on which the Bishop came to our rectory was for a meeting between Archbishop Desmond Tutu and Chief Gatsha Buthelezi. There was an increasing rift growing between the Zulu people and the ANC and it is possible the meeting was to discuss these matters. Not long after the Inkatha Freedom Party was formed complete with uniform. The Zulus were keen not to be side-lined by the fast growing support for the ANC; in fact they were still trying to get back their identity as a nation which had been lost to the British in 1879. In the 1970's Gatsha was under great pressure to conform to the Government's blueprint for Apartheid but they never formally agreed to become a 'Homeland' in the formal sense.

Apart from the visits from the Special Branch there were the usual petty Apartheid issues to deal with. One day a lady telephoned me to say she had moved up from the Cape and her servant had a problem. She couldn't go with Madam to church as it was for whites only and she didn't understand Zulu so there wouldn't be any point in her attending the Township church so could she please come to ours? Madam would drop her every Sunday before travelling the extra half-a-mile to her own church. We bought an Afrikaans version of our prayer book and Claude Donelly, who was fluent in both 'official' languages sat next to her to help her through the service. She once said that our hospitality was what had helped keep her faith in the christian church. Another shameful event was when the Catholic Convent School began to enroll 'coloured' pupils.

There was a joint swimming Gala in the town every year with all the schools taking part. Directly the Afrikaans speaking schools heard what had happened they withdrew from the competition. Something even worse happened at the High School! The Headmaster there, newly appointed in the mid-1970's, was trying to be even-handed between the two language groups and so he appointed the same number of prefects from each group. He also joined Rotary which met every week in the town. This was too much for the Afrikaans parents. After all there were twice as many Afrikaans speaking pupils at the school! So they trumped up charges against him. These included urinating in public - when he had been at a barbecue and had gone to the bottom of the garden and behind a tree. Kissing a girl in public - when she had received the top prize for academic achievement from him. Fraternising with a girl student – when one of the girls strained her ankle in a race and he carried her to the side of the track to sit down. And for organising a dance for the Top Class's end of term celebrations! The parents asked the Governors to convene a public meeting at which they accused him of these things and demanded his resignation. They included in their condemnation the fact that he was a member of Rotary which was of course an American front for Communism! When the vote was taken there was an overwhelming majority against him. The English Teachers at the school had been married at our church and came round to us after the meeting. They were suffering severe shock and said 'Tonight we have seen a public hanging.' The Headmaster resigned and took the Governors to court. Before the case they settled for compensation, not a lot but enough for him to buy a small farm and never to return to teaching again. No wonder someone I met in the town who had played full-back for the Orange Free-State Rugby team and you don't come much more Afrikaaner than that, said that Vryheid was the most narrow minded place he had lived in! There were other moments as well like the day I went to Durban with the son of a priest and decided that we would eat along the beach as we could have a tray passed through our car window. The Indian Waiter took our order and then returned to ask if the order included food for the 'boy' next to me. I asked what that had to do with him and apologetically he said that if he brought the same plates and cutlery for both of us he would get the sack. So wherever you went the apartheid laws affected you somehow. It was tiring and depressing but church life had its pluses. The year before we left I decided it would be good to end my stay with a 'mission' and somewhere I had read that Tom Goddard, ex-Captain of the South African cricket team, had become an evangelist. I wrote to invite him and he agreed to come for a week around Easter. There was a very good response. He was able to go into the High School and that was the only time I sat in their Hall. The church was packed out every evening as he proclaimed the good news of Jesus Christ and homes were full whenever we were invited for coffee, talk and questions. It was a fitting climax to my nine plus years there.

My mother came to stay with us for our last three years there. It happened like this. We had decided to leave in 1976 but a few months before this the Church Wardens and Treasurer came to see me. Why were we leaving? We gave it some thought and although there were a number of reasons for our decision the top one seemed to be that Mother had been living alone for over twenty years and as she was now 75 years of age it seemed only right to be nearer her. Father was settled in Portsmouth with Audrey. When they heard what I had to say the church officers offered to build a 'Granny flat' if we would stay on. We contacted Mother who wrote back and said that having thought it all over long and hard it seemed a very nice idea. We were thrilled to think that the church cared so much. Our rectory was ideal for an extension as the old unused study couldn't really be usefully used as anything else and so it was just a case of building on a bedroom and toilet. It was agreed that she would have her meals with us and use the sitting room as she liked. We left for long leave happily and hopefully. This leave we were based in the beautiful home belonging to U.S.P.G. at Bramshott near Liphook where we had already been in 1972 for some of our leave then. It had belonged to a Bishop who left it in his will to the Society. 1976 was the year of the drought and England looked more parched than South Africa! For our last two weeks we were sent to Bournemouth to a flat next door to St. Francis Church We took a taxi all the way to Heathrow which cost £30 – cheap even for those days. On the way we picked up mother and my sister Joy. It was reminiscent of that day when I left for Malaya, twenty years previously, except this time mother was coming too! We nearly missed the plane! Mother wanted some rands and I found out they could be obtained at Terminal four. What I didn't realise was the distance between the third and fourth Terminal! When I eventually came running back they had been calling for our family of five for some ten minutes or more. We ran for it with Mother panting behind 'I can't go any faster.' She had Angina! There was a great welcome for her at the rectory and soon she became known as 'Granny' to everyone except our alcoholic friend Harold who simply called her Gran! Her Doctor in England had said that it would be alright for her to have a tot of whisky as a 'night-cap' and before long we had people asking at the door how Granny's whisky supply was. If we said it was running out a bottle would appear within an hour or so outside the front door!

    Her arthritis improved dramatically in the warm, dry climate and she was able to reduce the number of steroids she had been prescribed in England. This was just as well in view of what they can do to your bones! She would sometimes wander off into town and got lost on one or two occasions. A phone call came one morning from the Catholic priest who had met Mother heading for the cemetery. She had asked him if he knew of a shop that sold almond paste! There were a few members of the church who found her friendship a great help. These ladies would arrive looking miserable and within minutes we would hear the sound of laughter coming from her room. In fact she sometimes found the atmosphere in the rectory a bit too serious. One lunchtime she left the table in a great hurry and we wondered what was wrong. After she had closed the door she opened it again and her little face re-appeared with the words 'Too little laughter in this house!' We still quote this to ourselves sometimes! She sometimes made 'gaffes' as was her wont. One day we had a couple come to church who wanted to be married and she looked much older than he. They came to the rectory for coffee after the service and I whispered to Mother that they had come about marriage. She couldn't have heard me properly as soon we heard from the kitchen her sweet voice saying 'Oh I see you have come to church with your son today.' On another occasion she was with us as a guest at a Wedding Anniversary celebration and sat with one of our acquaintances liberally drinking her champagne! Next day this new-found friend of Mother's appeared at the door with a large bunch of roses. We called Mother to the door where she was presented with this lovely gift and she peered through her glasses at the 'friend' and said 'Excuse me but have we met somewhere before?' She was much loved and not least by Harold the already mentioned alcoholic friend. He would come and stay in our outside room from time to time and always remained sober whilst with us. He would sit and watch telly with 'Gran' and although Mother couldn't stand him at first she gradually took to him and would even miss him when he would suddenly leave as he did. One Sunday night we were at church with only three or four in the congregation when half-way through the service Harold appeared rather noisily and slumped at the back. After a while he spotted Mother up at the front and started to call to her, quietly at first but then louder and louder – 'Gran!' She seemed to take it in her stride and it did liven up the service somewhat!

It wasn't the first time Anita met her when she came to stay with us. We had travelled to England in 1972 and Mother had a friend who ran a taxi service and she was there at Heathrow to meet us! It was in May and we had just left a beautiful Spring day in Switzerland where we had visited one of Anita's friends and it was also a fine warm day in England. Mother was nervous and 'interviewed' Anita about Hanna who was not quite one year old then. We had tea at her home in Sheet and I couldn't get over how small the house seemed after being away for the past three years. Hanna, being herself, put banana over the armchair and Anita was upset about this but 'Granny' disarmed the situation by saying with one of her charming laughs that it was of no consequence. Anita was also seven months pregnant with Mary at this time. We travelled around England in a hired Mini-Minor with Anita sitting in the middle of the back seat! We decided that Mary should be born in Sweden and by the kindness of the Swedish Church Mission we rented a flat in Uppsala and the birth took place in the large hospital there. As I left the ward at 1.45am on 20th July the first bird was beginning its song on a tree by the hospital gate. We hadn't decided on a name for our baby yet and the next day as I was walking to the hospital to visit them both it suddenly came to me as if it were a message that she should be called Mary. So I wrote a note saying 'Her name IS Mary'. The dear child soon came out in a baby rash all over her little body and was taken back into hospital. Anita walked the four kilometres to the hospital and back again twice a day to feed Mary whilst I tried to amuse the fourteen month old Hanna.

Once during our Swedish break we took a bus and visited Forsmark, a village 140 kilometres north-east of Stockholm and some 90 or so from Uppsala. In this famous little village, where once they mined iron and exported it to Sheffield as early as 1600 and where now stands the first nuclear power station to be built in Sweden, Anita's mother and stepfather hired a cottage for the summer months. It was originally built for the Blacksmiths who probably came from Belgium. There would have been five families living in this one house with its well in the garden and (still) the toilet in a little shed round the back about fifty metres from the door. Anita had been able to hire a flat in a similar cottage in the village in 1965 before going out to South Africa where she had put her furniture and other belongings. She had returned to stay there in 1968 for her long leave. Now it seemed sensible to give it up and the idea was to transfer her belongings into two rooms in her parents summer house. We stayed in her old cottage and Anita's sister's partner who had a van helped us to transport everything over.

It was my first meeting with Gunhild, Anita's mother. She was there alone as Sven was working and so came only at weekends. It was decided that we should go out fishing – very apostolic! She arrived by rowing boat at 7.00am on a balmy summer day complete with two long sticks, a fishing line with hooks and plenty of grubs. We set out on the lake which is really a dam made to supply the old forges with power. It is about four kilometres long and less than one kilometre wide surrounded by beautiful woods with just the occasional cottage peeping through. We had already had breakfast which is just as well because although she told Anita we would be back 'about nine' somehow we managed to stay out until almost 11am. Gunni caught seven and I caught four of the little flat fish which live in abundance in the lake. Anita could hear our laughter as we crossed the still lake on our way home as Gunni had suggested that I row us back. It was about twenty years since I had rowed and that was on Petersfield lake which is only the size of a playing field. The amusement was due entirely to my zig zag progress of sorts across the water. Gunni,or Mormor as we came to call her, had hit it off in spite of our difficulty in communication and she was always kind to me afterwards. In fact this was the start of a new and important chapter in Anita's life as she had never had the chance to bond with her mother as a child and now after all these years the grandchildren formed a bridge of love which grew stronger and stronger with the years. Anita had been conceived in Stockholm where Gunni was training to become a dressmaker, and the story is that her father was cycling out to her parent's home to ask for her hand in marriage when he got a puncture and gave up! Anyway he disappeared and Anita was taken to a Childrens Home where Gunni would visit her when she could get away from her work.. The Grandparents became worried about what their daughter was doing in Stockholm and visited. Anita was about nine months old at this time and when they arrived at the Home she was sitting on the floor crying with an ear infection. Her Grandfather picked her up and said 'You are coming home with us.' So Anita grew up with them in their lovely home near the river, where Anita spent many happy childhood hours. They were marvellous to her but not very kind about her mother's behaviour and so she never really got to know Gunni and rather feared her. Sadly Grandfather died at 59 years of age when Anita was only twelve and her Grandmother went into decline and also died after seven years of illness. This made Anita into a very independent teenager used to working, as indeed she did once at the age of thirteen, looking after children and doing most of the work for a family. She then studied to become an occupational therapist' living in different towns. Her creative temperament and growing spirituality have, over the years, made her into a mature and rounded personality.

    In 1976 we repeated our trip to Sweden travelling for the first time by ferry from Felixstowe. Christopher had been born by this time. Again I was present for the birth and the Doctor held him up and said 'No mistaking what this is then!' I went home and called on our friends the Nebels early the following morning. I tried to hide my excitement and said as casually as I could 'It's a boy.' Inger's response was to grab me by the arms and do a jig in the street. It was a great moment of course, not least because our surname was to be preserved although there is also a Duffett cousin who has a son. So this time there were five of us staying at Forsmark and the Grandparents loved it. Sven was a great photographer and was always taking snap shots of the children. They also took us to a lovely circus. I took up jogging again and would run for two hours in the lovely wooded lanes around the house finding new paths and sometimes getting lost! Never as bad as once in Gothenburg however when the Police stopped me just as I was entering a long tunnel when I was hopelessly lost and going in completely the wrong direction so they were really 'angels in disguise!' They asked for my address and of course I didn't know it. It took a whole hour for Anita to contact the local Police Station who had been alerted by my two helpers over their radio. We arrived back at Helga's house at 10.00pm with Anita very worried. The children had told her 'Daddy will be alright because God will look after him.' The police were amused but kind and advised 'Next time he goes out please put a card around his neck with his address on it!' The dam at Forsmark was beautiful to swim in if the weather was right and we had a fantastic August in 1976. It had been as dry and as hot as in Britain. Occasionally we would go to a lovely 'beach' called Kallero right on the Baltic coast. It was rocky but the water was very shallow so one could wade out for 400 metres and still only be up to your knees in the water. The water was never really warm but bearable for the children to frolic in. We would take sandwiches and coffee and stay there for hours. The seabirds were amazing in their variety and numbers and although we never saw anything we could identify as rare Hanna and I did see a couple of cranes one day. We had gone for a cycle ride along a forest road to get some exercise when we suddenly heard a squarking sound. We dropped the bikes where they were and crept slowly up a steep bank. There was a clearing where a number of the trees had been felled and here the ground sloped away into what looked like a sandy pan. Right there in the middle were two cranes eating from the ground! After a minute or two they must have become aware they were being watched as rather like clumsy airplanes they flapped their wings and noisily began to ascend. As they mounted their wings drew out to their full extent of about three to four metres and they gathered speed very quickly. Within seconds they were above the trees on the far side of the clearing and gone. It was an awesome sight.

Before this chapter of life ends there are some more stories to relate. One is about a confirmation at the Coronation coalmine about twelve miles from Vryheid. The candidates were all children of the workers who lived in the 'compound', a place of small concrete houses surrounded by a high wall. There was also a small church built by the Anglo-Americans, the owners of the mine. Here Bishop Alpheus was due to confirm candidates prepared by a 'cathechist', a man or woman licensed to teach. I went to see the mine Manager, himself an Anglican from Yorkshire, and told him that Alpheus was coming. 'I suppose you mean we should entertain him?' he said. 'Why not?' was my rejoinder. This posed a bit of a problem for him as he knew that some senior members of the staff wouldn't have a black man in their home. In the end it was decided to hold a barbecue in the largest garden. The Church Wardens from the Zulu congregation wouldn't come but there were about twenty or so who usually attended the joint Methodist and Anglican service there who would. They were very nervous but Alpheus soon put them all at their ease and there was much chatter and laughing. When he finally left they stood around in a circle to say goodbye and he shook hands with them in turn. About half-way round he stopped and looked at them with a characteristic glitter in his eye and said 'If you were Zulus you would all be dancing by now!'

Another story concerns Alex, a tall young man on the streets who turned up one day the worse for wear and asked if he could stay. He did although we had a lot of difficulties with him. we discovered he could get drugs quite easily in the town and on one occasion he harassed a nurse at the local hospital. He would come and go as he liked and often stay away for as long as six months at a time. One day there was a ring at the doorbell and on opening Alex collapsed at my feet. There was a Doctor's surgery across the road from us and I ran to ask for help. One of the Doctors came back with me and slapped Alex's face commanding him to get up. He did but immediately squared up to the Doctor as if to box with him. I was left standing in the middle like a Referee. A window opened and Anita shouted 'Take off your glasses!' She thought they might get broken in the ensuing fight. There was no fight fortunately as Alex collapsed once more and a stretcher was sent for to carry him to the surgery and thence to the hospital by ambulance. Alex eventually made good. He appeared one day at the door smartly dressed and carrying a brief-case to tell us that he was now married to a christian girl and went with her to church. He was a Representative for a drug firm of all things!

There was also another visitor whose name was Philip Viljoen who arrived one day asking for work. He claimed to be a skilled Carpenter. We needed some cupboards in the church hall and I asked the Church Warden if we could try him out. It was agreed and he did a first class job. As soon as he was paid he was off! We discovered some bottles left behind and as expected we had stumbled across his problem. He told us he had had a good job until one day his son was killed in a shooting accident when he was only sixteen. That was when he started to drink heavily and he took to the road. He returned to us six months later and he never drank in our presence or even appeared the worse for wear. The children loved him and provided him with much pleasure too. There were usually bits of work around the place for him but always he would leave suddenly without saying goodbye. After a few years of this routine he was leaving as usual one day but stopped to say goodbye and thankyou. As he left Anita came back from the gate crying. Somehow she felt so sad for him going off alone with his clothes and just a few pence. A couple of days later we received a phone call from a hospital in Ladysmith, a hundred miles away. He had been found bleeding and unconscious at the side of the road and had died a few days later as the result of a burst ulcer. He had regained consciousness and given our name as his next of kin. They told me that I didn't have to go to the hospital to identify him and that was the last we heard of him. He had come to the church once or twice but often said he felt out of place with his torn and grubby clothes although we did try to give him things to wear. We had told him what he wore didn't really matter anyway.

Because I had been Hospital Chaplain I was keen to keep in touch with that particular ministry. A letter arrived from a Lesley Lovely, then a Chaplain at Johannesburg General. Would I consider being the Secretary of the newly formed 'Hospital Chaplains Fellowship'? I felt highly honoured and after meeting with him together we organised a gathering for sharing about the work each of us was doing. Then we began to plan training courses for newly ordained ministers which proved to be very exciting. There was an American couple who had both taken a degree in 'Clinical Pastoral Studies' which was a three year course. They gave lectures on the training courses we ran and also supplied an instrument for measuring skill at visiting the sick. This was called a 'verbatim report'. The visitor had to choose one of their visits and immediately afterwards write up everything that was said during the visit. Observations about body language and what the visitor observed in the room/ward were to be recorded. Finally there was space for the visitor to write psychological and theological reflections. These reports were then presented to a group of five others. I was the leader of one of these groups and it was fascinating if demanding work for us all. This process was carried out for two successive years and we stayed in a convent and had joint worship every day as well as time off. The staff would meet to discuss progress and it was a rich experience.

During my time at Vryheid I had been asked to join the Bishop's Council and later his Chapter of six clergy. This meant being made a Canon and the ceremony took place in the Bishop's chapel in Eshowe. I had also been Rural Dean of the area and this had enabled me to continue working with the Zulu priests and congregations. When Bill Johnston was away on long leave this would mean my taking services in congregations as far as fifty miles away. One was in a very remote area on top of a mountain and another beside a school on farmland far into the country. Here it meant driving to a spot and then walking for two miles across the veld. Always I was met by two girls from the school whose job it was to carry the heavy suitcase with all the vestments and other things for Holy Communion in it. The first time it happened they stopped at a little stream and knelt by a rock. As I looked I saw etched onto the rock the shape of a cross. Was it a memorial I asked? No, and they giggled. What was it then? More giggles. I had to wait until I could ask the teachers. They laughed too! Apparently they had taught the children that they should pray at the start of each day but these particular girls had to get up at dawn and clean the house and prepare breakfast for the family before going off to school. They had decided therefore that the best way to pray was on their way to school and the chosen rock had been scratched with a cross to make it something of a trysting place. I wanted to cry when I heard this story and every time I went there the same ritual happened. The only difference was that then I joined in with them kneeling on the ground with the only noise being that of the wind rustling in the long grass. God met with us. Bill was away one Christmas and rather foolishly I agreed to cover his programme as well as mine. From midnight on Christmas Eve to 1.00pm on Christmas Day there were seven services. Never again! Not long afterwards I heard that Catholic priests are forbidden to take more than four services in any one day and since then I have adopted that ruling too!

So the years passed by and the time came for us to consider the children's future education. We winced at the idea of them being taught in the racist atmosphere of Vryheid and not at all happy with the prospect of boarding school many miles away in Natal. There would also have been a problem affording that. We decided to stay until the end of 1979. The year before a Bishop from Kimberly, Graham Chadwick had led the clergy retreat at Kwanzimela. Something he said had triggered in me a desire to have an interview with him. During that he had led me in prayer to express my disappointment about my father and then to forgive him. There had been some tears and I had left feeling much helped. In our last year I was asked to lead the clergy retreat. What a privilege and responsibility. Many hours were spent in the church hall kitchen (the quietest place!) preparing the addresses. I found it an exhilarating task. Some of the clergy came afterwards for interview and confession including one who later became a Bishop.

Anita had been amazing during the nine plus years there. Her first experience of life in a rectory, bringing up three children born so close together and almost single handed as my work took up so much of most days, having a mother-in-law to stay for three years which she called the happiest years of her life, going to her first ever Bible study and growing spiritually all the time. She had passed all her 'tests' with flying colours! There are other stories that could be told. Like the time when a Church Warden's sons was murdered. Or when I was told that a man who used to attend church at one time was having affairs with some of my confirmation candidates and how we had talked about it and he had decided to come back to church. He never missed a Sunday after that. But these details are really best left between God and me. Certainly the ministry in Vryheid had been most challenging and exciting.

We finally left Vryheid on December 18th 1979. There were two little aircraft flying from the tiny airport and we filled them both with our luggage and ourselves! What we hadn't expected was that the Church Wardens had telephoned around the congregation and as we arrived at the airport there was a crowd of about fifty people waiting to say goodbye. They stood round in a circle and sang carols! Oh the hugs, kisses and tears. Dear Harold was crying profusely unable to look at us. Mother had left a month before us and was staying with my sisters awaiting the outcome of negotiations for a room in an Abbeyfield House in Cambridge. I was glad. She would have been heartbroken leaving as we did. About six months before that I had written to the then Bishop of Portsmouth and asked if he had heard of me and if there was any place for me to go. He had replied that I was 'still on file' and he would be pleased to offer me the two parishes of Greatham and Empshott north of Petersfield, which also included the Army camp of Longmoor. It was a case of 'a bird in the hand being worth more than two in the bush!' and I readily accepted. I tried to remember exactly where Greatham was because that was where the rectory was. I vaguely remembered going through the village on the way to Farnham where Father's two Aunts lived. Mother and Father would sometimes play bridge with them or visit at Christmas. A strange thing happened soon after I had accepted this job. I had a vivid dream about six o'clock one morning! I had just been out to the toilet and fallen asleep again when this dream came. That kind of dreaming just before waking for the morning are the only kind I can ever remember afterwards. The dream was about the rectory where we were to live. I saw the Georgian front with a blue front door and a bush with red flowers to the left of the front door. I tried to remember whether I had been there before but couldn't recall. In fact I probably had been once before as my friend Andy Western, whom I had met at Ripon Hall when he had visited our chaplain, had gone to live in Greatham. We had been introduced because he had got a job teaching at Churchers and our chaplain knew I had been there. So during one of the vacations I had visited him there and I think we might have gone over to the rectory to meet the then rector. As it happened Andy had to leave his digs there and I arranged for him to go and live with Mother in Sheet. They became firm friends! So it is just possible that I had seen the house once about sixteen years previously. I described the house in my dream to Anita. The United Society for the Propagation of the Gospel recommended to all those returning to England to take six months leave and look around for a suitable parish. This was good advice but I knew that sometimes it didn't work. A friend, David Watson, who had been in the diocese for a few years went back and couldn't find anything and so was technically unemployed after six months. He took a job as a Taxi Driver! One Saturday on a 'wedding job' he was asked if he did many weddings! Not an easy question to answer he told me! So I decided to go ahead as the Bishop had offered. It never occurred to me that the Church wardens were taking a lot on trust by not seeing me first perhaps together with other applicants. I had written to the outgoing priest-in-charge as the Benefice had been suspended for re-organisation but his reply was guarded and unsatisfactory. I had asked him about all the different aspects of church life and he simply replied that he thought I should get there first and find out for myself!

It had been very different in the Church of the Province where the Bishop always sent a man to a new place only after talking to the Wardens first and wherever possible one priest took over from another in person. So my successor, Graham Marchington, who had been the Personnel Officer of a paper mill before his ordination came to stay for two days and I took him around and showed him all the files and other relevant paperwork. There was no doubt however that I was naïve! It had never occurred to me that I had not been a vicar before in the Church of England and that there might be differences in the way different church bodies functioned. There was a double misapprehension! I had been a curate in the Diocese and had been brought up in the area and had attended school just down the road. It all seemed so familiar and so I was deceived into thinking that it was a case of carrying on where I had left off! The expectations of the local people for this local lad were also high. Unfortunately we were both in for a disappointment! It started well enough. It always does! There is a kind of honeymoon period.

CHAPTER 10

OLD BLIGHTY!

So we flew from a hot South Africa into a very cold Heathrow! The same taxi as in 1976 came to fetch us and deposited us at Bramshott to the beloved Wheelers where we had stayed then. The furniture, such as it was, was yet to arrive. This consisted of a lovely old Swedish chest of drawers which Anita had discovered at Rorke's Drift belonging to one of the first missionaries, and a few other household items plus all our personal belongings.

After a day settling in we decided to go and see the churches where we would be living. Did we hire a car or had my brother Chris already sold me a second-hand Wolsey 18 for £350? I really can't remember. He had got it from a colleague whose mother was the only owner, he said. The problem was she had a dog who had eaten most of the upholstery in the back! This had been patched up and as it had done only 40,000 miles it seemed like a bargain. Anyway we looked in on the rectory and to our amazement it was the house of my dream with a fine Georgian front and yes a rose tree on the left of the door as you faced it! It's colour of course we couldn't guess. It was a dull and cold afternoon and the garden looked overgrown. At the back of the house was a Nursery School and their part of the garden looked cared for! There was also an occupant in the flat above the school. The previous Rector had been gone about nine months and the lawn which had been mown, was vast but there was no vegetable patch. To our delight there was a young lady raking the drive and removing the weeds. She turned out to be Serena Neave, daughter of Sir Arundell and Lady Richenda Neave who were living at Greatham-Moor in a large house just over the field from the rectory. She lived in London working for the Church Missionary Society and had become a committed christian through Holy Trinity Brompton. She had come home for the weekend and her parents had told her that volunteers were asked for at the Morning Service the previous Sunday to help tidy up the rectory garden for us. After a cursory look and encouraged by the feeling that God meant for us to be there we went across the road to see the church, which was closed! It was mostly Victorian and had a beautiful spire, one of the thinnest and most elegant I have ever seen.

Thence we proceeded up the hill to the charming village of Empshott with its 120 or so inhabitants and its jewel of a church built in 1187 as the French monks made their way from Portchester inland. It had an atmosphere of love and prayer. To our delight we found some of the congregation decorating for Christmas. It was a Saturday and the Carol Service was to be held the next day. It looked beautiful and the people were very welcoming. The Church Warden was Colonel David Aston whose father had been an Archdeacon of Salisbury. David had retired from the Army and eventually settled into one of the old thatched cottages in Empshott. The children were especially made a fuss of. When we left to our amazement it had snowed! It was the first time any of the children had seen snow. We were invited to spend Christmas, which was five days later, with Joy who was now living in Gosport. It was a sunny and cold day with the frost shining in the trees and along the telephone wires. Father and Audrey were there too.

St John the Baptist Church in Greatham

For two Sundays we worshipped at Bramshott whose priest had also spent a number of years in South Africa and was married to a South African. When she heard that the U.S.P.G. had allowed us only four cubic metres of furniture and we were therefore without the basics required to make a home she offered to organise a 'shower'. This was like the 'baby shower' we had experienced in Vryheid but this time the appeal went out to the congregation for anything to furnish the eleven rooms we had inherited. Then, providentially, Anita who was always interested in what may be hiding in cupboards or sheds saw some furniture through the window of the potting shed. We asked the gardener what they were and he showed us some beautiful antiques that had been there for as long as he could remember! We wrote to the Missionary Society and they replied that they had been left there by the owner who had left the house in his will for them to use. He was a Bishop and had been dead for about twenty five years. They said we could take what we liked and send a donation. We chose several pieces, including a couple of tables, a Windsor chair and a smaller card table. I had no idea about antiques and decided that £40 would be a fair donation! To our surprise when we moved in one of the men helping to decorate the house offered us £300 for one of the tables which by then was standing in the hall! On enquiry it turned out to be a Jacobean 'Gate' table made of oak. A little later a local second-hand dealer asked us where we got the card table from and then told us it was from the time of Charles 2nd and worth about £200. This was in 1980.

The licensing was fixed for Saturday, January 12th and in the meantime we moved into the rectory and met the Church Wardens and a few others. We also had an invitation from the Archdeacon of Portsmouth and his wife to Dinner at their home in Fareham. The rectory had been lived in by my predecessor and his family for over eleven years and it was really due for re-decorating for which the Diocese gave me a grant of £400! Even by the standards of those days that was not going to be nearly enough for such a large house. We were helped out by the Church Warden who brought along an ex-Marine, just retired, who offered to work for 50p an hour! Arthur became a dear friend as the years went by. His wife, some thirteen years older than he, was an eccentric but delightful American who had been a Ballet Dancer when the two of then had met in new York. Martha also played the piano and as the church piano had been moved to the rectory for safe-keeping would often knock on the door, sometimes as late as 10pm, and ask if she could practice! Another great help came from the Manor House just down the road from the rectory. The 'Lord of the Manor' had long gone and he had been very fond of the bottle and was eventually forced to sell. He had been a power in his time and at least one Rector had stayed but a year before giving up the struggle against his authority! The man who bought part of his farm told me that he had come to the church just once when he first arrived twenty years previously. He had sat at the front only to be told that his place was at the back by the aforementioned Lord of the Manor who was also Church Warden! His comment was 'He wanted my money but not me!'

Next door to the Manor was a rich widow who was a christian and helpful, I believe, to a christian organisation called 'L'Abri' when they wanted to buy the Manor. I had read about this organisation whilst in Zululand. We had a small Bible Study group on a Wednesday morning and to it came one or two ladies from other churches. One was the wife of the Headmaster of the German speaking Lutheran Church School. She mentioned L'Abri during the course of discussion and then lent me the book of that title written by the wife of the founder, Francis Schaeffer. She also lent me another book by him called 'The God who is there' and I found it very helpful amongst the increasing liberal theology we were being bombarded with in the late 60's and early 70's. Francis had been a Presbyterian minister in the USA who had left the church over the doctrine of the authority of scripture and had gone to Switzerland where he and his wife invited students to come and stay with them. It was a kind of basic christianity commune. Like a different experiment, Taize, they were over-whelmed with the number of 'drop-outs' who wanted to stay and find out what life was about. Soon it became so popular that they were able to spread and set up homes in other countries. One of those who joined them was a man from 'Rhodesia', Ranald Macauley, who had studied at Cambridge and was about to go to a Theological college to train for the Anglican Ministry. During a vacation he visited the Swiss L'Abri and was much impressed with their approach to Evangelical christianity. He was equally impressed with Schaeffer's daughter Susan and they eventually married. So it was Ranald and Susan who had negotiated the sale of the Manor House in Greatham to become the British Headquarters of L'Abri. When they heard that we were struggling with the decorating of the rectory they sent along a group of students to help. Students came to study christian life and doctrine and lived in community about twenty at a time with a staff of five or six. They also helped with all the chores associated with the running of such an institution. Some of these young men and women arrived at the door offering their help. Immediately they took over my study and completely redecorated it from top to bottom.

Apart from the chest of drawers we had brought with us and the four pieces we had discovered at Bramshott I had a Windsor chair which had belonged to Mother's parents and had been given to me for my last year at Churcher's. Sister Daphne had been looking after it and they brought it down with them for the licensing on January 12th. Naturally we needed a little more! Our first surprise was a visit by my sister Joy and her son Andrew. They had hired a van and brought over some pieces of furniture, including a bed, and some useful household utensils. My mind immediately went back to my ordination when Joy gave me sheets for my bed in the Clergy house Fortunately the Diocese had a grant of £3000 for those moving into rectories for the first time. With this we bought beds and some carpets, a cooker and fridge plus some cupboards for the bedrooms and a few other things. For a week we lived in one room which had a large gas fire! The oil was yet to be delivered and we needed to furnish as we could going from room to room. One marvellous find was an enormous desk which stayed with me until I retired and was far too large for any room other than rectory-like studies! The second-hand shop in Liss did quite well out of us. Then the little miracle happened! It was about ten days after we had moved in. Sunday, after lunch, we were resting in front of the coal fire in the sitting room when the door bell rang. Outside were four cars and at least one van lined up in the drive full of furniture. It was the result of the 'shower' held in Bramshott! We could hardly believe our eyes. There were armchairs and upright ones, beds, and pots and pans, and even a full-size 'tall-boy.' On enquiry we learnt that this had been given to someone who had recently moved into a small cottage and it would fit nowhere. It had therefore been housed in their mother's garage. She arranged that it should be sent to us on permanent loan and twenty-two years later it is still with us! One lady gave a stitching set with full cotton reels and needles. Then the phone kept ringing. One man was a member of the 'Gospel' Hall in Liphook whose daughter attended the parish church. He owned a second-hand business and asked if we could do with a settee and two large easy chairs. There was a couple in Liss who had moved into a bungalow from a house and wanted to be rid of the set. He said that they would pay us to remove it! I went to the house and there was this beautiful lounge suite and they were reluctant to take the £10 I insisted they have. It was just right for our large sitting room and when it was covered with loose covers it looked as good as new. How blessed we were.

 The day came for the licensing and the Bishop came himself. As the Benefice had been suspended I was to be Priest-in-Charge until such time as it was set up as the new combined Benefice of Empshott and Greatham. These things have to go through the Privy Council and Parliament. The church was full and the Bishop preached an encouraging sermon. At the reception in the village hall afterwards people welcomed us warmly. Two incidents stand out. I was sipping my wine when suddenly behind me the Zulu language was spoken meaning 'Good Day Minister'. I was flabbergasted! It was Ranald Macauley speaking. It transpired he had been born in Zimbabwe where the Ndebele tribe speak a dialect of Zulu having been chased there by King Shaka in the early part of the 19th Century. He had also been to school in Natal where the Zulus form the majority of the population. In fact his father had been born in Vryheid. It was an amazing coincidence! He told me that at the Manor House they had been praying for the right man to be appointed and they could hardly believe it when they heard that I had been working in Zululand. The other story concerns Lady Neave whom I have mentioned already. After greeting me in her 'Queen's' voice she immediately said something like 'I was bored with your predecessor, his sermons were always the same. I hope you will be more interesting and please remember no sermon need be more than ten minutes long!' My stomach pitched! Tomorrow's sermon was already prepared. It was with heavy feet and heart that I climbed the pulpit for the first time. As I glanced in her direction I saw her look at her watch. I made a great effort to get a move on. Getting down afterwards I furtively looked at my watch. I had taken nine and a half minutes. A quick prayer of thanks was silently uttered!

One of the first problems was that people wanted my predecessor to come back to officiate at Weddings, Baptisms and Funerals. There was nothing particularly unusual about this but I had been taught that it was not wise to do so if it could be avoided. He however seemed only too willing and I didn't feel it was my place to refuse. Indeed how could I? There was some justification when it came to Baptism. I was reluctant to baptise the babies of those who were not regular attenders at church. This was a difference between the church in Zululand and England and I wanted to help parents come to a more public faith. But not surprisingly it back-fired! One couple who didn't know the previous priest well asked if the neighbouring Rector of Liss could do it. Again it was difficult to refuse although I did stipulate that I should preach on this occasion. Partly my fault and partly not it was resolved when my erstwhile rector, Ben Forster, who was now Rector of Hawkley just up the road, wrote to him and told him to keep away. He didn't tell me he was doing this but could see how unsettled I was by what was happening. He later told me that he had a stinking letter back! It worked however. I guess there had been misunderstanding on all sides.

The next problem seemed to be L'Abri. I was invited to tea by a couple who had also asked another couple along. I had seen them all in church and three out of the four were Church Councillors. They warned me that those at the Manor House were a dangerous fundamentalist sect. One of the couples had been disgusted that one of the members had rented a room in their house and had started to try and convert them. Moreover he was, to their knowledge, a homosexual. These people, they warned me, were also 'sheep stealers' having organised a Holiday Club for children and encouraged children of Church of England parents to attend. As I had already made a friend in Ranald it was unlikely that I would sever all contact with the Manor House. Later one of them wrote to the Bishop and I received an unexpected telephone call from him. He replied to the complainant that he doubted whether I would agree with L'Abri in everything but as a parish priest it was my calling to nurture christian unity. One of the couples left the church after about six months.

The culmination of all my supposed errors came the following Christmas. The Midnight mass was partly my fault as I had actually selected the wrong readings. One Farmer walked out after the sermon and never returned. I later heard from Arthur that he had told Arthur that he had 'better do something with that priest of yours'! For the Carol Service no-one had told me the traditional form and I got on with it as I had done in South Africa. It has always been my policy to encourage newcomers by giving them something to do and so I asked some of those who had started coming to church during the year to read the lessons. By so doing I missed out the Leader of the Brownies and the Parish Councillor who had been asked to read in previous years. We also had a visitor for the Midnight Mass, the Godfather of one of those who had joined us. As he was a priest I asked him to help with the chalice. However I was told to my face that I had told him to sit in the wrong place and I should have known better! So I heard that the Church Wardens had called a special meeting of the PCC without informing or inviting me. At the official meeting the following week I was told a list of some twelve things I had done wrong or failed to do. I tried to explain but I was clearly on the defensive! One of the 'wrong things' was to do with the Confirmation Class for adults I had conducted. There were eight grown-ups in the class all of whom had started coming to the church. I found a course called 'Saints Alive', one of the predecessors of the Alpha Course, and it ended with a communion in the round where the participants pass the bread and wine to each other for communion. The course had been made open to anyone who wished to come and at the communion there were two of the leading members of the Church Council. Later I had a phone call from the Archdeacon to say that they had written to say that an illegal service had taken place! Fortunately it was in the chapel at the Cheshire Home and therefore strictly speaking a 'private' affair. The next Council meeting the following month was even worse. One of the members said that she couldn't think of anything good that had happened since I came. At that point I said that I had better resign and left the room. I was asked by the Church Wardens to go back in but I refused. The next morning I phoned the Bishop and told him of my decision to resign. He asked me not to do so as it might put me out of work altogether. The Church Wardens came to see me and also persuaded me to carry on. I had started to pray with three senior members of the L'Abri community once a week. They were very supportive and couldn't understand what the fuss was all about! Also it wouldn't be fair to say that everything was going wrong.

There had been some very enthusiastic people join the church. One couple became a sort of lifeline for us, praying with us and helping to guide us through the difficulties of some of the relationships. But because a number of people joined the church from outside the village and were elected onto the Church Council this also caused trouble between the old and the new members. We started coffee in the rectory after the Sunday service and that was critcised as forming a clique! There was obvious disagreement between the way I wanted to preach and teach and the traditional churchgoers view of what the church should be. This 'trouble' was mainly in one of the villages and at the other the small congregation seemed more ready to co-operate and glad that a few new members joined in the life of the church.

There was also the first ever Cheshire Home in the parish. To begin with I found it hard learning how to relate to people with severe disabilities. I made mistakes but was readily told so by them and gradually there grew up a rapport that was closer and deeper than anywhere else in the benefice. There were some deeply committed christians there wanting and giving support. Anita started to work there on Sunday nights when I could be home to look after the childern and she became much respected and loved there. Because of the tensions I began to look for work elsewhere.

There was only one place which gave me an interview and that was Lee Abbey where I had been as a student. It was marvellous to go there again and see how it had developed. The interview with John Parry, who later became Bishop of Cheltenham, went quite well but one other wasn't so good and we felt that we probably weren't right for the job. I wasn't offered it and we decided to struggle on in Greatham. A big break through came when one of the leading ladies in the parish went on a retreat and came back with a renewed vision of the faith and the church. She sent for Anita and there was a mutual forgiveness and she asked me if she could train as a Diocesan Reader. She became a great support in the parish thereafter. Things began to build up and the numbers attending services increased. Not all the newcomers were helpful however. At least two of them were pushy and tactless, very critical of the 'old guard' and causing great resentment amongst them. It was very difficult to reconcile the two groups.

Round about 1984 I tried to persuade the churches to hold a mission. We had David Steele who had taught the clergy in Zululand come for a weekend and do a workshop on personal evangelism. This was to be followed up by a whole week of 'mission' led by a group called the 'Village Evangelists' based in Hastings. They were an interdenominational group who went all over Britain to village churches, some Baptist, some Methodist, some Evangelical but the majority Church of England, to help members do their own evangelism. It was another instance where some of the PCC were ambivalent but on the whole the week went extremely well with meetings in various people's homes and even one in the pub! It was a glorious Summer week and the garden party with a clown and other attractions was especially popular. There was one family for whom it was life transforming. The mother had asked me the previous year if I would give her a lift the thirty miles to visit the grave of a baby who had been born prematurely and died. Perhaps that was what made her feel attracted to the week of mission. Anyway she came with her husband and four children and they were well and truly converted. The father joined an adult confirmation group and as they hadn't married in church they asked me to bless their marriage. The children started attending Sunday School and the Crusaders Group. They left the village not long afterwards but we still hear from them at Christmas and they are still very actively involved. In fact Shelagh, the mother, has been on more than one of Daniel Cousins' groups. He takes up to 1,000 at a time walking from village to village in large areas like Cornwall or The Isle of Wight.

The Crusaders Group mentioned above was a very successful group for as long as it lasted. They are a national young peoples movement and usually meet one night a week and include christian instruction in every meeting but with very healthy regard for young people's interests. Their outings and holidays are well recognised throughout the country. One year we took about fifteen of our group to a railway station on the way to London and joined 1,000 others on a special train which took us straight to Stoke-on-Trent and thence by fourteen double-decker buses to Alton Towers for a day out. The remarkable thing about our group was the leaders. I found no less than nine men who were ready to volunteer to lead. We usually had about thirty at our meetings and met in the Evangelical Church in Liss Forest about a mile away. There were also District meetings and for those we travelled to Petersfield, Havant or Haslemere. Other churches in the area joined us and for about five years it was great fun but like all young peoples groups it began to wither as they grew older and leaders moved away.

There were some noticeable events in the life of the church apart from those already mentioned. A Teacher who lived in the parish asked to be confirmed and as the lessons progressed it transpired she had never been baptised and she was asking to be fully immersed. We had a lovely Evening Service in the Evangelical Church where we used their pool for the baptism. Then there was all the drama! In Vryheid there never seemed an opportunity to put on any plays and now I was keen to get back to it.

In 1981 the Diocese of Portsmouth organised a Pilgrimage to Canterbury. There was a certain amount of disagreement about the way it had been organised, too much having been done centrally or by the Cathedral. It was decided that a 'Fringe Committee' be organised and the Rector of St. Mary's at Portsea was asked to convene it. Anyone interested could attend the first meeting and there were about fifteen of us there. I said that I would be willing to write something if people could be found to act in it. Coincidentally there was a Director of a Drama Group from a Fareham church present who said that he would willingly supply the people. I took this as God's way of saying 'Yes' to my idea. Going home I set about the writing. It was called 'To Be A Pilgrim' and was set in a church. The story was about a group of tourists who get locked in a church and during that evening and night relationships develop, confessions are made and lives are changed. In the morning when the surprised vicar unlocks the door the company realises that their 'interior' pilgrimage has made them better fitted spiritually to continue their physical walk to Canterbury which they had started together a couple of days previously. There were some nine people in the cast and I had to find two of them myself. One was obvious. The young man already mentioned who worshipped at L'Abri and had so shocked the couple in my congregation had always wanted to be a professional actor and had done some training. I approached him as I thought he would be ideal for the leading role. He was thrilled. Then there was the amazing way I bumped into an actress! One day the phone went after lunch and a female voice asked if I was the vicar. Please could I come to see her as she was at her wit's end. She lived in a small house at the end of the village and when I got there I had to let myself in as there lying on the couch was a lady of about thirty years of age with one leg in plaster up to her thigh. Around the room hung clothes on picture rails and it was full of furniture. She explained that she had had an accident whilst riding her lambretta and that whilst she was living in the same house as her husband they never talked to one other and lived in separate rooms sharing the kitchen. Divorce was imminent. She was very lonely and depressed and needed help. We talked about faith and it turned out that she had been a churchgoer before she married but her husband was against it. I suggested that someone gave her a lift to church next Sunday and she start again! Then the question came up about what she did for work and she told me, but then admitted that what she really wanted was to be an actress and had indeed done quite a lot in Repertory. This was amazing and I told her about my need for someone to act in my play. She never looked back.

We rehearsed on Sunday afternoons at West Meon Church which was half-way between Fareham and us. It was decided to do three performances – one at Greatham, one at Fareham and one at the big city church of St. Mary's whose vicar was Chairman of the Committee. The only thing which failed was the publicity. I should have found someone to look after it for all the churches. As it was it was poorly advertised and the audiences very poor except in Greatham where the church was packed. 30 in Fareham in a church holding 150 or more and in Porstmouth 60 in a church capable of holding at least 500 was very disappointing. The cast and helpers with stage and costumes, etc. enjoyed themselves immensely however. That inspired me to write something for the following Christmas.

It was based on something I had written for a South African radio competition and had been 'commended' without winning one of the three prizes. It tried to get inside the heads of Mary and Joseph faced with the news of the Virgin birth. It included some singing and dancing and one of our new members, a music teacher, wrote some lovely tunes in Jewish style. It was well attended and much enjoyed by all the cast who came from the two villages. This 'success' was followed by a play for Easter the following year. This was called 'Josh you are wonderful' (with the obvious reference to Joshua, Jesus) and it was based on the last chapters of St. John's Gospel beginning with the raising of Lazarus. The idea was to appeal to people who were outside the church and so we decided to stage it in the village hall. The problem was to find thirteen men! The part of Jesus I gave to our friend from L'Abri and they also supplied three other men. At last we managed to find them as long as I included myself in a minor part and 'Matthew' doubled up as the Undertaker in a scene about Lazarus' death! For the resurrection scene Jesus needed something to show a difference in his clothing and appearance. At Blackmoor, the next door village, lived a retired Bishop in his eighties and Anita and I were invited there to tea with him one day. He wore a beautiful white skull cap to keep his head warm and it occurred to me that this was just the thing for Jesus to wear as a symbol of his rising from the dead to a new life. The dear Bishop was only too pleased to lend it for the play. The opening scene was of a coffin coming in from the back door, through the audience and up onto the stage into a bedroom. Martha and Mary meet the coffin with much grief and Jesus arrives to comfort them. He goes into the bedroom and his voice is heard in prayer and command. Lazarus then appears on the stage from the bedroom. We wore modern day clothes and the whole play lasted about one hour and had a modern setting. Most of the action took place in the 'Upper room', a modern day sitting room with a big table for the Last Supper and so there wasn't much scene changing. The play ended with the audience being invited to sing 'Spirit of the Living God, fall afresh on me.' We sold tickets at about £3.00 each to pay off the expenses and we made a little money for the church too. It was performed on two nights to a full hall. There was a tremendous fellowship amongst the cast as the play was far from easy to produce and we all had to work very hard. The commitment was amazing as again most of the rehearsals were on a Sunday afternoon.

    Mother had stayed with Daphne and Jock when she first returned to England in November 1979. Coral and Chris found her an Abbeyfield Home in Cambridge and she moved in there in the New Year, quickly settling down to her new life. We tried to see her once a month travelling up through Farnborough and around London to Watford and then the A1 - pre M25 days! She also came to stay with us. During 1980 her health deteriorated with cancer found behind one eye. Eventually her angina became worse and she was hospitalised. We were called to see her during the first week of November and she was very sick, breathing with difficulty. The next day, Saturday November 9th, she died. It was the eve of Remembrance Sunday and somehow suitable for a great British patriot. A short service before cremation was held at the church round the corner from the Abbeyfield Home, where she had attended on Sundays, and later a lovely Memorial Service, with priests she knew and loved taking part. We sang, as she had requested one night after church in Sheet, saying 'Now you will all sing –'Now thank we all our God' – at my funeral.' She was 79 years and 8 months and had been divorced for 25 years.

    Father lived a couple of years longer. He and Audrey were in a 'not-so-wonderful' Home for the Elderly in Fareham. They also stayed with us a couple of times and we visited them both in their home at Lee-on-Solent and in Fareham. Once, on Boxing Day, I ran out of petrol on my way home and was helped by a very surprised priest in Hillsea. He had been a policeman before ordination and always kept petrol in his garden shed! It was 10pm and he was in his dressing gown running a bath. The car was about a mile away!

One evening in 1982 the phone rang to say that Father had had a Coronary whilst sitting in a chair and had fallen on to the floor. The Head of the Home said that he was badly bruised. We didn't go over to see. The funeral was taken by a kind priest from Alverstoke in the church there. Later I went to Portchester Crematorium to see the ashes scattered under the trees; not a nice experience!

Audrey was shattered and never seemed to open her eyes afterwards! When we went to see her she was in bed and hardly speaking. Anita asked if she would like an ice cream and, yes, she would. She sat up in bed and ate it with eyes closed! When she died some months later I officiated at her funeral in Portchester Crematorium. Her nephew looked after her estate and sadly he too died not long afterwards. She and Father had loved one another and been reasonably happy together I think. I was glad that, with Anita's help, I had accepted them both together in the end. Both Father and Mother had tried to do their best for me. They wanted their children to 'better themselves' with opportunities that they never had.

In 1987, although the church was fully active with a flourishing Bible Study and young peoples work, small choir and confirmations coming up regularly, a committed small congregation at the second tinier village and plenty of pastoral work to do especially at Lee Court, the tensions were still there. The Annual Meeting of that year was particularly tense with a couple of members filling the attendance with people they had canvassed but who seldom came to church in order that the candidate for Church Warden who had been suggested by the other Church Warden and myself wouldn't get elected! Instead Sir Arundell Neave was chosen and in fact he turned out to be a very good Church Warden.

Anita had recently attended a meeting for Clergy wives in the Diocese. The Bishop, Tim Bavin who had been brought over from Johannesburg to free that Diocese for Desmond Tutu, addressed the group. He started by saying that he was much happier speaking to them than to their husbands! He then went on to talk about Sabbaticals and said that if their husbands had been working for twenty-five years or more and hadn't had one they should apply quickly. I had been ordained for twenty-eight years and not had a sabbatical as such so the next day I wrote to Stephen Platton who was then in charge of ministerial training. I thought of St. Deniols in North Wales where they hold various courses for clergy and also have scholarships making the prices reasonable Stephen was quite willing to let me have the necessary for board and lodging for thirty days and I decided to do reading, which had become a pile of unread books. It was fixed up for May. About three weeks before the Sabbatical began there was a day organised at Catherington House for those interested in leading Quiet Days or Retreats. A priest from the Diocese of London led it. In the coffee break I mentioned to him that I was due to go to St. Deniol's shortly and he said to be sure to visit St. Benios about six miles down the road whilst I was there. This was the centre for Ignation spirituality for the Catholic Church in the U.K. Ignation was a word I had not used and probably not heard since my days at Ripon Hall when I tried to read a book about the different methods of prayer. It was so dry and diffuse that it had put me off the words spirituality and contemplation ever since! But I wrote to them to see if there was space on one of their courses. The answer came back that it was full but they could offer me a room to conduct my own Retreat. As I was already doing this after a fashion I declined with thanks.

The journey to North Wales was by train and bus. St. Deniol's is at Harwarden just inside Wales and about eight miles from Chester. The journey was quite straight forward really. The place itself boasts the largest and most comprehensive theological library in Europe. Originally it was the personal library of Lord Gladstone whose country seat was at Harwarden. He left his books to the Welsh nation, several thousand of them, and they were originally housed in a hut with a tin roof. Sometime after his death however it was decided to make this library his memorial and a splendid building was erected. Then at some stage the Welsh Tourist Board gave a andsome donation to furnish and redecorate rooms for residents. It had become a residential library rather like a college or small hotel. At the same time it also housed a group of about twelve students for the full-time Anglican ministry who had their three-week residential course there. There is a lovely little chapel where the daily offices and Holy Communion are held. It was indeed like being back at college again. The weather was lovely and food excellent.

Then after a few days God dropped a bombshell! I was sitting at lunch with those preparing for ordination and they were speaking about a Retreat which was to begin at the end of the week on Bardsey Island just off the coast of Wales. It is in fact a Bird Sanctuary. Two things attracted my interest. One was that the Retreat was to be an 'Ignation' one, eight days long, and the second was that it was to be led by a Bishop Graham Chadwick. That name was familiar to me because the last Clergy Retreat that I had attended in Zululand (apart from the one that I led myself) was taken by the Bishop of Kimberley whose surname was also Chadwick. I asked if the one leading the Retreat had been a Bishop in South Africa. One of the group was sure that he had. My next question was whether there were any places left on the Retreat. To this they were sure the answer was no! Places were taken up a year ahead particularly as it was possible to take only twelve at any one time. Well I thought it would be nice to make contact with the Bishop again. He was now living in St. Asaph about ten miles away and was the Assistant Bishop of the Diocese of that name. I decided to phone him. He was at home and yes he remembered me and said he would like me to come for coffee on Wednesday in two days time. I readily accepted not knowing how I would get there. At our next meal I asked if anyone was going to St. Asaph on Wednesday and although no-one was, one of them kindly offered to take me there. At chapel services for the next day and a half I prayed that the Lord would open a way for me if he agreed with the priest who had said that I should get on one of these Retreats. I arrived on time on Wednesday at the Bishop's bungalow. Almost immediately after sitting down and receiving my coffee I asked whether by any chance anyone had dropped out of the Retreat. He looked at me a bit oddly and said 'Yes, last night. Why do you want to come?' Of course I did and we began to see how it could be possible. He would lend me one of his sleeping bags and I would ask the Bursar at St. Deniol's whether the £80 needed for the eight days could be released. In fact the Bursar was reluctant as I was on a scholarship but he agreed to pay half of it. One of the clergy training group was taking his car to the port from which we had to sail and so a lift was readily arranged. It was all very exciting!

On the Saturday it took about two hours to drive to the tip of Wales. The boat was a packet vessel which crossed twice a week with the post and other necessities including up to fifteen passengers. The trip took nearly two hours because of the swirling currents. The island is just over a mile long and only a little more than half a mile wide. There are a few houses on it which used to be inhabited by a small population but are now used by bird watchers during the Summer. The Bishop hired them cheaply for the last week in May and the first one in June for these Retreats. There was one resident family, the Warden of the Bird Sanctuary and also a Nun living by herself. The island was covered by thousands of birds of course. Mostly shags and sheerwaters which flew in by night in their thousands with fish for the sitting females and the subsequent chicks. We also saw herons and choughs which had become very rare. There was also a variety of wild flowers and hundreds of resident sheep. When there was a small population a Methodist church had been built and the Welsh 'revival' had swept the island in the early 1900's. It had quite a big graveyard. There was also a beautiful ruined Abbey which had belonged to the Benedictines in the 12th Century but had been closed by Edward 2nd afraid that it was too near Ireland and a refuge for rebels! The island was also known as the 'Island of Saints' it being said that it was a place of pilgrimage in the 6th Century with up to 3,000 christians choosing to be buried there. Four of us priests were to occupy one of the houses for the eight days without speaking to one another! It worked very well in fact. My only complaint was that the Bishop's sleeping bag didn't smell very sweet and the east wind cut through one like a knife and never stopped blowing!

Ignation Retreats are 'one to one', that is to say that each individual had a personal director with whom she or he meets every day for about one hour. The director or 'soul guide' gives the retreatant a piece of scripture on which to meditate. The meditation follows a method which St. Ignatius found most helpful to himself and encouraged his followers to use. Mainly it consists of using the imagination. The reader of the passage uses his own senses to imagine himself into the scene. How does it look, smell, feel and to hear the noises, even taste the food if there is any, or simply the fruits on the trees or whatever. To feel the air, to hear the sea and so on. The scene is then dramatised before one's imagination with you in it. Such questions as where were you standing in relation to Jesus or the Disciples or the crowd. What did people do and say and how did you feel about it all are to be asked of oneself. At the end the idea is to see what God has been saying to you about your christian life, your thinking, feeling and active life as a follower of Christ. You then describe all this to your leader who comments asking questions helping you to see more clearly what God wants of you or to give you. To prepare us for this way of 'praying' we were sent on a walk over the island in order to train our senses to be alert, to look at the flowers, sea, birds and so on, to feel the grass, to smell the air, the ground and the sea. Silence was kept in order to concentrate the soul on God and worship at midday and evening helped to do this, as well as to foster a sense of community and closeness to God.

Breakfast and supper were in the different houses on a self catering basis but lunch was all together and cooked for us as the main meal of the day. Rest was also encouraged and most of us slept after lunch and then walked round the island for exercise. Because I like writing and find my imagination works best that way I wrote down my meditations in the form of a description. Things began to happen in a most stimulating and sometimes challenging, even frightening way. I found myself moved one day to lie on top of one of the 'tombs' in the graveyard and to contemplate what it meant to die to sin, and also my own physical death. On one occasion in the meditation on the crucifixion I found myself crying, not so much about the horror of it, but in how I was implicated in it happening and how I could treat such a good friend this way. So one can say that the whole Retreat is experiential and helps one to live a life in closer fellowship with God. Of course the first lunch and afternoon is not silent and also the last morning after worship silence is broken. My director was the Bishop himself and he was most gentle and encouraging all the time. The Retreat was a landmark in my spiritual development. I felt better able to pray and a delight in silence. It also made me want to lead other people in Retreats or Quiet Days. The priest from London had done me a great service. The journey back to the mainland was very different from the one the previous Saturday. The wind decided to blow a gale. My 'sealegs' worked but I was amazed to see one of the Catholic nuns who had been helping with the leadership sitting with her arms around the boat's fence-like sides screaming with laughter as every few seconds she was dipped under the water head and all!

Before leaving St. Deniol's another chance came up. This time it was a 'Fun Run'. I had been able to do some jogging around the place as Lord Gladstone's ancestral home had some lovely paths and tracks. Then I heard of this run from Flint to Mold in aid of some Childrens' Charity. There wasn't time to raise money but the entrance fee also went to the cause and so even if it wasn't much it was something. What was lovely about the run was that it was downhill all the way. It is about six miles and I was very pleased to complete it in forty-five minutes. Back home I had been running in the 'Butser Fun Run' and raising a little money that way. Because that was so hilly it meant keeping as fit as possible and I would go out at least twice a week around Longmoor, usually with our dog Jenny who covered three times the distance I did chasing rabbit or other animal scents! The time in North Wales had been a very refreshing sabbatical and I had done some useful reading. One book in particular, 'The New Wine' by Caroline Bax, about problems which arise when renewal gets going in a church, was full of useful advice but I felt too late for me. A pity it hadn't been pointed out to me a few years before! Other books I read were to do with baptism and a policy for parish priests and one on pastoral care written by a Hospital Chaplain which was full of insights taken largely from his long experience in hospitals. This was interestingly prophetic in view of what was about to happen.

Having arrived back at the beginning of June I scandalised parishioners by choosing a Diocesan event to do with mission, which I had helped to put together, rather than attend the yearly Garden Party which was our main fund-raiser. Not that I did it without informing the Church Wardens that I wouldn't be there. Anita bore the brunt of some anger about my decision! The event could of course run perfectly well without me but in some ways I was the host as it took place in the rectory garden. Our finances had in fact improved nicely since the end of the first year when we had faced a shortfall. That had been averted by God. One morning on our door mat a letter arrived containing a cheque for £2,000, a gift from an ex-parishioner whose father had been a Rector of the parish. She was now in her late eighties and said in her letter that she would have left it to us in her will anyway but we might as well have it now rather than later. It saved us from embarrassment and we didn't look back after that.

After our annual holiday in Sweden I received a phone call from William Sanders who was at that time the Honorary Secretary of the Zululand and Swaziland Association which tried to raise money for the two Dioceses. He said that I probably didn't know that he was also the Secretary of the Diocese of Ely's Patronage Board which was responsible for selecting priests for parishes which had no patron and would I be interested in a parish with a part-time hospital chaplain appointment. They were having difficulty finding someone as the Church Wardens had turned down the one they had sent. It sounded promising in view of the fact that hospital chaplaincy had meant a lot to me in the past. I was also looking for a move as after eight rather difficult years it seemed right to move on. The Archdeacon thought that there was nothing else available to me except in the Isle of Wight and we felt uneasy about being cut off again. However when the Bishop came to Hawkly nearby I asked my friend Ben, the Rector, if he could arrange an interview for me. The Bishop was kind but firm. Although there were six vacancies in the Diocese he didn't think any of them were for me. When I told Anita she cried. Actually I felt dejected myself. If none fitted me then what did? He did in fact allow me to apply for one of them which was my old parish church of St. Cuthbert's and although the interview went quite well I knew that another man who was a Rural Dean in the Oxford Diocese would get it. He is now the Archdeacon of the Isle of Wight and did a very good job at St. Cuthbert's for several years. After that the Archdeacon had written to say that perhaps I should look outside the Diocese. I then had a feeling that I had somehow blotted my copy book! So the phone call came as something of a sign and an answer to prayer. The name of the village was Papworth Everard and I must admit that I had never heard of it. It was arranged for the Church wardens to send me the Parish Profile and on reading it we realised that there was something different about this place. First of all it mentioned the hospital which had become famous for performing the first heart transplant in Britain, and specialised in heart surgery and chest diseases. Then there was mention of the Village having special character and history but it didn't mention specifically what this was! However it sounded most interesting and I went for an initial meeting with the Archdeacon of Ely and the Church Wardens.

One of them, a young man, was about to leave and in the sitting room of the senior Warden, a Yorkshire spinster in her early sixties, the Archdeacon admitted another man in his thirties to take his place. It was my first time to see this. The Archdeacon took me to a church situated on top of a hill and rather out of the village and then on to the rectory much better placed nearer the centre of the village and opposite the sports field. The house was built in 1950 and was of a good size without being over large. The garden was rather large but nothing like Greatham and somewhat neglected. It had been unattended for at least six months. Then we went to the hospital. It was my first time to see one of the old-fashioned TB sanitoria with their semi-circular wards facing south to maximise the sun, and balconies so that patients could be put in the fresh air, something which was done in the depths of winter as well as the height of summer. Some newer wards had been built and also some fine up-to-date theatres. The number of patients at that time was about 150. The chapel was a nice building, a memorial to the first matron, but was now in a totally unsuitable place. This was because unlike TB patients, many of whom could be ambulant, most of those who underwent surgery for heart by-passes, or suffered with severe chest diseases, certainly weren't. However it was used for a service during the week and sometimes visitors and the occasional patient came. The work paid for in the hospital at that time was one session – a three and a half hour period – a week, and I was told that my predecessor had worked much more than that. The Archdeacon took me to see the Unit Manager and immediately asked that if I were to come there, would he please double the hours paid for. He promised to look into it.

My next visit was to be for the formal interview and as I drove up through Hertfordshire and entered Cambridgeshire it hit me how I missed these open 'skyscapes' similar to those in South Africa. It felt good to be there. The interview was to be held at the suffragan Bishop's house in Ely. This is near the great Cathedral which is known as 'The Ship of the Fens' as it can be seen for miles around. I was ushered in to sit in a little side room near the front door to await the official time. Whilst there, a knock on the door was answered by one of the panel who welcomed the newly arrived with the words 'There is only one candidate left, two have dropped out.' I lifted up a silent prayer of thanks. The panel was awesome! I had been told nothing by my friend William. There were three Rural Deans and several laymen of the Diocese plus a representative of the Health Authority sitting in for the hospital. The Bishop was in the chair. The questions were mostly kind and courteous although I had to duck one or two about the hospital, trying to hide my ignorance about the present stage of transplantation in Britain. It transpired that one of the Consultants at Papworth had resigned because he didn't believe in the definition of 'Brain Stem death' which means that if scans of the brain show no activity on two occasions separated by about twenty-four hours then the person can be pronounced dead even if they are still breathing with the help of a respirator. But I think they were anxious to appoint someone whom the Church Warden had said she thought might be alright. There being no other candidates certainly helped my case! I went home quite encouraged and two days later the Bishop of the Diocese, Peter Walker, phoned to say that he had agreed to appoint me to the parish. Then the stomach-ache started! It must have been nerves about making the decision to leave. We decided to visit Papworth together. Anita liked the rectory well enough except for the galley-like kitchen. The Church Wardens had assembled the entire Church Council to meet me this time. They were very friendly and the discussion was straight forward except for one man who seemed a bit fierce! He said that the priest before the last one had always been at the hospital and they could never get hold of him in the village. They didn't want someone whose energy and time was taken up by the chaplaincy. The Archdeacon kindly took us out to a pub lunch and said he hoped very much we would agree to go there. When I got home I phoned the priest who had retired from Papworth to ask him about this aggressive speaker. 'Frank' he said 'He's a sweetie!' I took his word for it and indeed he turned out to be right. I had less than a week to decide.

The tummy-ache continued. After all we had begun to settle in the parishes. I had officially been made Rector of Empshott and Vicar of Greatham in 1986. Things were looking up following a glorious celebration of the 800 years of Empshott Church together with the dedication of new doors made from 16th Century oak, the same age as the original, and the new Reader was helping more and more in the parish. There was however yet another cloud on the horizon. The Diocese wanted to combine Hawkley as a third parish in the Benefice and sell the rectory in Greatham. The Church Warden in Hawkley told me that he thought their Church Council would like to have a say in who was to become their new vicar, which was fair enough. However I could see more hassle ahead especially as I thought the best plan would be to sell both Rectories and build a new one near the Cheshire Home which was right in the middle of the new Benefice and on the border of Empshott, the smallest of the three villages. The problem of Benefices with a rectory in one of the villages is that the people there still think they have a full-time rector and the other villages feel deprived. I decided to consult with Bishop Graham Chadwick who had agreed to be my spiritual guide since the Retreat at Bardsey. Over the phone I explained the situation. He asked me how long I had to make a decision. It was then Monday and I told him that Wednesday was the last day I had to make my mind up. 'So' he said, 'What's wrong with Tuesday?' meaning that I should say yes straight away. Once I had decided the tummy-ache stopped! I phoned the Bishop of Ely who said that he was pleased. Then the announcement had to be made to the churches. They didn't seem surprised! Two days later the phone went again and it was the Bishop of Ely. He apologised saying that he couldn't offer me the Parish until the hospital had seen me and agreed that it was alright with them that I should be the Church of England Chaplain. That meant another visit up there. It had already been agreed that we should move from Hampshire after Easter 1988 and this latest visit to Papworth happened on November 25th 1987. The Unit Manager was a man in his early forties and we discussed the hospital, it's history and it's uniqueness and he asked about any experience I had had with chaplaincy. The interview seemed to be going on a bit and so I asked when exactly he could let me know because we were preparing a Christmas letter and it would be helpful to put in information about a move and our new address. He looked surprised and asked 'Know about what?' It was then my turn to look surprised! Apparently he hadn't realised that he was interviewing me for the post but thought that he was simply introducing me to it as the choice of the Bishop of Ely. Perhaps if it hadn't been so near Christmas I would have gone away and never been told anything! A bit of a fiasco really but it turned out alright in the end. I asked the Manager to notify the Bishop and within a few days he had phoned again. All was well. The last few months went smoothly enough. We had had Canon Patton from the Cathedral to preach for Harvest and there had been a good meeting in the Village Hall addressed by one of the Diocesan Representatives at General Synod about the trends and movements within the Church of England today. There was a last confirmation and I heard our Bishop say to one of the Church Wardens at the reception afterwards 'So, you have got your way now with Paul leaving.' The reply was reassuring and a little sad 'No, we've got used to him now and are sorry to see him go!' I think the Bishop was also thinking of another little crisis a few months before when one of our new-comers, a very keen evangelical, had found out that this Church Warden was a Free-Mason. I foolishly agreed to let him speak to a group of others in the church. They came to the rectory as a body and asked me to denounce Freemasonry from the pulpit. Certainly I was not happy with combining the christian faith with Freemasonry but I knew a lot of christians did, including a past Bishop of Portsmouth, and I wasn't prepared to accede to their request. The poor Bishop had to put up with a long phone call from the protagonist about this particular 'problem'! Of course the Warden heard about it and was very hurt, but it soon blew over.

One of the aspects of the work that I would miss was what I had been doing in the Diocese. The Bishop in charge when I arrived had kindly offered me a place on the Diocesan Council for Mission and Unity. In this group I had been asked to help with a sub-group to work for evangelism in the Diocese. After a couple of years we organised a meeting in the Diocese for all those who were interested. It was a workshop and we had speakers from both inside and outside the Diocese speaking about aspects of this work from their different perspectives and their own experience. It was attended by over sixty people. This Council also had a Committee for a 'West Africa' link which was in conjunction with the neighbouring Dioceses of Chichester and Guildford. It meant raising money for Dioceses in West Africa and arranging visits to and from them. One year we had a splendid outdoor Eucharist in the Guildhall Square in Portsmouth attended by the visitors from West Africa and about 2,000 members from the church in the Diocese. It was followed by an equally splendid picnic in Victoria Park nearby. Anita and I hosted a priest from the Gambia for a week once, and another year a Bishop from Nigeria who had a Cheshire home in his Diocese and wanted to see Lee Court. The day we went, Leonard Cheshire was staying in his little cottage in the grounds and came over to see the Bishop. It was touching to see the great man genuflect and kiss the Bishop's ring. This same Bishop told us that in his Diocese when it rains the Catholic Priests who have Landrovers, look after the Anglican congregations because their priests have only bicycles and can't reach them! 'Why should the Church of England export the Reformation?' he said.

Then there was the Readers Board. Somebody asked me to join it. Readers have a proud history but the name is misleading as they are really Lay Ministers who are licensed to lead services and preach though many of them do very fine pastoral work as well. It was fun to be a member of a Selection Committee and to plan events for training, etc. One of those who came for selection at my first Committee I asked the question as to the difference between evangelism and mission. This obviously interested her and I have noted that she has become a priest now and also a Francican tertiary in charge of organising Parish Missions. Another candidate could barely read or write but we decided that as she was obviously very keen and a born leader the work would be tailored to meet her needs, for the training takes up to three years with several essays to be written for an assigned tutor. I was also asked to mark some essays and the standards of the ones given to me were enormously high.

Perhaps I shouldn't leave Greatham without telling about some of the more unusual aspects of the ministry. There was a young lady working at Lee Court who asked to see me. She had been having nightmares since dropping her boyfriend. These were always the same. He would tie her up and take her to a bonfire and be about to throw her on when she woke up screaming. She had told her Doctor who had said that he thought it was more my province than his. The really disturbing thing was that she had discovered that her ex-boyfriends mother was a practising witch! It was decided that there should be a form of exorcism. I knew from past experience that this should never be done alone and so I asked the priest in the neighbouring village to accompany me. We prayed with her and the dreams went away. Another similar request came through the man who had sold us our second-hand furniture. A customer of his had trouble with a male ghost who kept coming into her bedroom! After hearing the story from her I went to the house with 'Holy Water' and prayed for the tormented soul, blessing the rooms especially the bedroom. Similarly I was asked to exorcise a ghost in a house in our village, where a coach and horses were seen to drive through, but strangely only the upper half could be seen. The occupants had done some research and found that the original building was lower than the present and ended just before the spot where the 'coach and four' were seen passing by. Again I went with the water and the prayer book. One of the most moving of encounters was with a woman who had terminal Cancer. Her two sons came to the village Youth Club which I had stared and handed over to the local 'Bobby' and had incidentally been an enormous success with nearly one hundred teenagers attending at times. I visited her and when she was taken into Winchester Hospital went there as well. I offered her Holy Communion but she confessed she was a lapsed catholic. That didn't matter I said if she would like communion. She told me how faith had once been real to her and that she had thought of being a nun. 'The well ran dry' she said. As I left I asked her to look in the well because perhaps there was some water still there. The next week we spoke about this and that and as I was leaving she said 'By the way, there is still some water in the well!' I took her communion every week at home until she died about six months later.

We also had some interesting tramps coming to the door. Fortunately we had a room in the stable block where a Groomsman used to sleep and so we could put travellers up there. One man came to the door on a very wet day and was shown to the room and his coat taken into the house to dry off. At about 11.00pm the phone went and a voice said 'This is the Landlord of the Silver Birch pub. We have a man here who says that the vicar has stolen his coat!' He was brought down by car and the coat retrieved. Another man left me with a bad conscience. He was withdrawn and stayed with us for a few days more than once, eating breakfast and supper and looking after himself during the day. The last time he came the Nursery School Teachers complained that he was walking about in the garden where the children played, cursing and swearing. He denied this when tackled about it. Then after supper he asked Anita to fill up his flask, as she always did, with coffee saying 'Fill it to the top for us will you.' Was he having friends there to stay as well? As it happened the next day was Tuesday and it being Lent it was my habit to go to early service in the next door parish church at 6.30am. Coming back at 7.15 I listened outside the Groomsman room door and sure enough there were voices or at least our friend was speaking to someone. At breakfast I said that he had misled us and would have to be on his way now. He denied there being anyone else with him and, I must admit, looked sad and rather bewildered. Anyway he went off and a couple of days later I had a phone call from the Catholic priest in Petersfield. He said that our friend had been there and that he knew him of old and he had told the priest the story of how I had made him leave. The priest said that it probably was true that there was nobody there with him because he was a Schizophrenic and was probably 'talking with his voices!' He was now safely in hospital in Basingstoke. It only goes to show how careful one has to be.

Another traveller was rather different from the rest. He arrived one night with a friend and as they were well dressed and clean we decided to give them our spare bedroom. We also had to go out that night and left them in the house with the children. We didn't give it a thought really which was silly but fortunately all was well when we returned. Derrek, the younger one, told me that his wife had died suddenly and that he couldn't face going back into the house so took out his savings after the funeral and travelled until they had all gone. He claimed to be a Civil Engineer and certainly appeared to be an educated person. His friend didn't return but he did most weekends. Eventually he came to church and asked to be prepared for confirmation. One Sunday afternoon I was going to see a lady from the village who had learning difficulties but lived by herself. She had been taken into Winchester Hospital. To keep Derrek occupied I invited him to come as well. We saw her briefly and after that Derrek went on his way and never returned. A year or so later I was on Liss station going to London by train when who should be coming towards me but Derrek and Beryl, the lady we had visited. They greeted me and said that they were now married and living somewhere in London. I nearly fell over backwards!

One day I saw a man walking past the rectory. He was swaying dangerously across the road so I stopped him and he said that he was walking from Portsmouth to London, a distance of about seventy miles. He wasn't drunk. I invited him in for a sandwich and when he removed his shoes his feet were bleeding. We gave him plasters but after a rest he insisted that he must be on his way.

Eric, another man came to see us quite often. One day Anita was impressed when he started talking some Norwegian. 'Where did you learn that?' she asked. Casually he replied 'Oh I learnt that in prison'. He had only one leg but he seemed to travel all over Britain.

And of course there were the children. They had settled marvellously into school life. The Headmistress at the Primary School was rather old-fashioned and to begin with Christopher had to wear shorts in all weathers! Hanna was chosen to be the May Queen and there was some laughter when she said 'Let the fun begin' with a strong South African accent! They also wanted to run about without shoes in the Winter whenever the sun appeared. They all sang in the choir and Mary in particular had a lovely voice. She took part in one of the plays too. They were all confirmed. Christopher amused the Bishop when he was asked what he wanted to be when he grew up. 'A Lorry Driver' he said 'Because they could eat Mars Bars.' After a laugh there was a bit of a silence and then Chris said 'When Daddy grows up he wants to be a Bishop.' I was far too embarrassed to say that I had once been nominated to be Bishop of Zululand by a charismatic but rather eccentric friend when Lawrence Zulu had been elected. When it came to the day my friend wouldn't say anything in my support and the poor unsuspecting candidate from Vryheid had to put a few words together in haste. At the vote one was registered on my

Farewell at Lee Court Cheshire Home Greatham April 1988

behalf! Archbishop Burnett, the Chairman, was sympathetic at my request to withdraw but I denied that I felt hurt. Liar that I was ! Anyway I should never have allowed it to be put forward, it was a foolish conceit.

I had wanted to become more involved in the schools for the childrens' sake. I did become a Parent Governor of the village school and on talking to the Deputy Head of the Secondary he advised joining the Parents/Teachers Association and in my second year on that I was elected onto the Committee but that was my last year at Greatham.

Another initiative was a group of carers. A young man had committed suicide in the village caravan site. It troubled me that with some co-operation with his carers, he had been visited by a Psychiatric Nurse, this could maybe have been averted. I phoned her and we met. Of course there has to be patient autonomy and confidentiality but there are ways of co-operating although there are also risks. A Doctor and I had once misunderstood one another and the family were cross but still it was worth a try. So together with a Community Nurse who came to our church we started a monthly forum over a packed lunch and had speakers to tell us about their work. It had some support value I think. It was at the time Community Care was being launched and this had got off to a shaky start. For example, we had a young couple discharged from Basingstoke Hospital for the Mentally Sick into our parish and they both came to church and Bible Study. She was less well balanced than he and had got into trouble with her neighbours for swearing at them! We wondered why she always wanted to drink a lot of water at our meetings but were slow to understand the signs. One day she went to the Doctor who simply increased her dose of medication for Depression. At 2.00am one night the phone rang and it was her husband in great distress. She had been taken into hospital and had died of a Diabetic Coma. Could I take him there? It was about an hour's journey and one of the saddest moments in my ministry. He moved soon afterwards and we lost touch.

On a much happier note I was able to start a church cricket team. It began with 'Tip' who arrived at church one day with his new American bride. She wore a large hat! From a Southern Baptist background she had met Tip when he was on holiday. She had lived in a large house in Florida and he, a divorcee with no faith to call his own, had moved into a caravan in a rather run-down part of the next-door village to Greatham. She really must have loved him to move in there! She insisted on going to church and they ended up with us. Gradually I got to know them and found out that Tip was mad about cricket and together we decided to see if we could raise enough interest for a team. A pair of brothers were very keen and had some gear and they also persuaded some friends to join with them. They also arranged the games for us, mostly with Pub Teams on a Sunday afternoon. It was great fun and we won a few games as well. One Sunday match I had to retire from batting in order to get back in time to take Evensong. I asked Tip one day whether he would like to be confirmed and he agreed joining an adult class with about five members at that time. We watched some very good videos done by David Watson the famous evangelist. After a couple of years they moved to America and he got a good job driving the minibus for a home for the elderly. Then suddenly he died. Christine asked me to take the funeral as he had requested to be buried in England. By this time I was already at Papworth and I drove down one sad day and we scattered his ashes on the Liss Cricket ground where we had played a few times and where I had played for the 'Zombies' (a Portsmouth Football Club team) many years before.

Another scattering I did was for dear Clive. He was a great character and lived for his church and his golf. One day after the service he asked me if he could teach me how to play golf. He lived near to a large Golf Course and about once a month we would go out with a 5 iron on to the practice area. He was very strict with me and in the two years we played together he took me out onto the course only twice. Sadly he never taught me to drive. He died unexpectedly in his late seventies and after the funeral we took his ashes to the 18th green as he had asked.

Anita was glad to be leaving Greatham. It had been a hard time for her. The first time living in England and as a Vicar's wife in an English parish with many long-standing traditions and having the main part of bringing up children also for their first time in a strange environment. She had found some staunch support especially from one christian lady who had become a prayer partner but emotionally Anita had found it a draining experience. We had a member of the congregation who had a carpet business and he offered to go with her to Papworth to fit some carpets. For this he spent a whole day travelling there and back as well. He charged us only £150 for the whole operation. Such help was invaluable and always seemed round the corner like the couple who gave us £400 for a post-Christmas break on the Isle of Wight one year. But it was good to feel that we were on our way to another chapter in our lives. There had been a lot of learning, many mistakes and much patience shown for and by us! The farewells were very touching and with much sincerity shown. There were gifts of a glass bowl (made in Sweden) and jug, with the outline of the two churches etched into the glass done by a lady who lived in the benefice. Lee Court gave us a desk lamp which is shining at this moment! There were nice cheques as well to help in our new home. After all that had happened we were left feeling that we had contributed something and made some good friends. God had been at work all the time helping us and some others to grow in faith. Our removal firm was called 'Bishop's Move'! They actually needed two vans to take all our belongings. It was something of a parable of how we had been blessed since we arrived with such a little. And by the way when the rose bush to the left of our front door bloomed during our first Summer there, it was red!

CHAPTER 11

THE PLACE OF RESURRECTION

When we arrived before the pantechnicons at Papworth Rectory we found the house cleaned and tidy. The Diocese had decorated right through and put in new kitchen cabinets and mock tiled flooring. There was a lovely arrangement of flowers in each of the rooms and a few cards of welcome. One of them said 'When I arrived here at the age of sixteen I thought I was about to die. It felt as though I had been thrown on the scrap heap but Papworth turned out to be a place of Resurrection.' What was the history of the village we had come to? Someone lent me a book about it and as I read it my eyes grew wider and my mind boggled with the amazing place it had come to be! Until 1918 it was a tiny Manor Farm village. The Manor built only just before 1800 was a fine Georgian house with some Greek-like pillars at it's imposing front. It stood on a low hill with a valley between it and the Parish church that had been there much longer on the hill opposite. Otherwise there were about fifty dwellings, mostly farm cottages, scattered around the parish. In 1918 the Manor House was empty, the Lord having been found guilty of fraud was doing time! As part of his payment of many debts the house was up for sale. He wasn't a bad man as such, just too generous in giving away money he hadn't got! In fact the houses he had built for his farm workers were far in advance of anything else around at that time. The house caught the eye of the District Officer for T.B. as a potential hospital. At that time T.B. was the number one killer in Britain and there was no known cure. This Doctor, Pendrill Varrier Jones, later to be knighted for his pioneering and visionary work, had for a number of years being looking for somewhere to work out his plan. He had in fact already started in the village of Bourn about five miles away towards Cambridge but the house had quickly become too small. He discovered that Papworth Hall was going really cheap and so bought it together with the attached land and farm. At once he set out working for his vision to become reality. The idea was to select men and women who wanted to fight the disease and offer them hope through good food, fresh air, community living, and if they recovered a home to live in and work to do. The Papworth T.B. Colony as it was called was floated as a charity and caught the imagination of the public. Varrier Jones appointed the recently retired High Commissioner in South Africa, Lord Milner, as Chairman of the Trustees. It wasn't long before the Royal Family were involved and Queen Mary gave £10,000 in 1919. T.B. patients began to arrive and recover and houses were built in the village for them. When the Hall was full of patients little wooden sheds were built along the drive, rather like hencoops, where individuals would be housed. There was room for a bed, chair and small table. The light was a bare bulb in the ceiling. In winter it was known for snow to lie on the beds in the morning! No heating was allowed although many cheated by buying single bar electric heaters and plugging them into the light connection. Of course sometimes this would blow the whole system! But these were determined and strong-minded men. One of them told me how he would buy bacon and fry it for breakfast early in the morning, selling it to those who had ordered it. There are two of these huts still in existence used as garden sheds in near-by villages and in about 1996 a replica was built in the grounds of the hospital for visitors to see how their forebears lived. Hostels were also built for those who became strong enough to leave hospital. These were single sex houses run on semi-military lines. Meals were supposed to be adequate but sometimes left much to be desired. One man told me that he was the elected spokesman for the others and one day their supper was one boiled onion with gravy and bread and butter! He was asked to complain and went to the Matron's office. He was asked in. Yes Redman, (it was always surnames) what is it?' He complained about the paucity of the evening meal. She looked in her book. 'One onion, you say, yes I'm sorry it was supposed to be two.'

The village developed very quickly and the good Doctor introduced industry. Soon there was a leather goods shop producing the highest quality suitcases and other useful items. Before long the Royal Family was one of the customers. Another industry was vehicle bodybuilding. The Post Office would send the chassis of their vans and Papworth did the rest. Then there was the Printers and they got the contract for the cover on all the telephone books in Britain. Most of the workers were ex-T.B. patients. By the mid-1930's the work had expanded so much that the time had come to build a proper Sanatorium. In fact two were built, one for men and one for women. Some ex-T.B. Nurses were invited to work there so a new Nurses Home was built and the home built by one of the Lords of the Manor for the church Organist was taken over as a second. By the time the Second World War started Papworth was a thriving village of some 600 highly motivated people. The community spirit was fantastic. A large village hall had been built for weekly films and dances with music from their own band. Just before the War the Secretary of the 'Village Settlement' as it had become known, built an enormous stage at the back of the hall. He was very keen on Pantomimes, both writing and then producing them. The stage was the largest I have ever seen! When we arrived and were shown around it was a very strange feeling because the backdrop and lights were still in position from their last production in 1943! It was as though time had stopped. There hadn't been a production of any kind since then.

The War effort took over and soon after the War the Secretary died. In fact Dr. Varrier Jones had also died, worn out in his fifties, during the War. But not before he had been knighted for his work. He was indeed a remarkable man. As well as Pantomimes the village held mammoth Garden Shows. There would be prizes for just about everything under the sun and a great garden competition in the village so that people would come from far and near to look at the beautiful gardens lining the streets. These mammoth Garden Shows would quite often be opened by one of the Royal Family and there is a lovely old table in Papworth Hall with the brass signatures of many of them nailed to the top. The weekly film shows were an opportunity for sweethearts to meet. As there was strict segregation the men and women would queue and sit separately in the hall but with a bit of luck those who wanted to meet would clock in and then slip out. They would go off and come back just as the film ended slipping into their respective queues. There has probably never been any community quite like it. A cross between a Boarding School and an Army Camp! Of course the curing of T.B. brought a crisis and without new people the village would die. What could be done? The Trustees made a historic decision! They would turn their attention to the growing number of physically disabled people needing help in the community. This was in 1948 and a far-sighted change. Gradually new Hostels were built and the old ones adapted and so the character of the village began to change. Possibly the biggest mistake made was that the old constituents were never really consulted or informed about the changeover and felt sidelined. This feeling was prominent when I arrived and became more pronounced during the length of our stay there.

The hospital, of course, had to make enormous adjustments as well. Again there were visionary people around and a Chest and Heart Hospital began to emerge. In 1981 a South African Surgeon, Terence English, performed the first heart transplant there in Britain and later the first heart and lung transplant was carried out there also. The ethos of a high standard of tender love and care which had evolved in the T.B. era remained. There was good staff morale and patients began to talk about this ambience. After some years it became the centre for heart surgery for the whole of East Anglia and for certain diseases a National Centre as well. People for transplants or with Cystic Fibrosis, Pulmonary Hypertension, Emphysema or similar chest diseases would come from Scotland, Ireland, Wales or anywhere in England. This had made it into a very distinctive place known throughout the United Kingdom and beyond. When I met a man waiting for a heart by-pass who was Australian I asked him how he came to be there. He told me that he wrote books and lived six months in Australia and the other half of the year in Switzerland. When he had pains in his chest and went to his G.P. and then to a Specialist it was recommended that he have a by-pass. He asked where he should go for that and the reply was 'If you want the best hospital in Europe go to Papworth'! Most of this background we knew nothing about when we arrived there just after Easter 1988.

The Induction was set for nine days later and we were given to understand that this time was for settling in. The Trustees of the Village Settlement invited us to their monthly lunch before their meeting held in the panelled Boardroom on the first floor of the Hall, which was then used for Offices and Administration. The oil painting on the wall showed the first Matron of Papworth T.B. Colony, Miss Bourne, looking down on us in her white cap and mauve uniform, bust to the fore! Afterwards we were given an extensive tour of the whole Village, the Hostels where people mostly in wheelchairs greeted us warmly and the Industries full of noise and bustle. One man stood out. He was working on a wheelchair which Papworth was building, one of the first mechanised sort, and he stood up to greet us and explained what he was doing. He then said that he hoped we would be very happy in the Village. He was married to one of the regular church-goers and although a Catholic himself he came with her to the church and eventually after some badgering from me began to receive Communion. He had been born in Lithuania and had fought against the Nazis, was captured and sent to Belson. From there he escaped but was recaptured and forced, because he could speak German, to fight in the Nazi Army. He was then captured again and stayed in an American camp until released, found to have T.B. and sent to Papworth. He learnt English quickly and fluently. His health was never 100% but he lived a full life and he was full of joy when he could, for the first time since 1940, return to see members of his family in Tallin. He died in 2000 and is buried near his first wife who died of Cancer, in Papworth churchyard. Papworth was full of people with stories, not all as dramatic as that, but nevertheless full of interest, coming from all parts of Britain and the Continent, mostly Eastern European, for one reason only – to be cured of the deadly disease. And they were! Starting off in the hospital, then moving to the huts, progressing to the Hostels and finally to more and more modern houses as the Charity found money to develop. The same has happened with the physically disabled as ideas changed and more and more people found ways to live independently. Now Papworth Trust, as it became in the 1990's has sold lots of its land for private development and the Village is becoming a satellite of Cambridge although many commuters live further afield than that. The population was about one thousand when we arrived but in a few years time it will have trebled.

I had already visited the church. I had come with Christopher so that we could visit the local Secondary School and had stayed with Joy who was then living in Ely. The church service suited my way of thinking very much. It was a Sung Communion to a modern setting and there were other things which I would have liked to introduce in Greatham but had resistance against, such as a weekly typed bulletin with notices and a list of prayer requests. Then the 'Peace' was shared, something that Lady Neave had said in Greatham was the most unpeaceful moment of her week! The children in the choir also came to sit at the front during the sermon to help with their behaviour and their concentration! There was coffee at the back of the church afterwards to enable people to get to know each other better and to share with one another. It would have been difficult to do that in Greatham and Empshott where even coffee in the rectory afterwards was frowned on at first. Without exaggeration the Papworth congregation was the most welcoming and friendly that we have ever met. We asked ourselves why? On the whole we thought that it was to do with the nature of the whole community. People had come from different backgrounds and had to learn to accept one another. They had also been face to face with suffering and this had made them very tolerant and understanding of other people's problems. Of course there had also been the teaching of some very good priests, especially my predecessor who had built up the congregation and introduced new positive things. Especially, he had made room for wheelchairs by removing two pews in the front and two at the back of the church and carpetted the resulting flat area. This also made a good place to have coffee after the service.

One or two of the disabled community had started coming regularly and this helped us to build up the constituency. By the time we left there were about ten or twelve regulars in a congregation of fifty or more, many of whom had attended Confirmation classes and been confirmed. They set a good example to others because they were mostly willing to read or lead prayers at services even though some had great difficulty in speaking. No-one ever suggested that this was inappropriate and indeed I noticed how it made people more attentive to follow and hear what was being said. I think the best example of what I mean was Peter. The exact reason why he had been brought to Papworth was difficult to say. He worked as a Gardener for the Trust and everyone knew that he was what might be called a 'simple soul'. He lived in one of the Hostels and collected ornamental spoons as a hobby. The only time I saw him was when he would be pushing a wheelbarrow or sweeping up leaves in the hospital grounds. He would often greet me 'Morning Vicar' and sometimes 'present arms' with his broom. That was his way and he treated everyone the same and nearly always cheerfully. One Sunday he turned up at church. I never knew why he decided to do this. However he didn't do what everyone else would but stood by the door, at attention, welcoming everybody as they arrived and finally when there was nobody else to come he marched in and took a seat quite near the front. The next Sunday he stood with the Sidesman helping him to give out the books. He hadn't been asked but just did it. The following Sunday he was already there when I arrived half-an-hour before the service! The Organist also came early to practice and put up the hymn numbers. This Sunday he found the numbers already up! Peter couldn't read or write and after putting them up would stand reading the numbers out aloud to himself to check them. Then he would find me and ask for the numbers to be checked again. The next job he appointed himself to was putting out the cups for after church coffee and filling the urn with water. The ladies were very grateful for this help. He also liked taking the collection but the difficulty was his restlessness. He was excitable and would walk up and down to see if more people were coming. He would always talk loudly sometimes during the service as well as before and afterwards. One day he had been particularly tiresome and after the service our Head Server, a young man in his twenties, commented 'God got it wrong about Pharoah!' We had had the reading from Exodus about the plagues and so on. 'He didn't need to send plagues to Egypt, he could have sent Peter instead!' Peter eventually became confirmed and took it very seriously indeed.

Because of the nature of the Papworth community there were a number of the people who came to the church who couldn't live anywhere else. There was Michael who was an epileptic and had fallen under a train damaging his brain. His short term memory was very poor and his medication was so strong that he wobbled rather than walked. But he came to church most Sundays. The difficulty was that he would repeat himself hundreds of times and one got the story of his conversion every time one spoke to him. He could also be rather amusing, sometimes unintentionally. One day he said to me 'When you first came I thought you were a right plonker but now that I know you I think you are a bit of all right!' Unfortunately this comment would be repeated quite often.

Another regular churchgoer was James one of the most courageous people I have ever met His problem is Dystonia, one of the more rare neurological diseases. This had hit him when he was in his teens and therefore advanced quickly making him more and more paralysed. He insisted on walking although he would often fall like a ramrod as he was so stiff. The muscles of his throat stopped functioning which made eating difficult and speech impossible. Still he would force his mouth open and pour liquidised food down his throat and use a speech machine to communicate. He was always joking about something and loved to sing but didn't always stop when everyone else did! At the moment he is considering having an operation on his brain to release some nerve endings which would enable him to open his jaw better.

Amongst the older community was a man called George. He had served in the Army in Palestine before the war and came to Papworth as a Nurse soon afterwards. He worked there until he retired just before we arrived. He was a very keen member of the British Legion and always carried the flag at their events. He had been married for a short time and had known before deciding to get married that his wife-to-be had terminal Cancer. They actually had about two years together. It was war time and money wasn't easy to come by. One night in a pub he was talking to this man who asked him who his Best Man was to be and George admitted that he didn't yet know. This man offered to help. Then he asked where they were to spend their honeymoon and again George had to admit that nothing was planned. This kind man said that he had a flat in Brighton which obviously wasn't being used at the present and they were welcome to go there for as long as they liked free of charge. George could hardly believe his luck! At the end of the evening he naturally asked his new friend his name. It was, he said, Noel Coward! George had a fund of such stories. They included the time he was stuck in a lift with our Queen's Grandmother, Queen Mary. Then there was the time he had been an extra in a couple of films. Unfortunately George's health deteriorated and I was called to the hospital where he lay unconscious. I spoke loudly to him that he shouldn't desert his friends in this way and he recovered! On my next visit he told me that he had mystified the Chaplain by asking him for a torch. 'Why?' was the natural response. 'Well,' said George, 'I went down this long tunnel and it didn't have a light at the end like everyone says there is so next time I go down it I shall need a torch.' He often had communion at home but would always get to church if he could. He would sit near the front, immaculately dressed, and always with a red rose in his buttonhole. Again I was called to his room. He was dying I was told so I said the farewell prayers. Silence. No more news. I phoned the next morning to be told that he was sitting up in bed and talking! When I saw him he said that he would give anything for a custard tart. I offered to go to the store to buy him one. 'They haven't got any' was his rejoinder. 'So how do you know?' I asked. 'I phoned them' he said nonchantly. Anyway he did die eventually and we were on holiday at the time! It was one of the funerals I would have been most honoured to take.

One could go on but what has been said already is enough to explain the distinctive nature of Papworth community and church. As already mentioned when we arrived we were most impressed with how friendly the congregation was and how good they were at working together. There seemed to be very little bickering about who should do this or that and how. They had a wider perspective on life and a patience with other people beyond the normal and this applied to both the old and the new constituencies.

The work in the hospital took up more and more of my time and energy. Firstly the hours were increased to fourteen a week which meant most afternoons would find me there visiting or at some meeting to do with palliative care or Chaplains team work. The hospital paid the Chaplains and that meant a fair sum each month went to the Diocese to help with the payment of clergy stipends. That produced a disagreement with the office there. I reckoned that the parish were getting only two-thirds of a priest and that the Parish Share should reflect this. The Diocese didn't agree but we sent less than we were asked for anyway. It wasn't popular although there was only ever one letter of complaint from the office. It was the Deanery who had the actual responsibility of collecting it and they were always most supportive with our protest.

The palliative care group in the hospital actually started because a nurse in Intensive Care was appalled by the fact that there were no rooms on the wards for relatives to sit and relax in whilst waiting for something to happen. This was particularly bad in Papworth because relatives came from all over Great Britain and indeed beyond. On one occasion I had to try and console a mother whose son had died after a transplant out of a corridor window because she didn't want to be seen crying! The nurse spoke to me and we agreed that something had to be done. She then came back to me and said that she had permission to convene a group and would I join it. We met about once a month and dealt with such issues as procedures after the death of a patient, the mortuary, putting together a booklet on bereavement – this took nearly two years – and of course the relatives rooms. These were established on all the wards within one year of our first meeting. Some years later when the treatment of patients with Cancers developed and heart and lung transplants became more common a Doctor for palliative care was employed.

Some of the work I did was routine. I would sometimes return home after two or three hours and wonder whether it had been at all worthwhile. Perhaps there had been no conversation of any depth, interruptions had been numerous and perhaps some people had been indifferent or even opposed to my presence! More often than not however something of importance would happen. My first 'call-out' was my first mistake! It was the week after I started and someone in Intensive Care had died. I went and said the appropriate words and thanked the Staff. On my way home it suddenly occurred to me that I had missed the fact that both the Nurses in the cubicle had tears in their eyes and were obviously struggling with their emotions. Their needs too could have been attended to. It was a lesson from which I tried to learn. It wasn't often that the Staff asked for personal help from the Chaplain but when it happened it was always significant. It might in fact have to do with someone's death. People having transplants stayed longer than others and the Staff often became close to them and sometimes to their relatives as well. Once I met a Sister in the corridor, 'Just in time' she said, 'In room seven George is crying his eyes out.' Going there it transpired that a woman with cancer who had been in for some time had suddenly haemorrhaged whilst George was doing routine checks. At least a litre of blood had been vomited up and she had then collapsed and died. The terrible shock had left George in pieces. It took me some time to get him to sit down and eventually to calm down at which stage it was possible to say prayers with him and the dead woman after which he was able to go home early. Another was an emergency call on Boxing Day from a Nurse at home. She was in deep depression. We arranged to meet at the hospital that afternoon and I discovered all sorts of problems which made 'Casualty' on T.V. seem mild by comparison! She had in fact been to the Staff Doctor already and so we were able to consult and co-operate together in trying to help her. There weren't many 'official' opportunities although I was asked to bless a marriage and baptise one baby during the time I was there. There was also one very sad funeral. It was the son of one of the Staff. He had been a bit of a 'tear away', well known at one of the pubs in his home town and had tried drugs. It was even more sad because he was at last settling down and had come to live at home again after some years away. He was twenty-four and had driven his fast car off the road at 3.00am in the morning. The funeral was attended by over one hundred of his friends. Afterwards one of the girls said to me 'Nice one Vic.'! The only time I have had THAT compliment!

There was also one very moving wedding on the ward. A lady with inoperable Cancer had told me that she had only weeks left. Her partner and she decided that they wanted to be married. With the co-operation of the Registrar it was possible to arrange it on the ward where she was bedridden. The Nurses who were not immediately engaged in some work came into the small room. It was such a reverent and peaceful occasion. She died a few weeks later.

Another wedding which was hastily arranged never actually took place. A man who was to have surgery decided that he wanted to marry the mother of his grown-up children. He was seriously sick and the operation was scheduled for the evening of his request. One daughter asked me to help and we managed to get the Registrar to come in at 3.00pm. Sadly the poor man died at 2.00pm. I was sitting in the small relative's room with the traumatised family and as we sat almost entirely in silence it seemed to me they would probably be better left alone. I asked them if that was what they wanted. They thought yes. So I enquired if they would like me to pray before I left. The mother said she would like that. I was just about to open my mouth when the door opened and the daughter who had been trying to arrange the wedding whom I had not yet met came into the room. She asked what was going on in a rather aggressive way. Her mother said 'The Chaplain is just going to pray Dear' to which her immediate response was 'Too f...... late isn't it!' I tried to remain as calm as possible and suggested that as she had had such a harrowing day perhaps she could come and sit down for a moment. I had just started to pray when her husband who had been sitting on the window ledge with his face turned outwards jumped up and burst from the room with a remark like 'I can't stand this!' After praying I went out to my car as it was time to go somewhere else and I saw him sitting under a tree so I went over to him. I sat on the ground near him and said that it must be very difficult for him. He simply said 'Please leave me, I'm not ready yet.' Such are the intricacies of the work of any chaplain sometimes. Surprising encounters could come in all shapes and sizes.

Soon after arriving I was called to Intensive Care to see a priest. He had come in for an Angiogram which is a routine examination of the heart using a tiny catheter placed in an artery near the groin. For this procedure people usually come in one day and leave the next. However this poor man had a Coronary Thrombosis whilst in the theatre having his Angiogram and was rushed to another theatre for immediate operation! Consequently he woke up in Intensive Care not knowing what had happened or where he was. As I approached him he grabbed me by the sleeve and said 'Annoint me.' I said that certainly I would and would be back in a few minutes knowing as I said it that there wasn't any oil in the church or the chapel. My predecessor had left nine months previously and had left no oil as far as I could see and I had been there only a week and not thought about it. I rushed home and asked Anita if she had any olive or clear oil in the larder. Mercifully there was just a drop of clear oil in a bottle. This was soon transferred to the bottle I had in my 'sick communion set' and rushed to the chapel for a hasty blessing before going up to the ward again. Nobody knew about the crisis. The next time I saw him he was much better but something else unusual happened! He said suddenly 'Could you remove this for me.' It was a bed bottle. I had obviously arrived at an inconvenient time! That was the only time I was asked to do that!

Another time I poked my head round the door of a single room hesitating about whether I should enter. It was a young Teacher who had had a heart transplant. She said 'Don't go away. There is too little counselling in this hospital.' I asked her what it was she would like counselling for and she replied 'Why is it that I am afraid to die twenty-five times a day?' I swallowed hard and tried to ask the appropriate questions before saying anything in response. It is true that at this time there was too little counselling. I had spoken to the Transplant Co-ordinator about it but it seemed she had too much administrative work to do as well as any counselling. The Hospital Social Worker also found that she was called upon a lot by the transplant patients. Soon afterwards the Co-ordinator left and was replaced by three specially trained Nurses and the counselling improved a great deal. It wasn't only the patients who needed help.

One of the villagers who allowed her home to be used for Bed and Breakfast by relatives was a regular churchgoer and phoned me one day to ask if I could come at once to see someone. The lady I was called to see was Norwegian and her son was studying at Oxford University and had become such a good oarsman that he had rowed for Norway in the Olympics. He had been training in Kenya and running up Mount Kilimanjaro when his heart suddenly gave out. He was twenty-one. He had been rushed back to England at once and had come to Papworth. His mother had flown over straight away. She was utterly distraught. Her other son had also been rowing in the Olympics with him. Their photograph was on the breakfast cereal packets all over Norway! The bottom of her world had fallen out. She was a lovely lady and not altogether out of touch with the church and we were able to pray together before I left. Her son was transferred to an Oxford Hospital and when I phoned to find out how he was he had had a transplant and was doing well.

Once, parents of a dying transplant patient stayed with us and we have kept in touch ever since. Hers was one of the funerals I took part in. It was in Bolton. One of the most moving funerals was that of a man who had been born in Barbados. We had an interest in cricket in common. He had also been brought up as an Anglican and wanted communion every Sunday. His heart replacement never really took and he didn't return to his wife and home in a small town in the Cotswolds and that was where I went to the imposing church. His family had assembled from around the world and each of his four children came to the front to make a moving tribute to their father. He was still not sixty when he died. The daughter was a Nurse in Winchester and wrote me a very nice letter together with a cheque for my travelling expenses, something which was not always thought of.

Sometimes experiences were amusing. I was visiting an Indian gentleman, an Anglican from Suffolk. A Nurse came to his room and asked him if he would like a cup of tea. Yes he would and could his 'friend' have one too! She replied that they weren't allowed to give drinks to visitors. His response to that was to put down his cup and say 'In that case I couldn't drink my tea without him having one. It's against my religion!' I have never seen a Nurse move so quickly! When she came back in she saw us grinning widely and said that she thought we must be pulling her leg. Anyway I got my cup of tea.

One evening as I was on the way home I saw a lady coming towards me down a corridor. She was the mother of a transplant patient who had subsequently married and had a baby. I greeted her and she said that she didn't know what to do because the baby's food was in their suitcase and she couldn't find the key for the padlock. The baby was crying. I told her that I would go to the workshop for help. When I arrived there the door was open, lights were on, music was blaring but there was no-one inside. Nothing daunted I took a fret-saw and hurried back to the room where the baby was still crying and cut through the padlock. Then I returned the saw to the workshop still open and empty! No-one knew that I had been there. So much for hospital security! It was sometimes like that at night. Twice I had forgotten the security code for the front door and went round to a back entrance to find it unlocked.

I wasn't often called out at night. The first time was to a man who needed an operation in a hurry and his wife was delayed in coming. Instead he said that he would like the chaplain to say a prayer. When I arrived in the preparation room the surgeon came in shortly after I arrived and when he saw me said 'I knew he was ill but I didn't think he was that bad!' Once I spent twenty minutes in Intensive Care after a man had died. His wife was Greek and wanted some sort of 'Last Rites'. She placed a rose on his chest and spoke to him in Greek for about fifteen minutes with some tears as well before I was asked to pray. Another long session was with someone whose husband had died having lived with a transplanted heart for a year. She cried profusely for twenty minutes whilst

I sat in a chair by the bed. Amongst the most moving was a request at 10.30pm when a Nurse phoned asking me to see a young lady of about twenty-four. She was a Roman Catholic and well informed theologically and on more than one occasion I had had a stimulating discussion with her about her faith. She had asked to see me. I was surprised and reminded the Nurse that she was a Catholic. Yes she knew but Maureen insisted that it was me she wanted to see. On arriving I sat by her bed. She was rather more breathless than usual and asked between breaths whether in my experience christians died peacefully. I had to fight off the tears. Was she dying I asked? She had been told she said that it could be days because of a sudden deterioration in her condition. I tried to comfort and reassure her as best as I could and then prayed with her. Happily she didn't die and within weeks a transplant became available and she made a good recovery. She later married one of the Doctors who had been looking after her.

Another moving time was with a Church of England Deacon. I had a lovely letter from her Bishop commending her and we shared time together. There was great rejoicing when her transplant was done. She was the only transplant patient who came to tea with us in the rectory. She was glowing and as we sat by the fire she told Anita and me that the most wonderful thing was being able to chase the Autumn leaves in the hospital grounds, something she had been unable to do since she was a child of about six when the heart defect was discovered. Sadly she didn't live long and it was heart rending to see her boyfriend go through his own personal agony.

My predecessor had started the habit of taking communion round the wards on Sunday mornings between seven and eight am. This was the best time to do it. The patients were mostly awake already and drinking their first cup of tea of the day. Nothing much happened until breakfast at 8.00am apart from the 'blood suckers' wanting their daily dose from the patients arteries with whom I was sometimes in competition. During the week I would meet people who were accustomed to going to church every Sunday or others for whom taking communion had once been a practice and who now took the opportunity to bring to God their fears and anxieties feeling that they were up against it. In this way I met a large number of interesting and wonderful people. I always checked on a Saturday night whether the patients were still where they were the last time I saw them. Sometimes they had gone home unexpectedly or been moved elsewhere. One Saturday evening having returned from an all day meeting somewhere and feeling really tired I thought to skip it but nevertheless dragged myself to the hospital at about 9.00pm only to find that everybody on my list had moved! The numbers varied of course from fourteen maximum to just one, or occasionally none at all, but it always surprised me how many amongst two hundred patients wished to avail themselves of this ministry. It often included members of churches other than Anglican and on one or two occasions Catholics who had been too shy to admit that they were, perhaps fearing a visit from their chaplain, although in fact he was very caring.

The call which stands out most in my mind was to a ward of five men. In it were an Anglican, a Baptist and a Methodist and when I arrived on Sunday morning the other two, a Hindu and a Muslim asked for the card on which the service was printed, requesting to 'take part in the prayers'. It was, I thought, a microcosm of our present society. Occasionally I would be asked for communion by someone in Intensive Care. One had to be adaptable and sometimes it would be a case of a couple of prayers and then the communion. More than once I was impressed by the flexibility of the nurses who would go out of their way to make sure the ministrations were possible. I generally used candles and a white cloth to give some semblance to an altar and once in Intensive Care I asked if it was alright to light the candles with the oxygen hissing all around. The answer was 'Yes, of course.' I felt sure they burned with a bigger flame than usual! One man there was a Treasurer from a church in Suffolk and had been back to the theatre four times! After communion he wept and his wife who was a Church Warden said 'Don't upset yourself dear.' His reply will always stay with me. 'I'm not crying because I am sad but because I am so grateful to God and so happy.' He returned home but didn't live very long after that.

On another occasion a young lady who had had a transplant was sitting up in bed and I set out the bedside table and began the prayers. After the first one instead of 'Amen' she said 'Kidney bowl' and the inside of her stomach poured out! I began to clear the table to leave her but she asked me not to go and we completed the service. Such was the courage and faith of some people. We sometimes had priests in and it was a joy to minister to them and feel their deep appreciation for it. The Sunday there were most for communion was when one of our local clergy had had a by-pass at seventy-six years of age. It was Easter morning and he had gone round the whole ward and encouraged the men to join in. They all did. Once a Bishop was in. When I went to see him I also spoke to the man next-door who told me that he was a retired Wing Commander and a 'Bush-Baptist' by religion! When I came later in the week to fix up communion for the Bishop this other man asked for it too. Later I heard that he had died rather as expected from his terminal Cancer and that his wife had contacted the Bishop to thank him for the way he had helped him come to terms with it all. One Sunday the communicant was a Professor Butterfield, famous in Cambridge. He had had a triple by-pass at the age of eighty or more and had made a good recovery but it was less than a week since his operation. As we came to the time for him to receive communion he moved from his chair to kneel on the floor. I was terrified that he wouldn't be able to stand up again or do himself some permanent damage. He managed however but not without some difficulty of course, and sitting back in the chair again he said that he could never accept communion without kneeling!

God had prepared me for this ministry in a very practical way! When I was in Hampshire I met a priest of 93 years of age who had been instrumental in building up a Healing Centre nearby over the preceeding thirty years. His second wife was a great friend of one of our church people. When a year or so later he died his wife asked if I would like to have his cassock, surplice and stoles. Of course I was honoured and pleased. His cassock, which I still use regularly, has inside it a little pocket in which one can put the sacrament to carry it to the sick. I hadn't had one like this since my curate days in Copnor, the cassock which had been stolen in South Africa. The church in Papworth has an aumbry in the wall for storing the sacrament for use in the hospital and the method used is 'intinction' whereby the wine is put on the wafer by the finger at the previous Sunday service and then carried to the sick. It is by far the easiest way to work in the hospital where it would be difficult to carry wine. The briefcase I had been given by the nurses in South Africa was used to carry the cards, white cloths and prayer book for short readings and other appropriate prayers. Just occasionally it was difficult or impossible. Only once or twice was this caused by interference from the Staff wanting to do something or making a noise. They always responded to polite requests. Even the Doctors would occasionally agree to wait until later but not often! They would usually apologise for interrupting but not always. I would sit by patiently and if possible introduce myself to them either before they began or when they had finished. A colleague told me that once he was so fed-up with interference that once he responded to the 'Sorry Padre for barging in' with 'Oh you're not, I'll tell you when I've finished!' Only once can I remember being shocked by the attitude of the senior Staff. I was in Intensive Care when a new Consultant came in to see one of his patients. He was at one end of the room and I at the other when after a prayer I heard him say quite loudly ' And we could do without your nonsense in here.' My immediate reaction was that he must have been drinking. Anyway I said nothing until not more than a minute later I heard him say 'Oh my God.' I couldn't resist calling out to him 'There you go then!' The Nurse told me afterwards that the Staff were fed up with his bad manners. Days later I greeted him in the corridor and after a shocked look he said 'Good morning.' After that we got on better and on one occasion he called when I was with a patient and told me to carry on and he would call back later! As I said this was often the attitude of the senior Staff. One of my last visits before retirement was to a Professor of Ceramics from Khartoum. He had a son who was a Doctor in Germany who considered that his father wasn't getting the treatment he needed in the Sudan. He was told about Papworth and phoned Sir Terence English who told him that if he could get his father to Papworth he would treat him. It was my first time to see a bible in Arabic! He was a Coptic christian. On the day he was due to go home I visited him and asked if he would care for a blessing. I was just beginning when the door opened and there stood Sir Terence. I told him what I was about to do and he said 'Please carry on and do you mind if I stay?' That is the kind of professional co-operation that all chaplains wish for.

There is an organisation called 'The College of Health Care Chaplains'. Another organised through the General Synod is the 'Hospital Chaplains Council'. These bodies take the training of chaplains very seriously. The former divides itself into regions and for four years I was Chairman of the East Anglia branch. We organised meetings three times a year going around the various hospitals in the District. Once a year there was a National annual meeting usually at the College of Ripon and York. About 120 of us would meet and have lectures to do with some theme of our work and the National Health Service. They were of a very high standard and I always came away inspired and encouraged. The College treated us like royalty and on the last evening there was always a Dinner with a visiting Speaker. The countryside around Ripon is lovely too and I enjoyed some good jogging there. I didn't attend every year as I was only part-time and I thought it unfair to ask the hospital to pay for it too often as these things certainly don't come cheaply! They never demurred however. What a privilege it was to belong to such a group!

Meanwhile back in the parish! Our children were progressing through their teenage years in typical fashion. Hanna had stayed in Hampshire to complete her 'A'levels and was staying with a friend whose parents helped them to work hard and they both did well. After finishing Hanna decided to go with 'Au-Pair America' to the States. Unfortunately her first employer was very demanding and she was very unhappy. For sometime she had given up prayer and belief but found herself one night on her knees in desperation. The next day there was a party for all the Au-pairs and she found herself speaking to a girl whom she thought looked kind. She asked Hanna if she went to church. She was immediately struck by the connection to her prayer and agreed to go with this friend the next Sunday. The first we knew about it was an urgent request from her to send out her bible! Meanwhile Mary hadn't done so well in her studies in Cambridge. We discovered that she was playing 'hookey' to see a young Canadian man who was in the U.S.A.Airforce and several years older than she. It wasn't easy for us all and there were some difficult encounters! At last he decided to return to Canada. Eventually Mary got a job as a Carer for someone whose father turned out to be a Baptist Minister. Again God had intervened and after some time we were invited to Mary's baptism in Southampton! Christopher did well at the Village college and very well at the sixth form one. He was developing into a good Artist and got an 'A'. His room at home was painted mostly in black and mauve, ceiling included, and he had a couple of girlfriends, one after the other. The car began to know it's way to their homes and the bus stop outside Papworth for the last bus from Cambridge! He also got jobs for pocket money, one as a window cleaner and then as a help in the pub where he was taught rudimentary cooking – something which he has developed since. Once he was asked to clean the windows of a Roman Catholic Youth Centre which took him two days and sent him up to the top of his ladders but they paid him £60! He went off to Chester College and was soon involved in a Baptist Church. He told us that with his two sisters becoming committed christians he didn't stand a chance!

An exciting aspect of the work at Papworth was the way the Rector was expected to take part in the community life. We hadn't been there a week when one of the church members came round to ask if I would stand as a Parent Governor at the local Village college. It meant that I became involved with the planning and presentation of the school assemblies. This I did for four years and so it became natural for someone to ask me to be on the Papworth School Governors as well. When my time for being Parent Governor was up the next move was to ask me to be Chairman of the local school Governors, a job I did for five out of the ten years we were there. This gave me good opportunities to be in touch with the parents as well as the teachers and children. It was lovely how the school, which wasn't a church one, wanted to be in contact with the church as much as it did. Then there was the Parish Council. My predecessor was co-opted onto it and so it was taken for granted that I would be too! I enjoyed this although the meetings would go on for hours and sometimes, not being the Chairman, I found it very difficult to stay awake when one had to! The habit of going through every bit of business in detail and having to deal with clashes of personality was sometimes quite exhausting. One piece of work that needed attention when I arrived was the closing of the churchyard which had filled up. It required an Order in Council and the Queen's signature to do it! Then the Parish Council is required by law to provide a burial ground or if they can't the District Council must do it. Perhaps my being on the Council helped to decide what to do and we were fortunate that the Papworth Trust were willing to give a piece of their land adjacent to the churchyard for this purpose so it looked as though the churchyard was being extended. The cost of maintaining the whole lot fell to the Council and this relieved a poor Church Council of doing it. The Parish Council had to devise its own rules being no longer under the church and it was interesting being involved with this and finding that most Cemeteries were less restrictive and cheaper than the church. We followed suit and as I was made Chairman of the Cemetery Committee I was able to carry on dealing with the fees, etc. just as if nothing had happened. I was able to persuade the Parish Council to take on the

Village Newsletter. When I arrived the church magazine had just become ecumenical with the three churches in the village contributing an equal amount each year to run it. Our Church Warden was the Editor and worked very hard at it. Fortunately the school was willing to type and duplicate it free of charge and a number of willing volunteers distributed it around the village each month. The magazine was free. A couple of years after our arrival the Editor felt that she must give up and as no-one would take it on I had to do so myself. Unfortunately the school took this change as the opportunity of giving up as well! I found an old duplicator in the Trust office and was given it, and a kind lady would labour with this thing once a month after it had been typed by another kind lady. It was always a headache although we managed somehow to get it delivered more or less on time every month. I was looking for a way to get out of it and asked the Parish Council if they would take it on with me as Editor. Amazingly they agreed and also paid for a Printer to publish it at considerable cost. The churches were given their own page and articles by the Parish Clerk and others made an interesting village paper. I ran a competition for it's name and someone really unexpected came up with the idea 'News and Views' which is what it is still called today. After about two years I announced my intention of giving up the Editorship and managed to persuade a couple to take over. Ten years later they are still doing it and it is still delivered voluntarily to every house every month in the village. When we arrived in 1988 that meant 500 houses and now means more than 1.000.

When it came to fellowship with other christians and their churches things were very fruitful. After some six years we were able to make a 'covenant' with the Methodists where we shared as much as we could. One aspect of this was in Lent when we would have lunches together of soup and bread, pay £2.00 each and give the profit to some charity, usually Christian Aid. We had the covenant written out and published on our church notice boards and our local Art Teacher made an emblem which was put in each church in alternate months. We shared Sunday and Holiday Clubs for children together and the Methodists let us use their facilities for this. We often held joint services. Some of these included the Catholics and in particular we shared the Easter vigil when we gathered in the Catholic church. One year I did an adult Baptism during this and was always invited to help with the service in all possible ways. It was the communion where we had difficulty of course but the Anglicans and Methodists came for a blessing and the Catholics also were encouraged to do this after they had received communion. There was lovely fellowship and the three Ministers would meet to prepare for it in the Catholic Priest's house together with a lovely Catholic layman who acted as Organist and M.C. One year the Methodist Minister sang the Exultat, a long and difficult piece, but as he was a good singer that went down very well. It is probably almost unique for a Methodist Minister to do this! We all took turns to preach except the Catholic priest who always said that we should take part as much as possible. Not many of our people attended but it remained a symbol of unity. On Good Friday our respective congregations would walk together to the Village Hall for a short outdoor service at which one of our disabled members would play the trumpet or guitar and sing a solo. Again the turn-out was never great but it was a public witness to our common faith. At Christmas time I decided that it would be a good idea to have a community Carol Service near the centre of the village and invited the Salvation Army Band to come from Cambridge and play in the Village Hall. We usually got between eighty and a hundred people to this, more, probably, than in one of our churches. The Band and their Officers obviously enjoyed it and the Papworth Trust supplied the mince-pies to be shared with a cup of tea afterwards.

It wasn't always clear what my relationship with the Trust should be! The Governors were most welcoming when we arrived and I soon learned that they gave £500 a year towards my expenses, something which had started in about 1986 and remained the same all the time I was there. When it came to official recognition however it didn't seem to happen! We were never on their official guest list and when someone came to open a new building or project we were not invited. This I thought a bit odd and I did talk to the Secretary about it and things slowly improved which was nice. It wasn't that I myself wanted the recognition but that it gave me the opportunity to make pastoral relationships and put the church on the map! In fact I found that a number of the Staff who came from outside the village were connected to their local churches. Sometimes this happened by accident as it were. One day I was visiting in the hospital and met a very sick man. He couldn't talk much but repeated that he wanted to see Ben who I gathered was a Minister of a church where he lived. I made a number of phone calls and after three days I found out that Ben was the Pastor of a small Evangelical church about twenty miles away. When I tried to contact him his wife said that he was still at work but would be home later. Eventually I spoke with him and he told me that he worked for the Papworth Trust and had an office in the village! He was one of the Social Workers there. We struck up a good relationship and on two occasions he helped with Lent Courses in the parish. He went to see the man in the hospital who eventually made a good recovery.

Important visitors to the Trust included Princess Diana (twice), John Major to open a new Training Centre, John Gummer – another opening, of some new flats and the Princess of Gloucester who is Patron to the Trust. The Trust was always looking for new ways to be relevant to the needs of physically disabled people usually in the direction of independent living and working opportunities. Anita had as much contact with the Trust as I did if not more. For about eight of the ten and a half years we were there she worked in the Physiotherapy Department as an Assistant and became well known to a number of the Residents. This resulted in visits to the rectory for meals and chats. Every Christmas we had a lunch on Boxing Day for those who were alone over the festive season and made some good friends that way. In fact the rectory was the focus for a number of church events. The PCC always met there once a month and the garden was used for the summer party which would always raise about £500 in a couple of hours. We also hosted the 'Bluebell Tea' (Anita's idea) preceeded by a walk around the wood to see the amazing carpet of bluebells there and this often raised about £180. Of course fund raising was a constant challenge and we thought of various ways to do this. One good idea my predecessor had was to stage the annual Christmas Sale in St. Ives where many more people would attend than if it were held at Papworth. Anita began by having a new stall of Christmas decorations but after a couple of years also added a second-hand jewellery section to the stall which turned out to be very popular. One year her stall alone made nearly £100 and in all we would make at least £1000. This would be a great help with the 'Parish Share' to the Diocese which was usually in the region of £8000 and increasing every year. Another fund raiser would be simply called 'Gift Day' and I would sit in the Community Hall from 9.30am until about 3.30pm. The ladies of the church would provide free tea and biscuits and a number of people who never came to church on Sundays would come in with an envelope which had been delivered to their door by church members the week before. One lady I would see just once a year in this way although on one occasion I saw her a few more times as her husband had died. One year someone in a wheelchair came who had recently been married in her home church in Suffolk. Her husband pushed her everywhere and on this day she took out her cheque book to make a gift. At the end of the day the Treasurer and I shared the job of opening the envelopes and counting the total. I couldn't help noticing the cheque signed by this particular lady and it was for £100. I don't remember ever seeing them in church. That year we made a record amount of over £800. Between sixty and eighty people would normally respond and we usually made at least £500.

Our last year at the rectory will never be forgotten as in the course of thirteen months we had three weddings in the family! First Mary was married in Papworth Church to Alex Figgis who had been a friend of Christopher's at Chester College. Mary had worked for a few months at U.S.P.G. on a church placement in Wales and then as a Parish worker in Leicester. Alex had finished his degree in English and Theology and was working for a Christian Broadcasting organisation near Stoke. The wedding took place in August 1997 and the reception was held at the new school with its splendid dining hall. This fine building had only recently been opened by Sir Terence English who had become Master of St. Catherine's College, Cambridge. There were about 120 at the wedding including a number from Sweden and Anita was in charge of the catering and decorating of the Hall and so on. It was a mammoth task for her. I cashed in an Insurance Policy I had taken out in the 1980's to pay for it all and it was just about adequate. We had seen a wonderful old car on display at Wimpole Hall and our friend Margaret Miller, also Swedish, had asked if the owner would loan it to us for the wedding. He said he didn't usually do this but as it was for the Rector of Papworth he would do so on this occasion. How kind. Everyone admired this 1934 Daimler and we managed to keep it a secret until the day. Speeches were made, music was played by Britta, Mary's Great-Aunt, and members of the church came to have a drink with us when the cake, made by our Sunday Club Leader, was cut. What a glorious day it was! The singing was amazing and I had to preach on a reading chosen by Mary and Alex which gave me something of a headache but I enjoyed the challenge.

The next May Hanna married Tom Robson. They wanted a service in the church which they attended in Cambridge and for me to give Hanna away but they also wanted a reception in a marquee in the rectory garden. We managed to find one which would just fit – if we included the Silver Birch tree, and the price was not extortionate as the people who supplied it were a small family business. In fact we started off without a lining and ended up with one plus two enormous gas heaters which was just as well as it was a pretty cold May day! This time we managed to borrow a tiny Austin 7 belonging to a lady who played tennis across the road and I travelled in this car with Hanna the ten miles from home to the church. Again there was an enormous amount for Anita to do and I was wondering how I was going to pay for it all when suddenly out of the blue another Insurance Company wrote to me saying that there was an option for me to cash in their policy. It was a complete surprise to me and yet again just about covered the expenses of this wedding! We managed to find another 'Family Firm' for the catering who provided a marvellous meal for about £11 a head. In the evening they had a Barn Dance with their friends and some of the younger Parishioners from Papworth. Again it was a magic day. Many of the local church in Cambridge came to the service and packed the church with about two hundred people who raised the roof with the singing.

The last wedding was the following August in Chester. I commented afterwards that each wedding had been longer and louder than the previous one and I was glad we could stop at three! The church was packed with three hundred this time and the first part of the service was taken by me and the Baptists then took over with an amazing band! The 'going out' music was the hymn 'Be thou my vision' played as an Irish jig and just as fast! The reception was in a church hall in the city ending with another Barn Dance and Chris and Ruth - who is a Teacher and met Christopher through the Baptist Church he was worshipping at – danced out to their waiting car at 10.30pm! It was one of the most raucous days I have ever witnessed with such joy shining through. It was also the hottest day of the year and Ruth's mother said to me she thought it was the only wedding she had attended where the Bride and Groom had gone to the Bridegroom's home to shower before changing for the reception! The climax to a wonderful and exciting year.

It seemed right after that to make it known that I intended to retire in the Autumn. I was to be 65 in the October. The Bishop wrote a lovely letter of appreciation in his own hand and as always gave consent for me to have a month's paid leave before my actual date of retirement. There was so much going on in the village that the actual party was arranged for a few days after we had left. The village hall was packed with about 150 people including the local clergy and the Rural Dean made a nice speech to which I tried to reply. I don't think I have ever felt so tired in all my life the emotional strain being enormous. It was lovely to see my family there. Unfortunately Anita's family couldn't come from Sweden, nor indeed did we expect them to. Their turn had been in 1989 when I had organised a surprise fiftieth birthday party for Anita to which about thirty people came including several from Sweden.

I have said on a number of times since my retirement that I have been one of the lucky ones to have my 'best' job the last in my career. The church in Papworth was full of dedicated people who wanted to see the church grow and to minister to the needs of people near and far. For example the Christmas Carol singing around the village attracted up to twenty people who were willing to go out on two nights and then another night around the hospital. The results of these efforts would be a tidy sum for a children's charity and the Christingle Service would also attract a goodly number and raise another £100 for 'The Childrens Society'. The usual Sunday congregation would be about fifty although sometimes it would grow to eighty or more. The time of fellowship afterwards with coffee at the back of the church would be vibrant and often I would still be there near midday, the service having finished at eleven o'clock! The work in the village was challenging and interesting with nearly two hundred disabled people and over five hundred ex-TB patients living there. The hospital was a constant source of demand with ministry on the edge meeting people at the point of felt need. The 'Farewell' at the hospital was lovely too and although not many people came there were kind speeches from the Methodist minister and a handsome gift of book tokens and a computerised certificate of 'Service and Appreciation'. It really was the most blessed ten and a half years of my and I know Anita's life as well.

God had been good to us as well, in finding somewhere to live in retirement. Anita had taken up speaking at Mothers Union meetings in the Diocese and one day it was the turn of a group that met in Cambridge. The leader was a Priest's widow and on returning home she told Anita how depressed she felt because she had been trying to sell her house for six months and there had been no offers. In 1996 the House Market was quite depressed. She had already reduced the price by £10,000 but still no offers. Anita liked the look of the house. It was in a charming cul-de-sac just three miles from Cambridge with a reasonable garden looking out on to a field. It had an open fire in the sitting room, something we always enjoyed, and a large kitchen which had been added when she and her husband had moved in in 1972. Mary, the owner, suggested that I came to look it over the next day and on so doing I liked it too. The only problem was that the kind and generous Church Pension Board would give us a loan which reached only within £3000 of the asking price. When I mentioned this Mary said that she was willing to bring the price down to what we could afford. We were very happy and so was she as she had already made a bid for the house where she wanted to live nearer her children and grand-children. Soon afterwards she had other and better offers but she turned them away as she wanted us to have the house! We felt that God was looking after us. The only problem here was that we were still two and a half years away from retiring! Hanna was working as an Occupational Therapist in Cambridge and agreed to live in it with a couple of nice friends who came with her. We made the rent reasonable and they stayed happily there with one or two changes in tenants as time went on until finally Hanna and Tom lived there until we needed it and they were house-hunting.

Packing up the rectory was a mammoth task as we had much more than we could fit into this semi we now possessed even though we had already moved quite a lot when we first bought the house in 1996. It was hard to part with my oak desk which I had bought in Borden in 1980 and was the largest desk I have ever seen, but it had been damaged in the move to Papworth and was far too big for our new house. When finally we moved in, all of the plans which were in Anita's mind suddenly appeared and the house became transformed into a home as only she can make it. The old bathroom and toilet were made into one and modernised, the carpets came out downstairs and the beautiful wooden floor sanded and polished. The whole interior needed painting and was done by the same man who had helped us in the rectory. A stroke of genius was the attic. Anita had woken me in the middle of one night about six months before we moved in and said 'I've got it!' She had been troubled by the lack of storage space in the house. We got the local man who had done the bathroom to put in a floor and add a ladder for the attic and this has proved such a help since we moved here.

Retirement is one of those experiences about which one can theorise but it has to be faced and worked through to really understand it. Each individual has a different reaction although there are probably common patterns. I was determined to retire properly and not hold on to work as some clergy do, becoming defensive about retirement. But I was surprised by how much I had depended on the workload for my well being even when it was stressful! It was difficult to suddenly have to cope with choice when everything had been mapped out with too much to do every day. The family joke is now what I said to Hanna when she phoned one day soon after we came here. 'So what are you doing today Dad?' There was a palpable silence before I said 'Well the Refuse Collectors come today!' The sense of freedom was a great relief nevertheless and walking slowly along the streets of Cambridge or St. Ives was a pleasure I had never enjoyed before. Looking at my watch was another thing. After a while I hardly noticed whether I even had it on or not!

The joy of going out for the day and taking short breaks was enormous and still remains a pleasure plus the opportunity to discover new skills like a little cooking, a course in basic computing and developing a garden which have all been creative. Then there has been this piece of writing. I hoped to finish it within a year but it has grown like 'Topsy' and remained a stimulation. What to do in its place will be a challenge! I have also found it good to spend a bit more time on preparing sermons and daily prayer and enjoyed immensely the opportunity to go round different churches on Sundays and being the Diocesan 'Mothers Union' chaplain. It was a colleague who suggested joining the Third Order of the Franciscans which brings with it certain obligations and this has been an excellent way of keeping in touch with the corporate church. I have also been able to keep in touch with Hospital Ministry by doing 'On Call' at Addenbrooke's Hospital mostly at nights but occasionally for twenty four hours at a time to enable the chaplains to get a good nights sleep or take a much needed break. Anita has developed her public speaking, done some knitting for the first time in forty years and has just recently purchased a second-hand loom for weaving Swedish style mats. Each one takes up to fifty hours work! The garden has also been transformed under her hard work and planning. Removing old shrubs and making holes for new, even in concrete on one occasion, has been my contribution. We are able to to Sweden for longer now and this year (2002) Anita had her fiftieth anniversary of her confirmation on May 26th. It is a custom in the Swedish Church that candidates get together to celebrate this event and six out of the seven confirmed in 1952 came and the seventh wasn't able to make it only because she was a Godmother at a baptism somewhere else that day. In the event it turned out to be a most memorable occasion with our friend, a Swedish priest, being in charge. We had met him by chance on a walking holiday in the Swedish Lapp-land aand were equally amazed when we realised that he had been born in Zululand and that Anita had been to his birthplace. We have been firm friends since that day. Last year was the first time we have been to Sweden in June and the nature was so beautiful, like England at the height of Spring. It was even more glorious this year and I actually managed to swim in our little lake on the last day of May!

And now we have two grandsons! Being grandparents is a new experience and I'm glad it is happening first when we have retired because I don't think there would have been time for it whilst we were working. So all in all we are very blessed as we have been throughout our marriage and many years before when single.

In 1968 when I was on long leave I visited the Parish Priest where sister Daphne and her husband Jock were living. He was seventy years of age at the time and told me that he was feeling very disturbed. 'By what?' I asked. His reply – 'The church I was ordained into isn't the same as the church of today.' We discussed this for a bit and I encouraged him to carry on with what he knew and believed in. When I look back over forty years as a Parson the changes that have happened are much bigger than in the previous thirty or so years of which he was speaking. Synodical government with its Diocesan and Deanery Synods as well as the National General Synod came in about 1970. These of course had been in other churches of the Anglican Communion for about a hundred years as indeed in Zululand where we even elected our Bishops! This meant a lot more freedom to the church to determine its worship and the training of clergy amongst other things. So next came the liturgical revisions which have been going on ever since! Certainly the worship in the Church of England has changed enormously. Then came the 'Charismatic' movement with its emphasis on the place of the Holy Spirit in the life of a christian and the corporate church. Ecumenical activity has increased enormously with many local experiments becoming permanent. This has included the Roman Catholic church after the second Vatican Council. Perhaps the most significant has been the role of women and their ordination to the priesthood. Of course there has also been enormous changes in society generally over these years and this has affected the way the church has worked within it. On the whole I think it is a more healthy church, less reliant on the Church Commissioners for money and on the Establishment for the way it functions. Numbers may be down but it is leaner and more ready to move out into the world. I have been very impressed by the liveliness of little village churches, struggling, but ready to make enormous sacrifices in order to maintain and increase their life and I have enjoyed enormously the privilege of going round to take services and to preach in many of them in and around Cambridge.

We have also been privileged to make a holiday visit back to South Africa for a month in 1999. We stayed with our dear friends Bill and Pam and Bill had worked out a marvellous Itinerary for us. In fact we began by staying in Durban with friends who were in our Vryheid congregation and who had both become priests and then went up the coast to stay with the retired Bishop of Zululand, Peter Harker and his wife. Swimming in the warm Indian Ocean at Ballito Bay was like a fairy tale! Then Bill came to collect us and we spent happy days on a Natal farm with their daughter and son-in-law before returning to the heat of Matubatuba where I preached on the Sunday, a sermon for Easter which had been the Sunday before. Then as Bill had to attend a clergy conference at Kwanzimela where I had begun my time in South Africa we were able to go as well and meet many of our old friends from twenty years before. I was also given a slot for speaking after the eucharist the following morning. Then Bill loaned us his car so we were able to go up to Vryheid for a couple of days. Seeing old friends there was marvellous with much talking and laughter. Back to Matubatuba for a day or two and then we were off again to Pietermaritzberg to meet some friends who used to live in Vryheid but had moved there. Then there was the chance for a break by ourselves because someone had loaned us their flat and someone else a car! The flat overlooked the sea and once again we enjoyed the magic of the South African coastline. We were also able to visit Isandlwana and Rorke's Drift and see a Swedish friend in Dundee. By a most amazing coincidence we were in the country when a new school was being opened which had been built through money raised by Liz and Russ Sharp in the memory of the tragic death of a daughter aged eighteen years. Liz had been Occupational Therapist at Nqutu when I was chaplain there. She and her husband had become much involved with Helwel, a Community Development Trust started in South Africa in 1963 and developed by Anthony Barker into a British support group in 1976. The school is not far from Matubatuba and we were actually passing the turn-off on the day of the opening. It was a bit nerve racking getting there as we came upon the aftermath of a car-jacking but it all passed off smoothly. Finally Bill and I made a visit to to a Mission Hospital up in the mountains near Swaziland where I spoke at the morning prayers. But perhaps the most splendid outing was to the Game Reserve and lake not far from Bill and Pam's. We stayed in the Warden's home and they made a great fuss of us. We went for a night trip as well as seeing plenty of animals by day. On Lake St.

Lucia we were given a special outing and saw fish eagles catching their food as well as lots of hippopotamuses. The time simply flew away and we felt we should have stayed a bit longer really. We were aware of the dangers around now and some antipathy from the blacks but everywhere we found people in good heart and determined to make the new dispensation work. The church seemed in good shape as well. All in all it was everything we could have hoped for – the trip of a lifetime! Soon after returning we had a party at home to celebrate the fortieth anniversary of my ordination. It began with a lovely service of holy communion in our local church. Bill who had recently retired from Matubatuba led the service and got the congregation to say 'Hello' to me in Zulu! Ben Forster preached about the role of a priest in the church. He has been retired for twelve years or more and living in Malvern. What was really amazing was that six out of the seven parishes I have worked in were represented. Admittedly Isandlwana was included by the presence of Kate who actually moved there as a Nun after I left and strictly speaking Howard and Carolyn Mowbray were at Nqutu Hospital rather than the local congregation but only Inhlwathi was without somebody connected with it. Providentially David and Margaret Silva were on a holiday visit to family. They were the ones who were members of St. Peter's, Vryheid during their time there and who looked after us in Durban when we were on holiday. My niece, Trisha, who is also ordained led the prayers. Our local organist played the hymns and we were able to give £100 to the Zululand and Swaziland Association from the offering. Anita helped by our children and a few friends, put on lunch for thirty in the garden afterwards. It was the hottest day of the year!

In 2001 we made a memorable trip to Ireland, south and north. Bill and Pam took us and the crossing from Pembroke to Rosslaire took about four hours. We stayed in a Bed and Breakfast the first night before travelling on to Pam's sister who lives on a beautiful farm. The title 'Emerald Isle' is well deserved, the countryside almost glowing when the sun shines. And shine it did for us! Some locals said how unusual it was to have two clear weeks without rain. Whilst in the south we visited Killair which like most Irish towns has it's history of Cromwell's attempt to subjugate the people. It's also good for an Englishman to see memorials to the 'Rebels' but none to the World Wars! We also had an only too brief visit to Dublin but a memorable time in the museum at Trinity College. The coastline is magnificent both in the south and the north. Bill's brother-in-law has a house built on the beach of Belfast Loch with a magnificent view of the harbour. Giant's Castle was strange but beautiful. Indeed the man built castles seemed to be everywhere and some of them very much alive, as Hanratty where we had an evening meal followed by a demonstration of line-dancing and some traditional singing. A visit to a pub with live music had a typical Irish feel about it with the music at full blast and a waitress who disappeared for an hour and would only give the bill after insistence from me and then it was the wrong one! On our way back to the ferry Anita and I cycled for a couple of hours and picnicked by the water of the 'Ring of Kerry' with its stunning beauty. A visit to the seven churches of St.Kevin gave us some idea of the depth of the christian history of Ireland. The same day we went to the village where the television series 'Ballykissangel' was made which felt strange, as though somehow we knew it already! We covered enormous distances and stayed in comfortable Bed and Breakfasts with meals out at pubs and restaurants where the portions were usually enormous! It was a truly great holiday and we couldn't have had better guides.

Since then we have discovered the Yorkshire Dales when we attended a 'holiday' conference for retired clergy and partners. The magnificent hills striped by grey stone walls captured our hearts and we shall go again one day. The title of this four day conference was 'Think again' which as a friend said to me presupposes that one had thought before!

Indeed what do I think about the contents of this tale? Recently I was asked to give a talk to a symposium held at the church of Great St. Mary's, Cambridge on the subject of 'Growing old gracefully'. My reaction to the invitation was that I was not nearly old enough to do it! I was asked, I think, because I was the oldest of the Diocesan 'Spirituality Group' having been a member since its inception ten years ago. Feeling I knew very little about the subject I bought a book from S.P.C.K. by a retired Scottish Bishop and read another by a Jungian Psychologist lent to me by my sister, Joy. Both of these were very informative and stimulating. Then I did a bit of research writing to a Franciscan tertiary of eighty and interviewing a priest of eighty eight years. In the end I felt that I had learnt something. Part of growing old gracefully is reflecting on the past and appreciating it, giving thanks for it whatever its ups and downs may have been. Prominent in my mind is the Providence of God. His touch on my life, from schools who gave lip service to belief, but made sure that it was part of the 'system' through to a Godfather who wrote, encouraging me when I began to read the bible for myself curious as to what was in it. A mother who encouraged me to be confirmed and prayed for me, even a father who somehow 'feared' God and never stood in the way of my growing interest. Then there was that odd idea of feeling sorry for the R.E. Master and sticking up for him when he was 'ragged'. Going in for the essay competition and being the only entry, and the strange way that I replied to Mother when she asked me what I would do if I failed to get a scholarship for University, simply saying 'I think I'd like to be a parson' – a surprise for both of us! Perhaps the most unusual and indeed risky was the part that Owen, my communist friend played, by tearing my faith to shreds intellectually and forcing me to think though what being a christian meant, which sent me to christian meetings and missions to find out! Time and time again I have been aware of a guiding and guarding hand, and time and time again I have been forgiven and put up on my feet to start afresh. Significant people like Bishop Lancelot Fleming and Ben Forster have been there to encourage me. The decision to go to Zululand was so simply guided with such rich results for my life; a renewed faith, a loving wife and beautiful children. The maturing process back in England and at Greatham, where amongst other things I first was taught something about ministering to physically disabled people. And finally Papworth with the coming together of the twin interests of my ministry. All these have helped me to believe and relate to a God who is both Father and Saviour.

What I have tried to convey is how in so many ways my life has been ordinary. My background and upbringing were nothing special just like thousands of others of my generation and that I had no special qualities or gifts for being a priest. Yet on the other hand how extraordinary the life I have been led into with the rich pattern of different places and cultures. The final response can only be the words from a psalm that Jesus himself once quoted, and in the same words *'This is the Lord's doing and it is marvellous in our eyes.'*

POSTSCRIPT.

It seems almost unbelievable that it is almost five years since the completion of my 'Memoirs' to actually getting it committed to publication.

Of course a lot has happened. We have six grand children now all-growing apace. The chaplaincy of the Mothers' Union and the locum chaplaincy at Addenbrookes have finished, but instead I find my self the Area Minister for the Franciscan Tertiaries in the Cambridge Area, and in fact Anita and I have been on a pilgrimage to Assisi and Rome organised by one of the local tertiaries. Then last year out of the blue came a request to stand in for the Franciscan Chaplain in Assisi for ten days, which enabled us to look at that remarkable city in some depth. We have also paid a visit to the Shetlands where a church member from Papworth retired. So life goes on creatively, with some good surprises popping up now and then. Our friends Bill and Pam who spent over thirty years in South Africa have persuaded us to join them for six weeks there next year. We have a lot to look forward

Index

A

Abbott, Eric 63
Abingdon 55, 58, 59
Acker Bilk 33
Aden 43, 49
Alderman, Captain 50
Aldwinkle, Stella 35
Alexander, Elisabeth 23, 29
All Saints Church 22
Allen, Geoffrey 55
Alpha Course 138
Amsterdam 53
Anita 110, 120, 132, 139
Applesbosch 104
Archdeacon of Ely 146
Archdeacon of Portsmouth 135
Aston, Colonel David 134

B

Barker, Anthony 70, 107, 108, 110, 113, 115, 118
Battle of Britain 4
Bavin, Tim 142
Beer, Margaret 71
Bishop King 58
Bishop of Cheltenham 139
Bishop of Hong Kong 57
Bishop of Natal 92
Bishop of Oxford 19
Bishop of Portsmouth 28, 35
Bishop of Zululand 71
Blendworth Church 24
Boars Hill 55
Bramshott 134, 135, 136
Brittain, RSM 19
Brown, Jock 15
Buchanan, Duncan 57, 59, 61, 70, 75
Buthelezi, Chief Gatsha 92, 124
Butler Education Act 10
Butser Hill 22, 67

C

Cambridge University 28
Cape Town 79
Carlson, Ulf 116
Carry On films 19, 40
Cassidy, Michael 123
Catherington 11, 15
Catherington House 62
Chadwick, Graham 56, 131, 144, 148
Chandler, David 60
Changhi Beach 48
Charles Johnson Hospital 107
Chataway, Chris 32
Cheshire Home 138, 139, 148, 152
Chubb, Nicholas 39
Churcher, Captain 5
Churchers College 5
Clare College 16
College of Art 22
Courthold, Augustine 22, 24
Cramp, Rosie 31, 37
Cranford 33
Crawford, Hugh 52
Cuddesdon Theological College 64

D

Dad's Army 4
Dajocopa 3
Dale, Lance Corporal 46
Dartmoor 41
Dartmouth 36, 60
David Chandler 60
Dawlish 59
De Berry, Keith 57, 114
Dhladhla, Archdeacon 91
Dhlamini, Jacob 97
Didsbury 59
Dig for Victory 3
Diocese of Portsmouth 61
Drake House 19
Duffet, Christopher 124, 128

Duffet, Christopher 4, 7, 9, 13
Duffet, Coral 22, 33
Duffet, Daphne 5, 9, 13, 15
Duffet, Hanna 121, 122, 127, 129
Duffet, Joy 36
Duncan Buchanan 57, 59, 61
Durban 109, 115, 116, 125
Durban 78

E

Empangeni 79, 95
Empshott 132, 134, 137, 148
Emsworth 13
English, Terence 157, 166, 170
Exeter 41

F

Fielding, David 115
Figgis, Alex 170
Fisher, Dr. Geoffrey 55
Five Heads Lane 1
Fleming, Bishop Lancelot 35, 63, 67
Forsmark 127
Forster, Ben 35, 52
Fosseus, Helge 115
Founders Day 19

G

Gardiner, Dr. Margaret 38
Gilbert and Sullivan 16
Gilmore, Norman 101
Goon Show 59
Gready, Leslie 77
Greatham 132, 134, 136, 137, 139, 141, 147, 148, 150, 151, 152, 153
Griswold, Don 89
Guildford Cathedral 68

H

H.M.S. Fowey 43
Hamilton-Jones, Michael 67
Hampshire Regiment 39, 43, 50
Harker, Hugh 83, 112

Harker, Peter 69, 74, 89, 90, 174
Hawkeys 14
Hayling Island 13, 63
Headington 34, 37
Hlatshwayo, Maam 107
Hook of Holland 50
Horndean Tennis Club 9
Hunt, Corporal 47

I

Italianate Victoriana 29
Ives, Mr 18

J

Jali, Canon Wilmot 76
Jenkins, Professor 56
Johnson, Charles 107, 108

K

Keble College 17
Kershaw, Gus 16,
Khambula 119
King Sobhuza 81
King, Ernest 3
Knapp Fisher 55
Kraft, Richard 96
Kwaisa 101
Kwanzimela 79, 89, 90, 92, 95, 96, 98

L

L'Abri 135, 136, 137, 138
Ladysmith 114
Lancashire Regiment 81
Lee Abbey 35, 36, 38
Lee Court 142, 149, 150, 151
Light of The World 29
Lincoln College 56
Liphook 136
Lofroth, Kjell and Bertha 115
Longmoor 132

M

Macauley, Ranald Ranald 136, 137
Mafengayo, John 113
Magogo 93, 94
Major, Reverend Dr.Henry 55, 58
Malaya 42, 43
Manchester Diocese 60
Mann, Colonel 44
Marchington, Graham 132
Marks, Tim 97
Matubatuba 117
Merbeck 57
Merton 55
Modern Churchmens 28
Mombassa 49
Monroe, Mary 84
Moral Rearmament 30
Mulford, Liz 89
Munster 50, 51, 52, 53

N

Naafi 43
Nasser 55
Natal 81
National Service 30, 37, 39, 42, 43, 46
Neave, Serena 134
Nigeria 56
Nqutu 104

O

Ochiltree 15
Oriel College 56
Osborne, Audrey 8
Owen, Wilfred 32
Oxford 55, 56, 57, 58, 59, 62
Oxford Movement 29
Oxford Pastorate 35

P

Papworth 147, 148, 154, 155, 156, 157, 158, 159, 160, 163, 165, 166, 167, 169, 170, 171, 172, 176
Papworth Hospital 109

Parry, John 139
Paton, Alan 95
Petersfield 5, 16, 28, 29, 33
Playne, Doreen 117
Plymouth Brethren 20
Portsdown Hill 13
Portsmouth Cathedral 62
Portsmouth Evening News 5, 66
Poynton, Jean 96
Purbrook 13

Q

Qudeni, 93

R

Rabbitt, Kieron 88, 103
Ramsey, Michael 34, 124
Raven, Canon Charles 28
Red Door Club 64
Red Lion Hotel 27
Rees, Reverend Bill 23, 35
Reynoldson, Tony 106
Rhodes, Pamela 76
Ripon Hall 55, 56, 57, 58, 59, 61, 62
Robertson, Marjorie 105
Robertson, Robert 76
Robson, Tom 170
Rorke's Drift 102, 103, 112, 115
Rosevita 51, 54
Royal Hampshire Regiment 39

S

Sanders, William 146
Savage, Tom 71, 75, 76, 83, 92, 102
Schaeffer, Francis 136
Simelane, Father 92, 100
Singapore 43, 48
Smith, Robert 36
Southampton 43
Southend 28
St. Aldate's 57, 70, 71
St. Andrew's 73
St. Augustine's 97, 101, 102, 108, 109
St. Christopher 81, 83

St. Cuthbert's 61, 63, 72, 75, 147
St. James Milton 63
St. John Edwards 59
St. Mary's Parish Church 36
St. Stephen's House 56
St. Thomas's 86
Stevenage 61
Stevens, David 30
Stott, Dr. John 34
Suez Canal 49
Swaziland 81

T

Terblanche, Harold 86
Thulasizwe 104
Tibbs, John 82
Togolosh 108
Tolkein, Professor 31, 38
Topsham Barracks. 41
Tor Point Church 36
Transkei 97
Tribe, Miss 15
Tucker, Cyril 30, 35, 37
Tulitt, Chris 22
Tutu, Archbishop Desmond 124

U

University of Surrey 68
Uppsala 127

V

V.J. Day 13
Varrier Jones, Pendrill 155
Vryheid 117

W

Wade, Alf 119
Waterlooville 13
Watson, David 132
Watton, RSM 40, 47
Welwyn Garden City 111
West Meon 141
Whitele, Reverend Dennis 56

Whitney, Owen 32
Wilson, Mervyn 56
Winchester 29, 38
Winchester Barracks 38
Winchester Cathedral 18, 39, 40, 42, 50
Wood, George 74
Wycliffe Hall 30